What Every Software Manager Must Know to Succeed with Object Technology

Managing Object Technology Series

Charles F. Bowman
Series Editor

Editor
The X Journal
SIGS Publications, Inc.
New York, New York

and

President
SoftWright Solutions,
Suffern, New York

Additional Volumes in Preparation

What Every Software Manager Must Know to Succeed with Object Technology

John D. Williams

Knowledge Systems Corporation

Cary, North Carolina

New York • London • Paris • Munich • Cologne

Library of Congress Cataloging-in-Publication Data

Williams, John D., 1951–
    What every software manager must know to succeed with object technology /
John D. Williams.
        p.   cm. — (Managing object technology series ; 11)
    Includes bibliographical references and index.
    ISBN 1-884842-14-3 (pbk. : acid-free paper). — ISBN 0-13-227604-6
(Prentice Hall)
    1. Object-oriented programming (Computer science)   I. Title.
II. Series. 11.
    QA76.64.W554 1995
    005.1'1--dc20   95-35598
                                                                 CIP

PUBLISHED BY
SIGS Books
71 W. 23rd Street, Third Floor
New York, New York 10010

Design and composition by Kevin Callahan.
Cover design by Jean Cohn.
Printed on acid-free paper.

SIGS Books ISBN 1-884842-14-3
Prentice Hall ISBN 0-13-227604-6

Printed in the United States of America
99 98 97 96 95   10 9 8 7 6 5 4 3 2 1
First Printing September 1995

DEDICATION

To my patient and loving family—
Bette, Christina, Michael, Samuel, and Joseph

ABOUT THE AUTHOR

John Williams is the Director of Development Services for Knowledge Systems Corporation, an Inc. 500 company. Development Services provides Smalltalk development and object-oriented technology services to customers around the world. Mr. Williams has over 16 years of computer and management experience, having held senior management and technical positions with such organizations as the Space Telescope Science Institute, Imperial Chemical Industries, and Diversified Systems. His experience includes managing a division in two Inc. 500 companies, serving as project manager on international projects and leading the design and development of several systems.

Mr. Williams is best known in the object-oriented community for his seminars on object-oriented methodology, management of object-oriented projects, metrics for object-oriented projects, planning for and attaining reuse, and tools for object-oriented development. He has taught seminars in Japan, England, Germany, Switzerland, Canada, and the US.

Mr. Williams has published numerous articles on software development and business issues. Several of his articles have been reprinted in Japan and England.

In addition to his years of management experience, Mr. Williams has eight years of Smalltalk experience and five years of C++ experience. He is also the inventor of record for US Patent 5109479, "A Method of Designing Three Dimensional Electrical Circuits."

Mr. Williams received his BA from Milligan College and has done graduate work toward an MBA as well as in computer science.

SERIES INTRODUCTION

As its name implies, the Managing Object Technology series focuses on the managerial aspects of object orientation. Specifically, this series provides readers with timely and accurate information dealing with a wide range of issues related to managing object-oriented software projects. The books are written by, and for, the professional community and are aimed at individuals—managers, consultants, developers, and educators—who are involved in managing systems developed using these new, emerging technologies.

It is my honor and pleasure to introduce *What Every Software Manager Must Know to Succeed with Object Technology*, by John D. Williams. This book addresses important issues concerning both the preparation for and the selection of an object methodology. More important, it provides a migration path for organizations wanting to make a smooth transition to object-based development.

I am sure you will find it a welcome addition to your technical library.

Charles F. Bowman
Series Editor

FOREWORD

$\mathbf{G}$o into any large technical bookstore today and you will find several shelves of books on object technology. It was not always so. Just five short years ago, you often would find only a few language-specific object-oriented programming books and even fewer books on object-oriented development methods. More recently, several fine books on managing object-oriented projects have begun to appear. However, books providing both management and methodological information are still rare. This is especially true of books written not by consultants or methodologists but by managers who have successfully led real projects to completion. *What Every Manager Must Know to Succeed with Object Technology* is just such a rare find.

John Williams begins his book with the compulsory introduction to the object paradigm. However, he does so in a relatively unusual way by providing a simple example that is used to illustrate the important concepts and modeling techniques. This skeleton is then fleshed out in the rest of the book.

The most important contribution of this book is that it is based on and provides significant information about a real project: StarView, the user interface to the Hubble Data Archive, which stores all the information collected by the Hubble Space Telescope. In addition to including actual design diagrams showing the complexity of a real application rather than the typical toy models included in most books, John provides a wealth of information in the form of lessons learned and advice. A major concern of managers new to object technology has been the lack of metrics: how to estimate project size and staffing needs and how to know what percent of the project has been completed. Many projects do not collect metrics and do not properly analyze any methods that are collected—and good metrics are rarely published, because they provide a competitive advantage. This book documents such metrics from the StarView Project and advises the reader on how to apply them.

While it lays the necessary theoretical foundation, *What Every Manager Must Know to Succeed with Object Technology* is rare in that it is rooted in the personal knowledge of a successful manager of object-oriented development projects. This book therefore concentrates on such management concerns as staffing and scheduling rather than on what the manager must know about the developer's work. Having walked in their shoes, John has provided managers who are new to object technology with the guideposts they need to stay on the path to success.

Donald Firesmith
Editor-in-Chief, SIGS Reference Books Series
Knowledge Systems Corporation
Cary, North Carolina

PREFACE

Object technology is on a roll. Many companies are adopting it as the wave of the future, and projects of every type are using the technology. Along with this explosion in technology come the inevitable failures. The greatest cause of these failures is not technology but the unrealistic expectations of management: no technology can be a magic bullet. Of more concern are managers who work hard to adopt the technology but who haven't been properly equipped to succeed. Many companies do a good job of training their developers in the technology while ignoring the training their managers need. This book was written to address this need.

What Every Software Manager Must Know to Succeed with Object Technology takes a practical look at how to succeed with object technology. Managers don't need glittering generalities or pie-in-the-sky theory—they need practical help from those who've gotten their hands dirty in the technology and made it succeed. That's why this book includes the details of an actual multimillion-dollar object-technology project that was successfully delivered. The book uses this example to show clearly what works and what doesn't. The system architecture of the example and all types of documentation and project tracking reports are included to show how an object-oriented systems is developed and managed.

Understanding a new technology can be difficult. One of the most common problems in learning object technology is understanding how all the pieces fit together. A simple but complete framework is introduced early in the book to help the reader overcome this difficulty; it provides a skeleton showing how all the pieces are put together. The rest of the book adds additional meat to these bones.

One of the greatest hurdles faced by managers adopting object technology is understanding that it can't be successfully managed using traditional techniques. Object technology is different from structured development or information engineering in its approach to developing systems. New software development approaches and methods are necessary. Along with these new development methods must come new management tools and techniques: Old management practices will impede progress. Managers need to be in control of their projects They often feel that they lose control when they have to change their practice—that they don't have enough experience with the new techniques to feel comfortable with them. The good news is that this book shows you new techniques that have been refined in the fire of practice that will give you the information and control you need to successfully manage an object technology project.

THE BOOK'S ORGANIZATION

The book is organized into four parts. The first part is designed to give you a quick tour of the technology. The first chapter, Why You Need Object Technology, provides a high level look at the benefits claimed for the technology and contrasts it with more traditional development approaches. Current development approaches are reviewed to provide a common base for discussing object technology and understanding how it differs from these other approaches. Chapter 2, Designing with Objects: The Short Course, provides a complete framework for understanding object technology. It does this by following a simple example from beginning to end and showing how the various pieces fit together. It also covers the basic terminology used in the technology.

The second part of the book is designed to help you understand the bewildering array of choices in object-oriented methods and select one that works best for you. Chapter 3, Choices in Methodology: Booch, covers one of the most popular object-oriented methods. The Booch methodology is used throughout the book. The real project discussed later in the book was developed with this methodology. Chapter 4, Choices in Methodology: OMT, discusses Rumbaugh's Object Modeling Technique. This methodology is widely adopted by many information systems (IS) organizations because of the similarity of its diagrams to those used in traditional development.

Chapter 5, Choices in Methodology: Use Cases, covers the object-oriented software engineering method pioneered by Ivar Jacobson. This method is best known for its concept of use cases, but as the reader will discover, it is much more complex and involved. Chapter 6, Choices in Methodology: CRC and Responsibility-Driven Design, covers one of the most popular techniques for discovering objects in a system. While it is best known for its use of notecards, it has other techniques that are also very useful. Chapter 7, Choices in Methodology: Coad–Yourdon, highlights the key elements of another popular method. The Coad–Yourdon method is often used in magazine articles on object technology. Chapter 8, Making the Choice: Comparing Methodologies, compares and contrasts the different methodologies and helps you understand the issues in selecting the one that is right for you. It also delves into the issue of language choice and how language can influence how you use a methodology.

The third part of the book begins an in-depth look at object technology and its use on a real project. Chapter 9, A Pragmatic Look at the Development Process, discusses in detail the object-oriented development process. It provides a practical technique for understanding and managing iterative development. The chapter also takes a hard look at how the development process can be modified to facilitate the reengineering of legacy systems. Chapter 10, StarView—A Real Project, shows the details of a real multimillion-dollar object-technology project. It covers in depth the type of work and documentation that was needed to make the project succeed. The chapter clearly points out where practice differed from theory and why.

The fourth part of the book focuses on the practical details of managing object technology. Chapter 11, The Rest of the Object-Oriented Life Cycle, discusses the much ignored issue of maintaining object-oriented systems. It also discusses the many issues surrounding reuse. The chapter provides practical guidelines for developing reusable code. Chapter 12, Managing Object-Oriented Development, shows you practical techniques for managing object-oriented development. Practical guidelines are given for project selection, project estimation, and staffing. The chapter strongly emphasizes the techniques used for creating project plans and for tracking development. The focus is on practical tools and metrics that will be meaningful to both the project manager and non-technical business managers. Chapter 13, Making the Move, shows you what is needed to make the move to object technology. It discusses the risks involved in moving to the technology. It identifies the tools and skills that are needed to make a successful transition. It concludes by showing you how to pick your first object-oriented project.

ACKNOWLEDGMENTS

No publication such as this is ever written in isolation. The book is based on a course entitled "Object Technology for Technical Managers" that I developed and taught in the United States, Europe, and Japan. Feedback from the students was an important factor in shaping and molding both the course and the book. Also, long discussions with others who are using the technology provided valuable insights into the pitfalls and struggles that many face in adopting object technology.

A special thanks is needed for the magnificent StarView team. StarView was developed at the Space Telescope Science Institute (located at Johns Hopkins University) under NASA contract NAS5-26555. StarView is the offspring of a dedicated group of scientists and software engineering professionals. This group includes Joe Pollizzi, Jay Travisano, David Silberberg, Jeff Johnson, Shian Lin, Mary Ryan, Michelle Jackson, Mark Kyprianou, Joel Richon, Rich Kidwell, Tom Comeau, Ed Hopkins, Karen Lezon, Rodger Doxsey, Mark Johnston, Knox Long, Stefi Baum, Kirk Borne, and Tim Kimball.

Thanks are due to Don Firesmith for long discussions on object technology and for an interesting tour of Munich. Laura Veith and Jon Hopkins of Rational provided copies of Rose for creating the Booch diagrams. I also need to thank my editors at SIGS—Deirdre Auton (nee Griese), Charlie Bowman, and Peter Arnold—for prodding me and keeping this project rolling along. Finally, I want to thank my wife, Bette, and my children, Christina, Michael, Samuel, and Joseph, for their patience and understanding while I worked on this book.

—John D. Williams

CONTENTS

PART I
A Quick Tour

CHAPTER 1

Why You Need Object Technology

In 1887 Mark Twain wrote, "All you need in this life is ignorance and confidence, then success is sure." Confidence is necessary, but for the software developer, ignorance results in shoddy work, missed deadlines, and failed projects. Firms need every edge they can find to bring robust products quickly to market. Object technology can provide that edge.

The purpose of this book is to provide a no-nonsense approach to making object technology work. Everywhere you look hoopla abounds. It's difficult to tell the hype from the helpful. What today's software developer and technical manager need is a practical guide to understanding and managing object technology. This book tries to fill this need by presenting a concise introduction to object-oriented methodology and an in-depth look at how to manage projects that use object-oriented techniques.

Early in the book you'll see a simple but complete example of the object-oriented development process. This provides a framework for later chapters. This is followed by an overview of several choices in object-oriented analysis and design methodologies. This overview provides a foundation for examining development and project-management issues.

3

Simple pseudo-examples are not enough to provide practical help in using an object-oriented methodology. Later chapters closely examine how object-oriented techniques are applied to real projects. These chapters will show the strengths and weaknesses of the object-oriented approach. They will also provide new techniques to fill the gaps in existing methodologies.

As every practical manager knows, there are no silver bullets. Each development methodology has benefits and risks. The benefits of the object-oriented approach far outweigh the risks if you plan carefully and know what to expect. This book will show you how to manage and track the development of object-oriented projects. More importantly, it will show you the things you need to know to use it successfully.

THE ISSUES

There are problems that are common to all software development efforts. Every method tries in its own way to solve them. Experience shows us that some are more successful than others. It also shows us that any methodology can be poorly used. It doesn't matter how many tomes have been written on the subject, there are no complete cookbook approaches to software development. They all require thinking human beings who understand the problems they are trying to solve. Its not enough to be a robot executing a methodological algorithm.

Most real-world applications bear little resemblance to the simple examples we find in books. Complex systems are encountered everywhere. This is not simply algorithmic complexity. Most systems have numerous components. The relationships and interactions of these components are often subtle and nonintuitive.

System complexity comes about in two ways. The very nature of a problem may be complex. Imagine a system that handles the needs of an entire business. This kind of system tends to resemble a living organism in its complexity and interactions. Such a system will be complex by the very nature of what it is trying to accomplish.

The way a system is designed may add to its complexity. It is difficult, if not impossible, to determine if a design is as simple as it should be. During the design process, you break a system into subsystems. You try to maximize the cohesion of subsystems and minimize the coupling between them, but there are always tradeoffs. Your selection of what goes into each subsystem will always be somewhat arbitrary. As a result, the structures you build into your system may be burdened by artificial complexity. This is one of the problems with the structured analysis and design approach to system development. In the structured approach, related functions and processes are grouped together to form subsystems. How closely they are actually related is the crux of the problem. Some will be clearly related. For others, the relationship may not be so clear. Still, these functions have to be put somewhere. This often leads to subsystems that are less cohesive, have higher coupling to other subsystems, and are therefore more complex.

Users of object-oriented methods find that the conventional structured approach leads to an unnatural decomposition of a system. The conventional approach adds unnecessary complexity and makes the system less adaptable to change. They find that the object-oriented approach is better because it more closely models the problem to be solved. The complexity of a system designed the object-oriented way reflects the natural complexity of a problem. Cohesiveness is maximized, while artificial coupling is minimized. Thus, less artificial complexity is introduced into the system.

There is also complexity in the development process. Pick any serious book on structured development, and you will quickly find yourself awash in a sea of details. This is not necessarily bad. Simplistic approaches are often inadequate for designing real systems. Complexity arises in the interactions of design steps. The work done at different steps is disjoint in structured design. There is no clear mapping and refinement of information as you move from one step to the next. Different steps generate information that has little or no relation to information generated by other steps. For example, it can be very difficult trying to reconcile data flow diagrams and entity-relationship diagrams.

The traditional waterfall model tries to minimize this complexity by compartmentalizing each design step. In its most rigid form, once each step of the process is complete, you don't go back. If subsequent work reveals the need to revisit earlier steps, you still don't go back. Like a lemming marching to the sea, you keep moving forward until you fall over a cliff by delivering a system that meets initial specifications but doesn't solve the real problem. Some developers adopt a more flexible approach, but the results are often the same. Even those that allow some iteration are not using a process that allows iteration to be exploited to its fullest extent.

The object-oriented approach uses a whirlpool model. This is an incremental and iterative approach. At any point in the development cycle, you may find the need to revisit earlier steps. This is fine. The whirlpool approach lets you integrate changes at any point in the development cycle. This approach also makes it easy to make midcourse corrections to your development work. Later chapters will show you new tools to help you understand where you are in this cycle. They will help you make intelligent design and schedule decisions about when and how to accommodate changes. The whirlpool model does not make the object-oriented approach any less rigorous than the structured approach. It is still very thorough—it's just more amenable to solving real development problems.

A lot has been written about software engineering in the last decade. Most of it is an effort to bring traditional engineering order and methodology to the development process. In spite of all that has been written, software engineering is still less of a science than electrical or mechanical engineering. There is no fundamental physics of software development.

Yet object technology does bring additional engineering order to the process. It does this by taking a more natural engineering approach to analysis and design. More emphasis is placed on understanding and modeling the problem than on creating systems based on artificial and arbitrary structures. Objects can provide well-engineered components for building systems. Unnecessary interactions are minimized, and duplication of effort is reduced.

The object-oriented approach has additional benefits. It helps you create systems that are more manageable, maintainable, and correct. It supports an iterative approach that lets you catch and fix problems earlier in the development process. Using the whirlpool, you analyze a little, design a little, code a little, and test a little. You repeat this process until the system is complete. In the waterfall approach, the development process culminates in a cosmic "big bang" of integration and testing. Object-oriented systems evolve. They grow in complexity and functionality. You integrate and test throughout the cycle. The final step is system testing—there is no "big bang" of integration.

The result is a system that is more robust and adaptable to change. The whirlpool approach lets you adapt to changing needs. This means that systems are more likely to meet real needs and not just meet an ancient and out-of-date set of specifications.

WHY OBJECT TECHNOLOGY?

Why should you want to use object technology? Is it different from traditional structured development? Let's take a brief tour through part of the software engineering process to highlight where things are the same and where they differ.

The first step in the software engineering process is to discover the needs or requirements of a system. This is true regardless of the method you use. You must understand a problem before you can create a system to solve it. This means you need to develop a set of requirements for the system that encompasses the problem.

Discovering requirements is clearly a system engineering process. At a system level, requirements may cover far more than just software issues. Hardware, organizational, and operations issues may need to be addressed. Good systems engineering is needed regardless of your software methodology. For our purposes, we will focus on the software aspects.

There are several ways to uncover software requirements for a system. Talking to the users of a proposed system is always a good place to start. They usually have some idea of what they want, but it may not be very clear. Object-oriented methods often use rapid prototyping as a way to elicit requirements from users. This technique allows you to reduce the paper requirements documentation you create and lets you speed up this part of the work. Even when the requirements are clear, there are numerous holes that have to be filled in. This means you need to look elsewhere for additional answers.

Domain experts are another source of useful information. They can help you focus on issues that remain hidden to end users. They often have a clearer understanding of what a system needs to do than users do. They can often point you to existing systems for additional study. By analyzing existing systems, you can understand what problems have been solved, how they have been solved, and what remains to be done.

Once the requirements have been generated, it is time for software requirements analysis to begin. Many developers make the mistake of believing that the requirements are either complete, sufficient, or correct. Both end users and domain experts will make assumptions about what you know or understand. They'll be wrong. No matter how much time you spend, the list of requirements will be incomplete. You might as well recognize this in the beginning. New requirements can appear at any stage of the development. Of course, the closer the system is to completion, the more difficult it will be to accommodate those changes. What's important is to choose an approach that lets you accommodate these changes to the greatest degree possible. The more accommodating you can be, the more likely it is that your finished system will fulfill real needs and not just meet outdated requirements. This is where the incremental and iterative approach to object-oriented development provides much-needed flexibility. Later in the book, we will compare this approach with the more rigid and inflexible one associated with conventional software development.

When you analyze a system, you define the scope of the system and determine what its structure will be. One way to determine its structure is to break it into smaller parts that work together. This process is known as decomposition and is the heart of software analysis. What is the best way to decompose a system? How do you uncover the underlying components that make a system work? How do you discover the relationships between the components? What interactions are necessary to create a functional system? There is more than one answer to each of these questions.

Consider two basic approaches to decomposing systems. The first is a functional or algorithmic approach. In this approach, your first concern is with the flow of information in a system. As you study the flow of information, you attempt to discover those processes that transform the information as it passes through them. These processes may or may not correspond to some entity in the problem domain. Your focus is on the transformations. You are not concerned with who does the transforming. The fact that several entities may be involved is unimportant in this approach.

Where does this approach lead? One problem often seen is the creation of very artificial structures, which are often not very good or accurate models of the system you are trying to analyze. Artificial structures result in a lack of cohesion between the system being designed and the problem being analyzed. This disparity results in a system that is inflexible and has difficulty coping with change.

Another important step in the functional approach is to break the system into modules. Modules usually reflect a major portion of a process. Modules will perform part or all of a transformation. You build a system by connecting modules. Software engineers have believed for some time in the benefits of modularity. It has numerous advantages over a spaghetti-style approach to design and coding. Still, there can be problems. If the underlying system decomposition is faulty or inflexible, the modules will suffer the same problem. Modularization is not a sufficient solution to overcome system inflexibility.

For a more complete view of a system, the information flow view should be supported by data models. These are usually created when constructing relational database systems. These models let you look at the organization of data and their relationships with other data structures. These are analogous to objects in an object-oriented design, but they are not identical. Objects are not just data. The need for data models indicates that the information flow view is inadequate to show all the important aspects of a system's design. The information flow view needs supplemental views to complete an analysis.

Another way to decompose a system is to use the object-oriented approach. This approach analyzes a system by creating a model of the problem domain based on elements of the system that cause change or make events happen. These agents of change are not the same as processes. Processes could involve several of these agents. These agents are referred to as objects, hence the appellation object-oriented.

As part of the object-oriented development process, you discover collaborations between objects that cause higher-level behaviors. These collaborations are known as mechanisms, idioms, or patterns. They may reflect actual interactions in the problem domain, or they may be artificial. Usually, an object-oriented analysis more closely matches the problem domain than one created by functional decomposition or event partitioning. This allows it to be more robust and flexible when confronted with changes.

This object view is supplemented by looking at the flow of events in the system, which are defined by the interaction between the objects and their sequence. This is analogous to the information flows of the functional approach. It should not be surprising that this is needed, because multiple views of a system are required for a complete representation. No single view can show all of the information needed to design a system. The important point to remember is to use whatever representations you feel are necessary to get the job done. It doesn't matter if they are officially supported by your methodology or not.

It appears that the functional and the object-oriented approaches are opposite sides of the same coin. In a very real sense, they are actually orthogonal views. Think of them as being oriented 90 degrees from one another like the x and y axes of a graph. Neither view is sufficient in and of itself to tell the whole story. Unfortunately, you cannot create a system using both approaches simultaneously. Depending on which one you start with, you will end up with very different architectures. What you want to do is select one to start with, and use that approach as a framework to express the other. This will give you a complete view of a system.

Does it make a difference which one you start with? Absolutely. Your choice of approach for analysis makes a big difference in where you end up. It results in the major differences in system structure seen between the object-oriented approach and structured analysis and design. This initial choice shapes your development benefits and lays the foundation for long term maintenance during the system's life cycle.

The object-oriented approach gives you the ability to build more powerful and complex systems. Since this approach closely models the problem domain, the resulting system will be more robust and easily maintained. It can also lead to shorter development times. These are not egregious claims.

The object-oriented approach is not simply the functional approach done in reverse order. The change in emphasis leads to very different results. You model the problem and the entities in it instead of constructing artificial processes. This approach results in a more flexible and robust design. Part of the robustness comes from the information captured using object decomposition. Object decomposition is more thorough than simply creating an entity-relationship (E-R) object model, because objects are more than data. You capture not only the structure of the objects, you capture their capabilities and relationships as well.

Of course there are similarities in the approaches. Both objects and processes can be partially described by state diagrams. Even if functional information flow is not the same as the flow of events through a system, they both provide a similar view of a system. The objects that compose a system still need to be seen, whether in object or E-R diagrams. Because of these similarities, it is helpful to have some understanding of the traditional structured analysis and structured design (SA/SD) methodology. It provides a context for understanding how the object-oriented approach provides the benefits claimed for it.

THE STRUCTURED APPROACH

The purpose of structured analysis and design is to capture the flow and structure of information in a system, with the emphasis on flow. This is done by decomposing the system into processes that transform the information, determining the order in which these processes take place, and capturing the content of the information. You may also use event partitioning. There are many steps in this process. There are also variations to the SA/SD process. For example, Ward and Mellor provide real-time extensions.

Regardless of the variation used, structured analysis and design provides three basic views of a system. The first of these is the information flow model. The purpose of this view is to capture the basic inputs and outputs of a system as well as the processes that transform the information flowing through the system. You don't try to determine who in the system transforms the information.

You simply try to discover the transformation processes.

This is one area where the structured approach differs from the object-oriented approach. A process may be contained within an object or may span several objects. It may be the interaction of several objects that create a higher level transformation. The structured approach would not capture this relationship. In structured design, it is the process that is important. There is no real sense of an object performing a transformation.

The information flow model is captured in two ways. The first is a data flow diagram such as that shown in Figure 1.1. This example shows a small portion of a system where a person engages in a bank transaction through an automatic

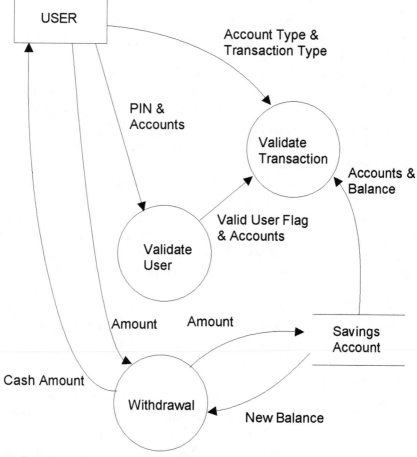

FIGURE 1.1. Data Flow Diagram

DATA ELEMENT:	SAVINGS ACCOUNT	IS ACCOUNT NUMBER
	AND OWNER'S NAME	
	AND OWNER'S ADDRESS	
	AND BALANCE	
ALIASES:	NONE	
VALUES/MEANINGS:	BALANCE	VALUE OF THE ACCOUNT
DESCRIPTION:	THE SAVINGS ACCOUNT IS	
	OWNED BY A CUSTOMER. IT HAS A	
	UNIQUE ACCOUNT NUMBER.	
	ITS VALUE IS ITS BALANCE.	

FIGURE 1.2. Data Dictionary Item

teller machine. The box labeled USER represents a terminator, an entity external to the system. This entity may be a producer or consumer of information. In this case it is both.

The circles represent processes. These processes take input information, transform it in some fashion, and output the new information to another process or an external entity. In this case we see processes for validation, selection, and updating. These processes are a decomposition of a larger process we could call a transaction. If we were to do a complete design of this system, we could decompose these processes even further. In this example we have created three processes: Validate User, Validate Transaction, and Withdrawal. The title tells us which process is performed.

The arrows represent the flow of data, with the arrowhead showing the direction in which the data item or information is flowing. Data flows may be incoming to a process or outgoing from it. They are temporary and exist only until acted upon by a process. Here we see data items for PIN and Account numbers, Transaction type, Valid User Flag, Accounts and Balance, New Balance, and Cash Amount. Each of these data items might in fact be a collection of data items. If this were the case, we would show the individual data items in a collection when the processes were broken down further.

The final item on the diagram is a data store. This is represented by the two horizontal lines with the label in between. In this case our data store is called Savings Account. A data store is a place where information is stored for use by one or more of the processes. It may be a simple buffer, database, or something in between. Note that no explicit sequence of events is given by the diagram. In this case we know from experience what the sequence is, but this diagram does not capture that information.

Validate User Process Specification
1. Customer enters card
2. Validate card
3. Read account numbers
4. Validate PIN
5. Set valid user flag
6. Set account numbers

FIGURE 1.3. Process Specification

Although our data flow diagram captures some information about the data items in the system, it tells us nothing of their nature. This is captured by the second part of the information flow model—the data dictionary. This serves the same function as a data dictionary for a relational database. It tells us what the data item is, who uses it, and what its constraints are. Figure 1.2 shows a data dictionary for our ATM system.

A data item entry will contain a name, aliases, values and their meanings, where and how it is used, supplementary information such as data types, restrictions, etc., and finally a description of the data item. Not all of this information may be known during the analysis phase. You want to postpone deciding about some information such as data type until the design stage. Other information you want to capture as early as possible. This is especially true for data items that are shared by multiple processes. You want to identify the common constrains and potential conflicts as quickly as possible.

In this example, we have captured some of the information about the Saving Account data element. There are four parts to this element: the account number, the owner's name, the owner's address, and the balance. This data dictionary entry tells us that balance is the value of the account. The description provides us with the information we need to understand the data element.

These two parts of the information flow model may be supplemented by a process specification, which describes how processing occurs within an identified process. This specification may be in the form of a written statement, or it may use a program design language (PDL) to describe the process. The use of PDL makes it easier to capture algorithmic information. Figure 1.3 shows a sample process specification, including the steps that occur during the validate user process. This is the sequence of steps, in chronological order, that transforms an input into the desired output. This example shows the sequence for validating a user and his or her accounts so that a transaction can begin. When the entire system is documented in this fashion, the PDL shows the sequence of events for the whole system.

This information flow model provides the framework for the other two models. At this point the mold is cast. Processes rule. It makes no sense within this context to talk about objects, which are scattered throughout the DFDs, never to be put together again. What exists are processes and data items. These are two distinct parts of the system. The concept of an object that would blend these two in a meaningful way is not valid in this approach.

This is why it is foolish to try to do object-oriented design as though it were a simple extension of the conventional structured analysis and design methodology. Such an approach is doomed to failure. The process of creating an information flow model is the antithesis of the object-oriented approach. If you start with an information flow model, you cannot possibly end up with the same result you would get with an object-oriented approach.

The behavioral model is the next basic system view provided by structured analysis and design. It is not used in all versions of the methodology. Its function is to provide information about the state of a process and the events that cause it to change state. It also shows what actions a process takes when it changes state. This is a more dynamic view of the system, which is captured in state-transition diagrams.

State-transition diagrams show what is happening within a process. They do not show system-wide state and behavior. In Figure 1.4 information is transformed and routed to a different destination. The process is Validate User. In this example, you can see how a request to validate a user is transformed into a request to validate a transaction. Conditions for continuing or aborting validation are shown at each state. Notice that the processes within the state diagram reflect the steps seen in the process specification for the validate user process. The arrows show the possible valid actions that take place as the state of the process changes.

We see that the process starts in the idle state. To change this state, the user must enter his or her card. When that happens, the process enters the state where it attempts to validate the card. If the card is not valid, the process returns to the idle state and the card is returned to the user. If the card is valid, the process then attempts to validate the PIN of the user. The process only moves to the next step if the PIN is valid. Then the process sets a valid user flag and sets the account numbers for a transaction, at which point the process is complete. The data flow diagram shows that this process passes the valid

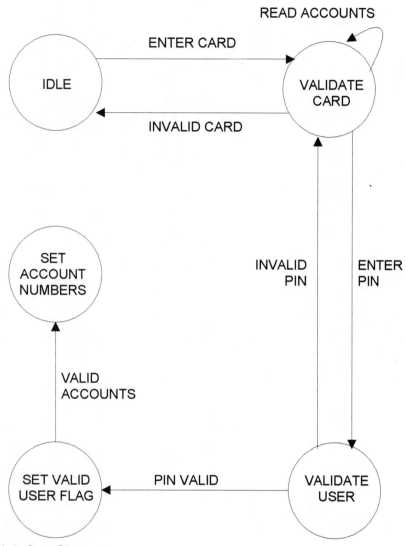

FIGURE 1.4. State Diagram

user flag and account numbers on to the validate transaction process. It will have its own state diagram.

The third system view is the data model. This model shows the relationship between data stores found in the data dictionary and shown in the data flow diagram. It is used most frequently in scientific applications where the relationships

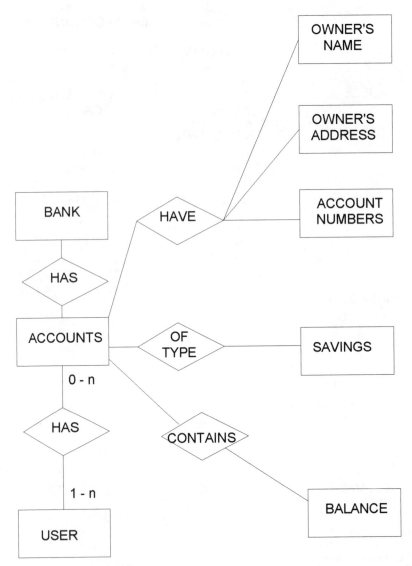

FIGURE 1.5. Entity Relationship Diagram

between different complex pieces of data is important. These relationships are captured in E-R diagrams, which not only show the relationship, but provide some information about it.

Figure 1.5 shows an E-R diagram. In this example, we see a relationship between a person and a bank account. We also see what is called the cardinality of the relationship. The symbols in the diagram tells us a person may have zero or many accounts. We also see that an account will have at least one or more persons who owns it. E-R diagrams can also show how complex data items are related to one another. Accounts have account numbers and may be of different types. In this case we show the savings type of account. We also see that accounts contain a balance. Accounts also contain an owner's name and owner's address. This structure reflects the information we captured in the data dictionary for the savings account data element. This type of diagram is often used to model the structure of data in a relational database. It provides insight into how the data should be structured in the database and can show how to model the data for most efficient storage or more efficient retrieval.

This model has the closest correspondence to object-oriented methodology. You will see similarities between this notation and that used by both James Rumbaugh and Peter Coad. The difference, however, is more fundamental than making the pictures look a little different. The real difference from structured design is that E-R diagrams are based on data flows, and not objects in the problem domain. Data have values; objects have identifiers, attributes, and operations. This distinction leads to a very different structure for the diagram.

There are other issues with SA/SD. The whole approach is organized around volatile functional requirements. This leads to systems in which structure will change radically as functional requirements change. There are major transitions you need to make in moving from DFDs to ER diagrams. It is difficult to find correspondence between the two. As a result, you often design data twice—once for the application and once for a database. This approach leads to common global data as a mechanism for data exchange and results in systems with highly coupled components. An added effect is system inflexibility, which makes it difficult to change systems. This inflexibility is the opposite of what you need when creating a system tied to volatile functional requirements. This dichotomy leads to system architectures that are not robust nor maintainable.

Another important aspect of implementing a system is the order in which steps are done. With the conventional approach, the "waterfall" method is standard. You start with analysis, move to design, then implementation. The system is then completed by going through integration and testing steps. It is called the waterfall method because the usual approach is to proceed from one step to the next without ever moving back to a previous step. This is usually disastrous. Issues can arise at any time that necessitate going back to an earlier stage and reworking the system. This is forbidden in many development groups. As you will see, the object-oriented approach is quite different.

NEW ISSUES

Object-oriented methodologies were developed to overcome the shortcomings of structured analysis and design. This is not to say they are perfect, complete, or wholly self-sufficient. However, they do offer a number of benefits that can pay off in both the short and long term, and firms that adopt an object-oriented approach will usually benefit. Switching to a new technology is often disturbing and painful, and it would be foolish to minimize the problems involved. It is important to understand what is involved in making the move. This book will help you with that. Those who make the move with their eyes wide open will gain an economic advantage over their competitors. In the long run, this will be the motivator that moves most development teams to adopt object-oriented methodologies. It will be a matter of economic survival.

What are the benefits of using an object-oriented methodology? First, it lets you build more accurate models of your problem domain. You might say "Yes, yes, but I don't do simulation, so why should I want to model the problem?" Creating a system that reflects the nature of the problem you are trying to solve lets you build a more flexible and robust system. Models that accurately represent the problem are easier to modify as the problem changes. Systems, burdened with artificial structures that reflect a narrow view of a problem, are less amiable to change.

This is the complaint about many systems created through structured analysis and design. Their fundamental structure, based on information flows, does not robustly model the problem domains. They have a restricted view of the problems they solve. This leads to the problems we have heard about for years. A system needs to change when the problem changes. Structured systems can often be changed only by tacking on a peculiar collection of appendages there and there. Often, the system has to be redone from scratch to accommodate the changes. Some developers throw up their hands in despair and simply say the changes can't be made. They then have to find a new way to tackle the problem.

Systems created with structured techniques are certainly adequate in some cases, but the history of structured design is littered with the bodies of systems that failed to live up to their promises. Why have they failed? Often, the techniques have been misapplied. Creating a system and all of the associated documentation with structured techniques is not a simple undertaking. System designers take shortcuts where they shouldn't. They also stick slavishly to rigid techniques when flexibility is called for. There are other cases when the structured approach is simply inadequate. In these cases, a system design is accomplished only by stretching or limiting the design. The structured approach is further constrained by adherence to the waterfall model of development.

Object-oriented systems are more adaptable to change. Instead of tearing down artificial structures and building new rigid ones, change is accommodated by modifying existing classes or adding new ones. The fundamental nature of a system does not need to change. Most changes to systems are changes in function. Grouping things into functions is the fundamental approach of structured design, and these designs tend to fall apart when functionality changes. Changes in function mean changes in flow, which translate into changes in system structure.

On the other hand, the object-oriented approach keeps functionality well encapsulated within objects. Functions can change without changing the external interfaces. If a change occurs in an existing function, external interfaces remain the same. When new functionality is needed, additional interfaces can be added without changing the old ones. A change in one part of the system has less impact on other parts of the system in an object-oriented design.

Systems created with structured techniques usually have clear boundaries. When a system needs to do additional work, it can be very difficult to extend the system boundaries. This is similar to the problem of changing functionality. It differs only in degree. The boundary problem is more of a systemic problem and refers to significant additions or changes in functionality. We see that it is difficult to change system structures. They are often too intertwined to make significant changes to a system. This is one of the main reasons structured systems are often redone from scratch.

Systems created with object-oriented techniques are more resilient. In this case, new functionality can be added by adding new objects to a system. You can define new interfaces without making radical changes to existing interfaces. It is often possible to leave the existing interfaces untouched. If you do need to make changes to the existing system, then encapsulation proves its worth by isolating functionality and keeping interfaces clean.

Finally, decomposition of structured systems is somewhat arbitrary. This is most noticeable when trying to group functionality into modules. Information flows do not reflect the natural structures in the problem. This results in the tightly intertwined structures that are inflexible when change is needed. It is difficult to avoid this problem with the structured approach, as this pitfall is inherent in using information flows and functions as the basis of a design.

The structure of object-oriented systems more closely reflects the objects and structures in the problem. The object-oriented approach to decomposition starts by identifying the basic objects and structures in the problem domain. With this as a starting point, additions and changes are made with the problem's structure in mind. The resulting system may have artificial structures, but they usually provide support to those structures that are discovered within the problem domain. This means that the structures are not as inflexible as they are in the structured approach. It is easier to accommodate changes in the problem domain.

NEW ANSWERS

What answers does the object-oriented approach try to provide to the problems we have seen with the conventional SA/SD approach? The object-oriented approach provides a more accurate model of the problem domain. This means that you are shackled by fewer artificial structures when the inevitable system changes occur. It also means that systems are more flexible and resilient, which makes them easier to maintain. Since most systems spend the greater part of their life cycles in maintenance, this is very important.

The object-oriented approach provides cleaner interfaces in three ways. Objects with clean interfaces are the basic components of systems. Encapsulation provides the necessary data hiding and visibility control necessary to create clean interfaces. This approach also provides better interfaces between subsystems. Subsystems are often defined by the interactions of a collection of objects. These subsystems can be treated as objects in a system design. Finally, this approach provides better interfaces between systems. This applies to interfaces between object-oriented systems and between an object-oriented system and a conventional system.

These capabilities make it easier to design complex systems. Cleaner interfaces and fewer artificial structures make it easier to manage complexity. Viewing the system as a collection of objects supports good modeling. Resilient systems are more amenable to changes that will occur in developing complex systems.

As you read through this book, keep in mind your own goals for system development. Evaluate the capabilities of object-oriented development in the light of these goals. There are several goals you might consider. Do you want more reliable systems? Object-oriented techniques provide cleaner interfaces and more robust systems through encapsulation. Do you need to build more complex systems? Object-oriented technology supports this capability by more accurately modeling the problem domain. Object-oriented methodology provides techniques that help you understand the problem and express the solution in terms of the problem. Encapsulation resists the artificial complexity found in the functional approach.

Object-oriented techniques can provide shorter development times. In later chapters we will see that a different development cycle emerges when you use an object-oriented approach. We will also see a different development process. This process is more flexible than the conventional approach. It allows for changes during the development cycle and lets you deliver a system that accommodates changing functionality. You will not be restricted to delivering a system based on an incomplete set of requirements.

Object-oriented technology shortens development times through code reuse. This consists of far more than simply reusing a function library. It provides a way of reusing the same code within multiple objects. In a later chapter we will see how to plan for code reuse. This a strategic business decision and requires careful planning. We will also cover the issues that are important for writing reusable code. Finally, object-oriented technology lets you develop more robust and easily maintained systems. We will see how the life cycle of object-oriented systems mirrors the development process and differs from the traditional life cycle. We will also see how to plan for maintenance and what is needed to support this part of the cycle.

CHAPTER 2

Designing with Objects: The Short Course

The purpose of this chapter is to provide a brief overview of object-oriented analysis and design. We will cover the major steps in the development process from analysis and design to diagrams and code and use a simple example to explain different object-oriented concepts. We will also highlight the different techniques used in capturing a system's design and show how they relate to object-oriented concepts.

There is a very real need for this type of overview. Newcomers to object-oriented technology often get lost when they hear the process explained. They are often confused by how you move from analysis to implementation. They just don't understand how to put the pieces together. What's worse, it's often not clear to them what pieces are necessary to create an object-oriented system. Newcomers may think they understand a concept, but they still cannot figure out how to turn it into code. They have trouble closing the gap between how a system diagram looks and how the code really works.

The purpose of this overview is to provide a framework for understanding the entire development process, which will provide a context for understanding the details of development provided in later chapters. The example in this overview is not intended to be a complete design. (The details of a real system will be presented later in the book.) Instead, this framework is a skeleton that we will flesh out as we move through the rest of the book.

We start the overview by introducing some basic object-oriented concepts and terms. These terms are the lingua franca of the object-oriented world. It is essential to understand them. We will then show the basic steps in the design and implementation process. The example provides a gentle introduction to some of the diagrams and documentation we will see later in the book. The notation used in the example is the one introduced by Grady Booch in his book *Object-Oriented Design with Applications*. The Booch methodology was chosen for this example because it is used to document the StarView system examined later in the book. We go beyond the design steps by showing code fragments written in C++. These snippets of code will show how the concepts and diagrams relate to the actual code.

This chapter will be easy going for those who already have a basic understanding of object-oriented methodology. However, it will introduce some new concepts that are not found in the standard methodology books. We will examine these concepts in greater detail later in the book. In this chapter, we provide a bit of the rationale for their existence and show briefly how they work.

WHY USE OBJECT-ORIENTED DESIGN?

There are some unique benefits that come from using object-oriented technology. These benefits are the things that make object-oriented systems object-oriented. Too often, advertising hype clouds the issue, obscuring what is meant by the term object-oriented. Many firms claim that their product is object oriented without any valid reason. It's easy to get lost among the muddled claims. Four features make a system object-oriented:

- Abstraction (modeling the problem domain)

- Encapsulation (information hiding)

- Inheritance (code and form reuse)

- Polymorphism (run-time decision making)

Without these, a system is not truly object-oriented. Unfortunately, this list is not very meaningful by itself. We need to take a close look at see how each of these features contributes to making a system object-oriented.

ABSTRACTION

The process of modeling the problem domain is known as abstraction. It is the art of concentrating on the essential and ignoring the nonessential. This capability is a fundamental part of object-oriented technology. Abstraction is not a new concept. You could view the history of software development as a record of tools that let developers create systems using ever-increasing levels of abstraction. Originally, computer programming was indeed a matter of 1s and 0s. The development of machine language was the first step in creating an abstract view of these 1's and 0's. This trend continued through the creation of higher-level languages such as Lisp, Fortran, and COBOL.

Still, this level of abstraction was not enough to manage the myriad details of complex systems. Methodologies, such as structured analysis and design, added additional tools for functional and data abstraction to the developer's tool kit. They added a system level of abstraction on top of program abstraction. The problem with structured analysis and design is that its abstraction model is artificial. It is based on perceived information that flows through arbitrary transformation processes, which introduces unnecessary complexity into a design.

Object-oriented methodologies take a different approach. They model a system by using the entities and interactions discovered in the system. We need to be careful at this point not to confuse object-oriented entities with Information Engineering entities. In Information Engineering, entities are only data. In the object-oriented approach, entities include both data and their associated functionality. These two items are bound together in a structure called a class. A class will often closely correspond with some real entity in the problem domain. For example, in a transportation simulation, the class Car would encompass both data about how many tires it had and what its engine's characteristics were as well as the functionality to carry out the car's behavior in the simulation. This does not mean that in the final design there will be a one-to-one correspondence between the objects in the system and the objects in the domain being modeled. Rather, the problem's entities are the starting point for modeling the system. Others are created to model interactions or other supporting structures.

The interactions of objects often provide much of the high-level behavior seen in a system. These interactions are usually ones that control or govern the behavior of the system as a whole. It is helpful to think of some of these interactions as objects in their own right. They may not have corresponding entities in the problem domain, but they are less artificial than structures created through analyzing information flows because they are built on real-world objects and serve to support the behavior the system must show. An exception to this are classes that simply provide utilities for other classes. These do little more than provide an object structure for the equivalent of a subroutine library. You will usually not find many of these classes in a system, but they can be helpful.

Let's return to our car example. If you were to model a car in the object-oriented way, you would begin by modeling the components that make up a car. The engine, wheels, transmission, steering wheel, and driver's seat are all entities that could be modeled as individual classes. Once you created your set of objects, you would start modeling their interactions. For example, after the driver has put the transmission in a forward gear, the car moves forward when he feeds more gas to the engine by depressing the accelerator.

These interactions could be modeled by other classes called a drive train and a fuel system. The level of abstraction you go to in modeling these interactions depends on what you are trying to accomplish. The SA/SD approach would have you transform the flow of fuel into the car, into the exhaust of gases from the car. This type of abstraction does not go very far in describing the fundamental components of a car or their interactions. The structure of object-oriented abstraction is tied more closely to the structure of the problem it models.

ENCAPSULATION

Encapsulation is the way in which object-oriented systems perform information hiding. Information hiding encompasses hiding both data and operation implementation. Data hiding is not new. It was created to handle problems that arise when information is too visible. When information is global in a system, one part of the system can modify it while another part expects it to remain the same. This can and does cause unintended interactions in systems. These unintended interactions can lead to system failure. The discussion of this issue in structured analysis and design usually takes the form of local versus global variables. In structured design, you attempt to limit the scope of variables by using them only within a function or a module. Local data is good—global data is bad. Unfortunately, simply grouping things into modules is not enough. Depending on how they are structured, several functional modules may need to make use of the same information. This interaction between modules is difficult to control.

Object-oriented encapsulation provides a new level of modularity. Encapsulation groups together data and the functions that work on that data. The only access to the data is through these functions. This is more comprehensive than just grouping things into modules or function calls. The set of data and functions together can be treated as a whole. The definition of this conglomeration becomes, in object-oriented terms, a class. A running instance of a class in a program is known as an object. An object keeps track of the data it can work on. What it can do with the data is defined by the functionality it encapsulates. External access to the data is allowed only through defined visible functions, otherwise it is hidden from the outside world. If another object wants information, it must request it through a function designed to return the information. The other object is not allowed to access it on its own.

This makes an object much like a black box. To return to our earlier example, we can think of a car as a black box. You can drive or "use" a car without knowing all the details of how it works. The steering wheel, pedals, ignition, etc., provide the interface to the black box. They are equivalent to the functions that other objects can call to make an object perform some specific behavior. The driver of a car does not care about all the details that go into making a car run. The driver just wants the car to run. Likewise, the calling objects do not care how the called object performs its functions. They only care that the function is available.

Encapsulation has the effect of localizing implementation decisions. Since access is only available through explicitly provided functions, the details of how work is done can be hidden from the view of other objects. This reduces the impact of internal changes to a class definition. If you are working on a graphics class and choose to use a vector class as opposed to a point class inside it, a calling object will not care as long as you return what it expects. That is defined by the function you allow the object to call.

Encapsulation can work at different levels in a system. Later in this chapter, we will see how it works at the class level. We will see classes with functions that provide clearly defined interfaces for other classes. Encapsulation can also work at higher levels in a system. It is one way to support higher levels of abstraction. The interactions and functionality of a group of classes might be grouped into a new class. The new class can be thought of as a subsystem. The access to this subsystem has the same restrictions that access to a class has. The only access is through defined functions, and no other access is allowed.

This approach sounds like class encapsulation, which it is. It is mostly a matter of perspective. If you look at a system at a very high level, you may see only a few classes. These classes may in fact be complex subsystems with myriad classes and their interactions hidden within them. It really depends on your point of view. Encapsulation can provide the same benefit regardless of the level of abstraction. Encapsulation is a powerful technique in helping the system designer model the problem domain.

INHERITANCE

Inheritance is a capability in object technology that has multiple uses. The most common use is as a mechanism for taking a general class and creating specialized versions of it. This use is known as generalization-specialization. This particular use of inheritance has the added benefit of providing a helpful form of code reuse. A related use is to create families of classes, through the mechanism of inheritance, that are similar in their use. This is reuse of form. Since code reuse is one of the items most often associated with inheritance, we will use it to explain how inheritance works.

For object-oriented systems, code reuse means something far more than reusing a subroutine library. Inheritance can be a mechanism that lets objects share code. It does this by supporting multiple levels of abstraction. This means that there can be different versions or refinements of a class. Later abstractions are built on earlier ones. The base abstraction is known as the ancestor. An abstraction that inherits from the ancestor is called the child.

Imagine you are working with a system where the idea of a car is a basic abstraction. If you were tracking the inventory of a car dealership, you would need to track different types of cars. Although the cars may differ in their details, the basic concept of car is the same. It can be reused. Now imagine that all of the cars could use the same parts. By this, I mean more than just using compatible parts. Envision a dozen cars driving down the road all using a single engine at the same time. This is the way inheritance allows code reuse. Each child that inherits from an ancestor makes use of the code written for the ancestor. It is not duplicated. It is the exact code written for that ancestor.

Inheritance supports the refinement of classes. It does this by allowing you to add new functionality or modify existing functionality while still reusing the code you want to retain. Often you do both. Let's go back to our peculiar cars for a moment. If we changed a car so that it had an automatic rather than a manual transmission, we would have modified its existing functionality. In this case the code for the new functionality is only found in the child class. It serves the same function and is called in the same way the old code was. The only thing that has changed is how it accomplishes its job. If we take that same car and add wings so it can fly, we add new functionality and attributes. In the same way, when new functionality is added to a child, that code is found only in the child or children that inherit from it.

Different object-oriented languages support different types of inheritance. Smalltalk only has single inheritance. This means a child can only inherit directly from one ancestor. Our car with the modified transmission could be an example of that. The ancestor was the basic car. The child inherited all of the basic characteristics and behavior of the ancestor, but modified one of its aspects. The child did not directly inherit from any others. Other languages such as C++ support multiple inheritance. With multiple inheritance, we could create an object that worked as both a plane and a boat. By inheriting from an ancestor plane and an ancestor boat, the new child would be a seaplane, which has the functionality of both. In software, the child contains all of the code and attributes of both ancestors. To help keep everything straight, inheritance makes use of another feature of object-oriented systems—encapsulation.

POLYMORPHISM

Polymorphism is one of those slippery and abstract object-oriented concepts. Most newcomers' eyes start to glaze over when they first see the word. Basically, polymorphism is the capability of the system to make choices at run time rather than compile time. Its purpose is to make it easier to create interactions between objects. Conventional languages require the developer to be aware of exactly who is doing what to whom at all times. Polymorphism lets decisions be made at run time through a mechanism known as late binding. With late binding, when the developer uses one class function (called a method), the developer may not know the exact nature of the class that will respond to that method. There may be a number of classes that respond to the same method. Late binding ensures that the right function for the right class will be called at runtime.

Polymorphism is related to inheritance. It is a means of providing common interfaces to different classes in the same inheritance tree. Inheritance provides the common interface by ensuring that all children can be called with a given method. However, each child class may implement that method differently. There may be a common level of functionality only at the lowest level of the ancestor class. With polymorphism, the classes inherit from the same base class and implement methods using the same name for them.

Polymorphism lets you achieve different results through a common interface. For example, if you tell a sphere to draw itself, it might do all sorts of shading and ray tracing as part of its display process. If you tell a text to draw itself, it might simply display each character on a screen. You sent the same message to each class, but the response of each was different. This type of behavior is valuable in providing a mechanism to uniformly handle heterogeneous objects. If you had a list composed of a mix of graphic and text objects, you could tell them to display themselves and expect each to do the correct thing. You don't need to know ahead of time what kind of objects are in the list.

In our car example, we could use a variation on polymorphism to choose different engines at runtime. The only requirement is that the interfaces to each engine be identical. You do not have to design a particular engine before you compile and run your car. You can dynamically choose what engine you want at any time. You could even change the engine while running the car. This is known as overloading.

In a practical sense, polymorphism lets you avoid some of the type checking you have with strongly typed languages. It's a mechanism that makes the developer's life simpler and provides more dynamic capabilities. As a common characteristic of object technology, it has several variations, and the specific technique for implementing this capability differs from language to language.

This chapter's example system will show the four characteristics of object-oriented systems we just covered. It will also illustrate all of the basic elements needed in a real system. We will not see just objects or information flow, but the union of both. Earlier, we stated there were two approaches to analysis and design: the object-oriented approach and the functional approach. Our example will show that often real systems are not all one or the other. Both views are needed. We will see how the object-oriented approach provides a framework for understanding the flow of events through a system. The example is not fully fleshed out, but provides examples of the steps needed to create a design and turn it into a real system.

DEFINITIONS

There are some definitions you need to understand if you are working with object-oriented technology. Some of the terms we have already bandied about in a loose way, but now we will become more specific. The rest of the book will be difficult to follow if you do not understand these basic terms. It's worth putting in the extra effort at this point to make sure you do understand them. Use this chapter's example as a check of your understanding.

Object: An object is a collection of data structures or other objects (called attributes) and procedures (called methods) that operate on those attributes. Each object is distinct from all other objects. Each has its own identifiers. Each object can have its own values in its data members. For example, different points in a drawing would have different x and y values. The objects may all be points, but each point can be treated individually. I sit in a chair as I write this, you may be sitting in a chair as you read this. Both are chairs, but they are not the same chair. They may be the same make, model, color, etc., but they are not the same entity.

Class: A class is the definition of an object that enumerates the common attributes and methods that each instance of the class will have. Objects are specific instances of a class. We can revisit our chair example and think of the concept of chair as the class definition of a chair. It defines "chairness." The chairs you and I sit in are specific instances of that concept. Classes define the structure of an object and what it can do. For example, one class could define a point with x and y coordinates. Another class could define a line that is made of two connected points.

Attribute: An attribute is part of the data structure definition of a class. Standard variables fall into this category. The x and y values of our point object would be standard floats. An attribute might also be another object. A line could have two points as data members. A chair would have a seat, back, legs, and screws as object data members or attributes.

Method: A method is a procedure or function that is part of a class definition. It is the implementation of an object's operations. Methods work on the attributes defined within the class. They provide an object's interface for other objects. They tell an object how to perform a particular function. For example, we could create display or move methods for our point or line objects. These methods tell the objects how to display themselves or move to a new location.

Visibility: Visibility describes which parts of an object can be seen by those external to it. It applies to both attributes and methods. This is one area where object-oriented languages differ. Some give you more control than others. C++ provides specific controls for visibility. Smalltalk provides none. Since our example code will be in C++, we will concentrate on the basic types of visibility available in C++. In C++, if something is visible, it is accessible by outside objects. If it is not visible, outside objects cannot directly access it.

Public: Public attributes and methods in an object are accessible by other objects. An example of this for our point object would be the method that tells the point to display itself. The object that wants the point displayed calls this method. Most classes also provide public accessor methods. These methods let other objects learn the value of hidden attributes without being able to manipulate them directly. For our point object, we may have a method that returns the x or y values, but does not allow an external object to look at those data members directly.

Private: The structure of private attributes and methods of an object are known only to objects of the same class. However, external objects of any class do not have access to them. Classes of an unrelated type will not even know they exist. In C++, all attributes are usually made private. The only way for an external object to learn or change their value is through public accessor methods. Methods that are declared private are those that perform internal calculations that external objects do not need to know about. For example, our point object may have private methods for doing coordinate transformations. Other objects do not need access to them or need to understand what they do. This is one form of information hiding.

Prototype: For our purposes, this is the formal definition of a class in C++—another C++ism. Other object-oriented languages do not require prototypes, but C++ requires them for both classes and methods. It is similar to what may be found in a header file in conventional C programming. In fact, that is where you will find it—in a C++ header file. We will not use this term to refer to an evolving or otherwise incomplete implementation as is traditionally done, however, we will see that this traditional view of a prototype has a valid place in object-oriented development.

Object State: This is the set of values contained in an object's attributes at a specific moment in time. For the point object, this would be the x and y values at a specific place and time. State is one of the three aspects of each object.

Object Behavior: Behavior is the methods possessed by an object. It is what an object can do. All of the methods that a point object has to display, move, etc. define its behavior. This is the second aspect of all objects.

Object Identity: Each object is unique, and the tag that makes it unique is its identity. When a program runs, each object in a program is unique. Its tag is the handle a program uses to find a particular object. For example, to find a particular point for display, we would first have access to its tag. It may be a variable name, or it may be an address within a complex structure. In any case, it is unique to an object.

CLASS SPECIFICATION

The class specification is the first bit of object-oriented documentation we will look at. It is one of the main documents we use in development. A class specification captures the details of a class's design. It will show us the structure of a class and let us track the other information we will need to implement it. Our first coding examples will show how to take the information in a class specification and turn it into C++.

The class specification is not entirely standard object-oriented methodology. Most methods have standard templates to track the details of each class. The exact form differs from method to method. Some methods add or delete items found in the templates of other methodologies. Having found the templates of other methodologies lacking in two respects, we have taken the liberty of doing the same thing. None of the standard templates in the methodologies we will discuss refer back to the requirements that a class helps implement. They do not show what other classes are needed for testing. I believe that these are serious oversights. This particular form of template, used in the StarView project discussed later in the book, has the basic information you need to collect for every class.

Part of a class's purpose consists of how it supports system requirements. If it does not, then why does it exist? Tracking requirements is one way to ensure that your design has the functionality you signed up to provide. Some classes cover several requirements, whereas others may support just part of a requirement.

Once you have written the code for a class, you need to test it. Most classes interact with others and need them to exist to fully test code. Tracking these classes is made more convenient by keeping this information in one place—the class specification. It would be possible to gather the same information by scouring numerous class diagrams, but it is more convenient to keep it where it can be quickly accessed.

An example of a blank class specification form is shown in Figure 2.1. The class specification is divided into six sections. Other methodologies' templates have different sections. My advice is to take this as a working prototype. Adapt it as you will—there is nothing sacred about it. The purpose is to have in one place all of the information you need to implement a class and to track its development. This class specification form has worked well for large and small projects.

The first section of the form explains the purpose of the class. This is where you record why this class exists. Some information should be given about the functionality it provides and the responsibilities it has in the system. This does not need to be a long-winded explanation, but it must be adequate for a programmer to understand what he or she must make this class do. It is better to include too much information than too little.

The second section identifies classes from which this class will inherit. How much information you put here varies with the language you use. C++ supports multiple inheritance. This means that a class can inherit the methods and attributes of multiple classes. Smalltalk only supports single inheritance, that is, a class can inherit directly from one and only one other class. In any case it is important to note any initialization issues that may occur with the ancestor classes. It is also valuable to note what parts of the ancestors are most important or used by this child class.

The third section of the form is the requirements reference. Here is listed the requirements a class addresses in full or in part. We will see this informa-

---

Class Specification

Class Name

1. **Purpose** (explains the reason for creating the class and describes its functionality)

2. **Inheritance** (identifies what other classes it is copying attributes and methods from)

3. **Requirement Reference** (a list of the requirements this class fulfills in whole or in part)

4. **Data** (a list of the attributes (data structures) that are part of the class.

5. **Methods**
   Public (list of methods that are visible to other classes)
   Private (list of methods that are known only to the class itself)

6. **Testing Dependencies** (a list of other classes and appropriate methods used by this class)

FIGURE 2.1. Class Specification

tion cross referenced in future documentation. The important point is not to lose track of how the system requirements are being addressed by the classes in the design.

The fourth section is where we list the attributes that are the data members of the class. These may be declared public or private, but by convention they are assumed to be private. This is part of encapsulation. For each attribute, you want to describe what it is and what it does. You would do the same in commenting on variables in a C++ header file.

The fifth section lists class methods and is divided into two parts. Since we are using C++, we will have public and private subsections. The number of subsections you need depends on the language you use. It is helpful to use these groupings even with languages that don't enforce private methods. Your intent for a given method usually falls into one of those two categories. They define the visibility you want the methods to have.

Public methods are those visible by external objects. They define the interface to the class. How much detail you record depends upon where you are in the development cycle. Initially you may capture the bare essence of information about the class. As the design progresses, you will add more detail. When the design is complete, you should have enough information to implement the class.

The private methods are those that you want only the class to know about. Even in Smalltalk, which does not support private methods, some are put in a private category, so their use is clear and other objects will know not to call the method. These methods provide a supporting role to the class. They are not part of the interface.

The final section of the form lists the testing dependencies. These are classes that are needed for a full testing of the class. This information is helpful in scheduling the order in which classes should be implemented. You begin by working on classes that don't have dependencies and follow up with those that need others that were just completed. It is often necessary to use stubs in methods early in the development cycle. These are eventually replaced by fully functioning classes.

Testing dependencies can be grouped into two categories. First, there are objects that a class needs as part of itself to function. These will be found as attributes in the data section. The second category is the external classes that this class calls, known as collaborators. It is helpful to list which methods of these external classes are being used.

EXAMPLE

The goal of this example is to provide a brief overview of the terms, notation, and process used in object-oriented analysis and design. It will add flesh to the skeletons of our definitions and provide a framework and context for our deeper explorations of object-oriented methodology later in the book.

We will do three things to provide this framework. We will show examples of object-oriented diagrams using the Booch notation to capture object-oriented concepts. The Booch notation was selected for this example because it is also used in the real system example later in the book. These diagrams will show us the overall structure of our system, and we will use the class specification form to capture information about individual classes. We will then show how to turn this specification into code. We could use any object-oriented language for this example, but the large system shown later in the book was developed with C++, so our code examples will be in C++. Using it for this example sets the stage for the more complex work seen later.

EXAMPLE

37

We begin our example with a statement of the problem we wish to solve:

> We will create a simple banking simulation. A bank has many types of accounts. A savings account is one type. A person will use an automatic teller machine to make a deposit to his savings account.

Our first task is to find the objects in this statement and uncover the methods they need to interact. A simplistic approach is to find the nouns and verbs in the sentences. The nouns become objects and the verbs their methods. Several nouns are obvious candidates for becoming objects: person, account, savings account, automatic teller machine (ATM), and bank.

Does this account for all the objects we will need? No. From our own understanding of the problem, we know that other objects are implied. If there is a bank transaction, money will probably be involved. If you use an automatic teller machine, you will need an personal identification number (PIN) and an account number. We can see that the simple noun-verb approach is a nice starting point, but it is inadequate to uncover all the objects our system needs. This is why we will later talk about more powerful techniques for uncovering objects.

You might think that the problem statement was simplistic and a more detailed statement would have let us discover all the objects. No problem statement is ever complete. No real system I have ever seen has ever been fully described by a problem statement or set of requirements. Requirements change and understanding grows as development progresses. The discovery of classes is an ongoing process and cannot be completed by simply underlining nouns.

The same thing is true for methods. The one found in the statement is "make deposit," but others are implied. When you use an ATM, you must enter your card, enter a PIN, and select an account. Let's see how far this start takes us.

The Person class will be one of the main classes in our example and will serve as a representative of the class specifications we would create for each class in the system. The Person class specification is shown in Figure 2.2. Let's begin with the purpose of the class. We see that this class represents a person who will conduct a banking transaction through an ATM. If we were creating a complex system, we might want to be more detailed than this. Notice that the Person class does not inherit from any others. It will be one of the base classes

Class Specification

Class Person

1. Purpose

This class will simulate a person interacting with an automatic teller machine in a banking simulation.

2. Inheritance

None

3. Requirement Reference

None

4. Data

int PIN	// Personal Identification Number for account transactions
String Accnt	// The account number
Money Dollars	// The money used in the banking transaction

5. Methods

Public

//Constructor for the Person class
  Person(PIN, Accnt, Dollars)

//Destructor for the Person class
  ~Person()

//The method for making a deposit to an account
  void makeDeposit(Money, ATM, AccntType)

//The method for making a withdrawal from an account
  Money makeWithdrawal(Money)

//The method for writing a check on an account
  void writeCheck(Check#, Money)

Private
  None

6. Testing Dependencies
  ATM, Account

FIGURE 2.2. Specification for Class Person

EXAMPLE

39

in the system. We also see that the Person class has no requirements reference. If our problem statement was a numbered requirement, we would put that number in this section.

The attributes in the data section include both those discovered in the problem statement and some found by implication. Accnt is the attribute that holds the account number. It is an object of class String. The two implied attributes are PIN and Dollars. PIN is an attribute of the standard data type int. Dollars is an attribute whose type is a class called Money. These attributes begin to define the structure of the Person class. We now see what information a Person object will carry internally. Other information will be passed into the object as parameters.

In the methods section, we have defined only public methods. No private methods have been identified at this point. As with the attributes, the methods are those discovered in the problem statement or implied by our understanding of the problem. The makeDeposit method was discovered in the problem statement. The data type of this function is void, which means it returns no value. It has three parameters. To work correctly, it needs information about the amount of money for the deposit, the ATM the person is using and the type of account to deposit in. At this point we have not assigned data types for any of these parameters, we have only identified the information needed. In a full-blown design, we would note the data types needed later in the design cycle. This information will be needed to implement the method.

Two other methods, makeWithdrawal and writeCheck, are examples of the kind of implied methods we would discover as we analyzed the system. In fact numerous methods could be added to create a complete class. The makeWithdrawal method is a little different because it has a data type of Money. This means that it will return an object of type Money when it is complete. The Money parameter is the amount of cash the person wishes to withdraw. The writeCheck method has two parameters. We can let Money be a class while Check# is a standard int data type. It is perfectly permissible to mix standard data types and classes as parameters to a method. This method also has a void data type and returns no value.

Methods can return any valid standard data type or an object for any class defined in a system. You might think of returning an object as analogous to returning an initialized structure. You essentially return a lot more information by returning an object than you do by returning a single data value. Of course, in returning the object you also get all the methods of the class as well as the attribute values. The returned object can be accessed and treated as you would any other object of the returned class type.

I have left the first two methods for last because they are peculiar to C++ and are not needed (at least in this form) by other object-oriented languages. The first method, which has the same name as the class, is called the constructor. It is what is called when a class is initialized. In this case, the three parameters passed to the constructor match the information needed for the class's three attributes. We will see how this initialization works when we look at the code. The second unusual method is ~Person. The tilde means that this method is the destructor for the Person class. It is called when the object is deleted. It makes sure all memory allocated by the constructor is freed when the object goes away. Making sure these two are in sync is very important in C++ development. If they are not, you end up with memory leaks—memory that is used and lost.

Our final section is testing dependencies. We assume you already know about the classes needed for attributes. In this section we focus on those classes that are external to this particular one. In this example, the Person class needs to work with the ATM class and the Account class to test its methods. These are the immediate classes, with which it interacts. The ATM and Account classes may be dependent on other classes. These other classes could be stubbed out if they haven't been developed yet, and you want to begin testing the functionality of the Person class.

Let's take a look at how we turn this class specification into code. We'll do this in two steps. First we will create the C++ class prototype—C++ requires this for every class. We will then show you how to implement one of the methods. The process is the same for all methods, and we only do one to serve as an example. Our purpose here is not to implement the full system but to show you the basic pieces, where they come from, and how they relate to one another.

The C++ class prototype for the Person class is shown in Figure 2.3. This is how you define a class in C++. Other languages have different requirements, but the basic information is the same. We begin with what looks like standard C include statements. We would include any of the standard header files and the header files for any classes we reference at this point. You can also include various define statements as you would in a C header. If you refer to an external class but do not include its header file, you will get an error.

The rest of the code is the formal definition of the Person class. It begins by stating that we are creating a class named Person. We would add other at this

EXAMPLE

41

```
#include <string.h>
#include "money.h"
#include "atm.h"

class Person
{
private:
            int PIN;
            String Accnt;
            Money Dollars;

    public:
            Person(const int pinum, const String &accntnum,
Money cash){
                    PIN = pinum;
                    Accnt(accntnum);
            }

            ~Person();

            void makeDeposit(Money cash, ATM machine,
String &transtype);

            Money makeWithdrawal(Money cash);

            void writeCheck(int checknum, Money cash);

    };
```

FIGURE 2.3. Class Person C++ Prototype

point if we were inheriting from another class. The body of the definition is divided into two sections: those things we want private to the class and those we will make public to external objects. As stated earlier by default we will make all our attributes private. You can see that the attributes listed in the private section are taken directly from the Data section in the class specification.

The attributes we declare to be private include both standard data types and classes. The PIN attribute is of the standard type int. You declare it as you would in any C program. The Accnt and Dollars attributes are classes and are declared in the same way. Nothing peculiar must be done to use classes as attributes. If we had private methods from section 5 of the class specification, we would put their prototypes here. Since we do not have any private methods, this section is complete.

The next section creates function prototypes for all of the public methods of the class. We could make attributes visible here as well, but that would thwart the encapsulation we want in object-oriented development. The methods shown here are the ones found in the Public section of the class specification. The first is the C++ class constructor for the Person class. The three parameters that are passed in are used to initialize the attributes. The first parameter is pinum, or the PIN number. It is declared to be of type int and to be a constant. This means that it will not change. It is passed in by value, which means a copy of pinum is passed in not pinum itself. The second parameter is accntnum, or the account number. It is of the class String and is also a constant. It is passed in by reference. This means that the actual object accntnum and not a copy is passed in. The final parameter is cash. It is of class Money and is passed in by value. Don't worry about all this talk of "by reference" and "by value" at this point. These are C++isms, and you don't need to understand them to appreciate how to turn a specification into code. I mention them only to account for all of the information that seems to be involved in stating what the parameters are for a function.

In the constructor, we see how these parameters are used. PIN is initialized in the manner you would expect for the int data type. The next two statements are equivalent ways of initializing an object. In the first we call the constructor for the Accnt attribute. In the next we use the = sign to accomplish the same thing. This is not always possible in C++ without some extra work. When you see these statements in code, you can assume that any necessary extra work has been done and these statements are equivalent. In this example, we have included the details of the constructor in the header file. This is not always done. If the constructor is complex, its implementation would be done in another file along with the implementation of the other methods.

The destructor is the next method. Since no memory is allocated by the constructor, no extra statements are needed by the destructor. It exists simply so that a Person object can be safely and correctly removed from the system.

The next three statements are the function prototypes for the other methods

EXAMPLE

43

the Person class needs. Their format is the ANSI C prototype format. Notice that its form closely matches that found in the class specification. This is intentional. When we developed the class specification, we knew we would implement the system in C++, and for this reason, we made the specification notation closely match C++. This minimizes the amount of work needed to translate the specification into C++. If we were developing in another language, we would change the specification notation to closely match it.

Let's look at makeDeposit first. Note that this is a prototype specification for the method. It shows specifically what the parameters are and what it returns. The details of the method's implementation are not shown in the function prototype. We will see those details later. MakeDeposit has three parameters, all of which are classes. None of the parameters are found in the Person class attributes. They are external to the class. You do not need to pass a class's attributes to its methods. They are directly accessible by name from within a method. The first two parameters are passed by value; the third is passed by reference.

The makeWithdrawal method is a simple prototype, which has a parameter of class Money and returns a Money object. The writeCheck prototype shows how we mix classes and standard data types as parameters. Both parameters are passed by value. Notice that classes are treated just as if they were a data type. This is true wherever classes are used in C++.

Let's next look at how to implement a method for a class in C++. We see how to implement the makeDeposit method in Figure 2.4. The first part looks very similar to our function prototype in the class definition. We see that the method has a return data type of void. We also see that the three parameters match those in the function prototype. The difference is that the method is now named Person::makeDeposit and not just makeDeposit. This is another peculiarity of C++. The :: characters are the selector mechanisms that tell us which class the makeDeposit method belongs to. Here it is the makeDeposit method of the Person class. Other classes could have a method of the same name that performed a different function. This lets us know which definition of makeDeposit to use if we call a Person object with it.

Once we get past the parameters, we see the actual implementation of the method. It is fair to ask at this point how we knew what steps to take in the method? The steps are shown in other documentation that we will get to at the end of our example. At this point, we simply see what C++ looks like when one object works with others to accomplish a given function.

```
    void Person::makeDeposit(
            Money cash,
            ATM machine,
            String &transtype){
        machine.enterCard(Accnt);
        machine.enterPIN(PIN);
        Account savings = machine.selectAccount(transtype);
        savings.deposit(cash);
    }
```

FIGURE 2.4. Person makeDeposit Method

The first statement shows something happening with the ATM machine object we passed in as a parameter. What the code tells us is that the machine object is being called with its enterCard method. The Accnt attribute of the Person class is being passed as a parameter to the machine object. To call an object's method you use the notation object.method. The . serves as a separator between the object and its method. Notice that we did not pass Accnt in to the method as a parameter. Since this is a Person method, the attributes are available to us by their name. We do not have to do anything special to access them. The methods we call for the ATM machine object would be noted in the class specification for the ATM class and prototyped in the ATM class C++ definition. This method returns no value.

The next statement is similar. We call the machine object with its enterPIN method, and we pass the Person class attribute PIN as a parameter. It also returns no value.

The third statement is a bit different from the other two. The code to the right of the = sign looks familiar. We call the machine object's selectAccount method. The parameter we pass is the transtype object that was passed as a parameter into the Person's makeDeposit method. The difference is that this method returns an object, which is of the Account class. We will use this to initialize a new object. We have named the new object savings, and it is also of the Account class. The = statement performs the initialization of the savings object. It is now accessible as any Account class object would be. We will use this object as the actual account into which we make our deposit. The final statement shows this happening. We call the savings object deposit method. We pass it the cash parameter the makeDeposit method received. When the savings

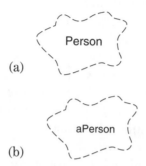

(a)

(b)

FIGURE 2.5. Class and Object Notation

deposit method returns, the deposit is made and our Person makeDeposit method is complete.

This type of process is repeated for each method defined in the class prototype. Header files usually have a .h ending. The C++ file where the methods are implemented usually has a .cc or a .cpp ending. All of the methods of a class are grouped together. It is best not to mix classes in these files. If you keep them separate, you will be able to make changes without needing to recompile multiple classes.

We've done a lot of work so far, but we have yet to see any object-oriented diagrams or notation to represent this work. Let's remedy that. Figure 2.5a shows the Booch notation for a class—a dashed cloud outline with the name of the class within the cloud. This example shows the representation of the Person class. I once heard someone ask Grady Booch why he didn't use boxes or rectangles for class notation. He replied that his drawing was a rectangle—he just didn't draw them very well. Figure 2.5b shows us the notation for an object, in this case, the object aPerson. Notice the difference in name. The class notation uses the name of the class, whereas the object notation uses the name of a specific object. It is drawn the same as the class notation except that the cloud outline is solid and not dashed.

CLASS RELATIONSHIPS

Classes are related to each other in various ways. These relationships govern the types of interaction that can happen between classes. The three main types of relationship are inheritance, contains, and uses. These are basic relationships.

Higher levels of system behavior are created by various combinations of these relationships. These three relationships provide all the interaction we need for our example. Let's examine each in more detail.

Inheritance is a major source of code reuse in object-oriented languages. It defines a relationship where one class shares the attributes and methods of another class. It defines an A as a "kind of" B hierarchy. For example, we might say that an automobile engine or a jet engine is each a "kind of" engine. We could say a rose or a daisy is each a "kind of" flower. For our example, we could say a savings account is a "kind of" bank account.

Using inheritance is simple. We begin with a base or ancestor class that provides fundamental capabilities. What these capabilities are depends upon what you want the class to do and share with others. When a new (child) class inherits from this base class, it is created to add new functionality missing in the ancestor. There are two ways in which it can provide this new functionality: the child class can override a method provided by the ancestor and make it do new things, or the child can also add new methods. This new functionality will not be available to the ancestor class. However, if the new class is inherited from by another new class, all of its methods will be available to the newest class. The value of inheritance is that you don't need to redo existing work. If the ancestor class provides most of the functionality you want, you only need to add new methods to the child class.

Let's consider what we know about our Account and Savings classes to see how inheritance works. (We won't create a class specification for these classes, but you might do so as an exercise. Use the information we discuss and see what you come up with before looking at the code fragment for the two classes.) We know that Accounts hold money. This money will become an attribute. You can make a deposit into an account. This process will become a method. An account will do you no good if you can't get your money back, so the withdrawal process becomes another method. This class will be a general type of bank account. It will provide the basic functionality that you would expect of all accounts.

We know several things about our Savings class. It should have all of the basic behavior of the Account class. To get this behavior, we will inherit it from the Account class. This means that we inherit the money data member and the deposit and withdrawal methods. The withdrawal process will not change. The Savings class will reuse the code from the Account class. We will expand this class in two ways. First we will create a method to calculate interest on the savings account. We will also add new functionality to the deposit method by making the account calculate interest every time a deposit is made. To do this, we will reuse the old code, but add a little more of our own.

In Figure 2.6 we see a C++ code fragment that has class prototypes for the Account and Savings classes. It also shows some detail on the deposit method for each and a small example to show how inheritance works. We begin with a class prototype of the Account class, which has one attribute of the Money class. Its name is Balance. Account has two methods: deposit and withdraw. The deposit method is declared to be virtual. This means that a child class can override it if necessary. We see in the deposit method definition for Account that money passed in as a parameter is added to Balance. Withdraw would subtract and return the desired amount if available. We will not provide the details here.

We next see the class prototype for the Savings class. Notice the declaration class Savings : public Account. The colon separates the name of the new class from the names of the classes from which it inherits. We have only put two methods in the class prototype. The calculateInterest method is new, and the deposit method is one we will change from the base class. We did not have to redeclare the existence of the attribute Balance or the method withdraw. These remain unchanged from the Account class.

Following the class prototype, we see the changes made to the deposit method for the Savings class. It has two steps. The first is to call the ancestor Account class's version of the deposit method. This puts the money into the Balance attribute. The next step calls the new calculateInterest method, which adds interest to the Balance. This is what will happen every time a Savings object is called with the deposit method. An Account object will only add the money to Balance when its deposit method is called. We see this in the final section of code.

In this last section we create a simple program to show the differences and similarities in the classes due to inheritance. We have created an object of the Account class named general and an object of the Savings class named nestegg. When we call the deposit method of both using the same amount of money as a parameter, we get different results. General simply adds the money to its Balance. Nestegg first calls the same code used by general to add the money to Balance. It then calls its own calculateInterest method to add interest to Balance. The end result is that the two classes have different amounts in their Balance attribute when the deposit method is complete.

We then call general and nestegg with the withdraw method. Their actions are identical. Inheritance lets nestegg use the withdraw method even though it

```
//Savings Inherits from Account

class Account
{
private:
            Money Balance;
public:
            virtual void deposit(Money Dollars);
            Money makeWithdrawal(Money Dollars);
};

void Account::deposit(Money Dollars){
            Balance = Balance + Dollars;
}

class Savings: public Account
{
private:

public:
            void calculate Interest();
};

void Savings::deposit(Money Dollars){
            Account::deposit(Dollars);
            calculateInterest();
}

main(){

Account general;
Savings nestegg;
.

.

general.deposit(132.75);
nestegg.deposit(132.75);
general.makeWithdrawl(50);
nestegg.makeWithdrawl(50);
nestegg.calculateInterest();
}
```

FIGURE 2.6. Savings Inherits from Account

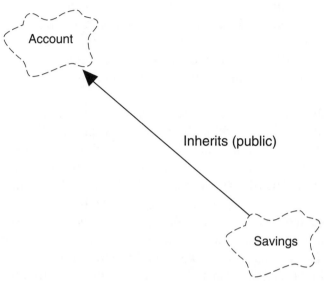

FIGURE 2.7. Inheritance Notation

is not found in the prototype for the Savings class. As long as it is defined in the base class, it can be used. We finish by calling the calculateInterest method of nestegg. This is valid because this method was defined for the Savings class. We could not call general with this method because it is not defined for the Account class and the Account class does not inherit it from anyone.

Figure 2.7 show the notation for inheritance. We have two classes, Account and Savings. The arrow pointing from Savings to Account says that the Savings class inherits from the Account class. The arrow always points to the base or ancestor class. When you see inheritance in a class diagram, you can infer what object-oriented languages might be used to implement the system. Smalltalk only supports single inheritance, and diagrams for Smalltalk will show a class inheriting from one and only one other class. C++ supports multiple inheritance. If you see multiple inheritance in a class diagram, you will not be able to implement that relationship in Smalltalk.

The contains relationship is important. This relationship says that one class contains another class as one of its attributes. For example, we could say a car contains wheels, a rose contains petals, a database contains records, or an account contains money. The contains relationship occurs when a class finds that the behavior of another class is essential to the functioning of itself. It is one way to add functionality to a class without inheritance or writing lots of new code. The containing class can provide an interface to the functionality of the contained class. This is often seen at a high systems level. You could have one class that is the equivalent of a subsystem where the classes contained within it provide the subsystem functionality. The high-level class provides the clean interface to the functionality. This happens on the small scale as well.

Let's think about what we know about our Account and Money classes and their relationship. Again, we will not create a class specification, but you can if you wish. We know that the Account class must be able to contain Money for a deposit to work. We also know that Money must be contained in an account to make a withdrawal. The Money class is the basis for all bank transactions. It may be handled differently by different types of accounts: a savings account will add interest, and a checking account will not. Money may also be handled differently by different automatic teller machines—some ATMs may charge for their use. The Money class may also need methods to manipulate itself. It needs to handle round-off errors appropriately. It also needs to ensure the accuracy of all calculations it is involved in. It may even need to handle currency from different countries.

We see an example of how the contains relationship works in Figure 2.8. Part of our Account prototype shows a Money object Balance as a private attribute. We have modified the deposit method to show how we let the Money object Balance worry about correctly adding a new amount to itself.

```
class Account
{
private:
            Money Balance;
public:
            virtual void deposit(Money Dollars);
            Money makeWithdrawal(Money Dollars);
};

void Account::deposit(Money Dollars){
            Balance.credit(Dollars);
}
```

FIGURE 2.8. Account Contains Money

Here we call the Balance object with its credit method. We pass the deposit amount to it as a parameter. In this way, the money object can handle round-off errors or conversion to other currency. We don't have to wonder if the correct thing will happen when we simply try to add it in at the Account level.

We see the notation for the contains relationship in Figure 2.9. We have two classes—Account and Money—connected by a double line. There is a solid circle on one end. The solid circle tells who contains whom. In this case, the Account class contains the Money class.

The final relationship we want to consider is the uses relationship. We can state that one class uses another (external to itself) to accomplish a particular function. For example, we could say a car uses the road, a carpenter uses a hammer, or a person uses an automatic teller machine. You might think that the contains relationship is a type of uses relationship, but we use this term exclusively to describe a relationship between one class and another external to itself. This is the main type of relationship you will see in class diagrams. It can be used to represent class interaction on many levels, for example for a one-on-one interaction between classes, or to characterize a higher level of interaction between several classes that will describe higher-level system behavior. We will see an example of this later in the book.

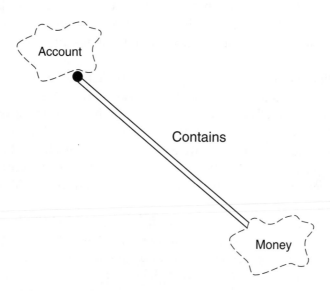

FIGURE 2.9. Notation for the Contains Relationship

```
// Person uses ATM:

void Person::makeDeposit(
            Money cash,
            ATM machine,
            String &transtype){
        machine.enterCard(Accnt);
        machine.enterPIN(PIN);
        Account savings = machine.selectAccount(transtype);
        savings.deposit(cash);
    }
```

FIGURE 2.10. Person Uses the ATM Class

Let's consider what we know of our Person and ATM classes and their interaction. If a person has an account at a bank, he must interact with the bank to do anything with that account. An ATM provides a mechanism for a person to interact with a bank. As we stated in the original problem statement, a person will use an ATM to conduct a transaction with one of his or her accounts. We also know that the ATM class interacts with a bank; specifically, it provides access to the accounts in the bank. The type of transactions it makes available to a person may be based on the type of account being accessed. An ATM may charge for use if an account is not held by the bank that owns the ATM.

We see how a Person uses an ATM in Figure 2.10. This is the implementation of the Person class makeDeposit method we saw earlier. We now want to look at it in a different light. The makeDeposit method provides the way a person interacts with an ATM. The ATM object machine is external to the person and is passed in as a parameter. Once we know about the machine object, we can call any of its public methods. In this case we use three: the enterCard, enterPIN, and selectAccount. These methods provide all of the ATM interaction we need.

We see a class diagram for this relationship in Figure 2.11. This diagram shows two classes—Person and ATM—connected by a double line with an open circle at one end. The open circle indicates who uses whom. In this case, the Person class uses the ATM class. Notice that this is very similar to the notation for the contains relationship. The difference is that the uses relationship has an open circle and the contains relationship has a filled circle.

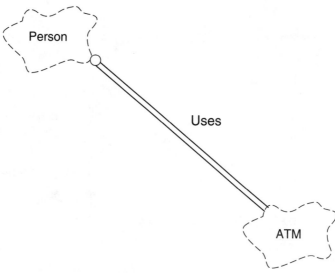

FIGURE 2.11. Notation for the Uses Relationship

EXAMPLE SYSTEM

You now know enough about classes, their relationships, and notation that we can create a meaningful system-level class diagram for our sample problem. We see such a diagram in Figure 2.12, which shows all three types of relationships discussed earlier: inheritance, contains, and uses. We also see the five classes we identified as we discussed the various aspects of the system.

Person: This class simulates the person interacting with an automatic teller machine.

ATM: This class simulates an automatic teller machine. It provides the mechanism for the Person to interact with his Savings account.

Money: This class simulates money and appropriately handles round-off issues in financial transactions. It also handles any other conversions that must be done.

Account: This is the base class that defines the basic behavior of all types of accounts. In our case it provides the base behavior for the Savings class

Savings: This class defines the specific behavior of a savings account.

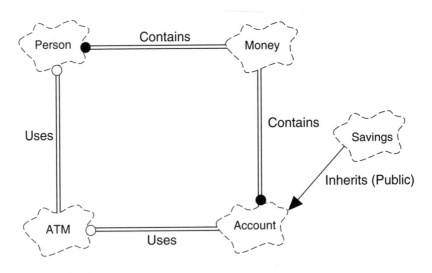

FIGURE 2.12. Class Diagram for the Banking Example

Let's look at how these classes fit together as a system. Figure 2.12 documents the relationships we discovered earlier. We first see the contains relationship between the Person and Money classes. This is the same relationship we saw in the class specification in Figure 2.2 and the Person class prototype in Figure 2.3. We next see the uses relationship between the Person and ATM classes. This relationship is part of the Person makeDeposit method documented in the Person class specification in Figure 2.2 and the implementation of the makeDeposit method in Figure 2.4. The ATM and Account classes have a uses relationship. Since we did not fully document this design, you won't find this relationship documented in the earlier figures. It is actually part of the ATM's selectAccount method. This method will return an object whose type is Account. There is a contains relationship between the Account and Money classes as shown in the Account class prototype in Figure 2.6 and in the implementation of the Account deposit method in Figure 2.8. Finally, we see the inheritance relationship between the Account and Savings classes. The corresponding code for this is seen in the Savings class prototype in Figure 2.6.

This diagram gives us a static view of our system: We see the basic relationships between our classes. The class specifications, class diagrams, and others yet to come also give us a static view. What is not yet clear in our design is how they work together. We need a dynamic view of the system to show how our

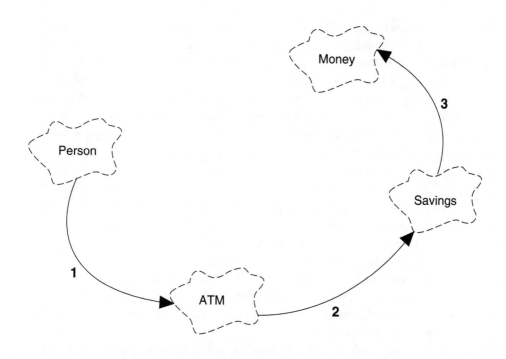

1. Person.makeDeposit(Money, ATM, AccntType)

   ATM.enterCard(Accnt#)

   ATM.enterPIN(PIN)

   ATM.selectAccount("SAVINGS")

      return Savings(Accnt#, "SAVINGS")

2. Savings.deposit(Money)

   calculateInterest()

3. Balance.credit(Money)

Arrows denote sequence of events

FIGURE 2.13. Event Flow Diagram and Language

design supports a requirement or action as well as to validate a sequence of events. We need something similar to a state diagram. Most methodologies support state diagrams, but they only show what is happening within a class. They do not provide a system-level dynamic view.

This is one area where I find most methodologies weak. My solution is to add to the standard methodologies by creating a dynamic system view. I call this view an Event Flow Diagram, an example of which is shown in Figure 2.13. There are two steps to creating the dynamic view. The first is to create a scenario or a statement of the action you want to document describing the events you want to follow in the system. This could come from your system requirements or from a description of user interaction. The second step is to create the diagram that documents how the system will carry out the scenario.

The diagram has two parts. The first is the event flow diagram itself, which shows the flow of events from one object to the next. It is used to illustrate what happens in a scenario. We use the Booch notation for objects and supplement that with numbered arrows that show the event flow in the system. This diagram is supplemented by an Event Flow Language (loosely based on C++), which is used to annotate the flow of events from one object to the next. The numbers on the statements match the numbers on the diagram arrows. The Event Flow Language serves much the same function as PDL in structured design. We use it to document the algorithmic steps needed to execute an action. Let's examine how this works.

Earlier it was stated that another diagram would show the steps necessary to put in the Person makeDeposit method from another diagram. Figure 2.13 is this diagram. As you look at it glance back at the implementation of the method in Figure 2.4. Now let's create a scenario by using the fundamental requirement in our problem statement.

> **Scenario:** A person will use an automatic teller machine to make a deposit to his savings account.

We see four classes in the diagram: Person, ATM, Savings and Money. These are required to document the scenario. The arrows show the direction in which events flow. The numbers tell the order in which they happen. We see that there are three sections of flow in the diagram. The first shows the steps in the Person–ATM uses relationship. They show specifically how the ATM object is used. The first step is to use the enterCard method. This is followed by the enterPIN and selectAccount methods. These are all the interactions needed with the ATM object. The last method call sets us up for the next flow.

When the person selects his account, the ATM object returns a Savings object. The person uses the savings object to make a deposit by calling its

```
#include <string.h>
#include <iostream.h>
#include "banking.h"

main()
{
        Money pocketchange(100);
        Money cash(137.46);
        Person paul(1234, "14326-12", pocketchange);
        ATM atmachine;

        paul.makeDeposit(cash, atmachine, "Savings");
        cout << "Transaction Complete\n";
}
```

FIGURE 2.14. The Main Banking Program

deposit method. This sets the stage for the final flow. After the person calls the Savings object's deposit method, it takes the Money it received as a parameter and adds it to the balance contained in the savings object. It also calculates interest on this new amount. At this point the money is deposited in the person's savings account and the Person makeDeposit method can end. The flows match the algorithms needed to implement these methods. Compare this diagram to the implementation of makeDeposit in Figure 2.4. The Event Flow Language provides the annotation necessary to implement the method.

We've seen many steps up to this point. We've seen how classes are documented and implemented and how to use different system diagrams to document the structure of a system and how the classes work together. All that is missing is the final piece. How do you actually create a stand-alone program that does this function? The answer can be found in Figure 2.14, which is the main C++ application program to do the deposit. It starts out with all of the include statements one would expect for this program. The requirements for using includes is exactly the same as in standard C development.

Next we see our main() section. This is the body of the program. We begin by initializing the object we need to do the deposit. We have two Money objects: pocketchange and cash. Pocketchange is used in initializing the person object paul. Cash is the amount to be deposited. After initializing the Person paul, we initialize an ATM object atmachine with which he can interact. We are then ready to make the deposit. All we do is call paul with his makeDeposit method. When this method is done, the program tells us the transaction is complete and the program ends. That's all there is to it.

The application program looks awfully simple for all the work that has to go on. The complex activities are hidden below this level. How do you know that this will work? How do you know a deposit is actually made to a savings account? It is documented in our Event Flow Diagram and Event Flow Language. Notice that we did not initialize a savings object at the top level. We see the ATM object takes care of this for us in its selectAccount method. This is also documented in the Event Flow diagram.

In this chapter, we have seen the basic process for creating an object-oriented system. You begin with a problem statement. You work with this to develop a class specification for all of the classes in the system. Next, you document the relationships of these classes in a class diagram. This is followed by creating event flow diagrams, which provide the details for implementing each class's methods. You begin the coding process by creating a class prototype for each class. To finish the development, you implement the methods of each class according to the event flow diagrams. Finally, you write the highest level of your application program.

It is clear how the pieces of the process relate to one another. The problem statement is converted into class specifications and is the basis for the scenarios that will describe the events in the system. The class specifications provide the basis for the class diagrams, which provide a static view of the system. The problem statement and class diagrams are combined to produce the event flow diagrams that document the dynamic view of the system. Finally, the class specifications provide the information necessary to develop class prototypes, and the event flow diagrams provide the information necessary to implement their methods. This is a very high-level overview. In the following chapters, we will look at several methodologies in depth and see how they fit into this framework for object-oriented development.

PART II
Picking a Methodology

CHAPTER 3

Choices in Methodology: Booch

In the last chapter we looked at the major development steps for creating an object-oriented system. In our example we developed a framework for the process of object-oriented development. We've seen briefly how you analyze a system with object-oriented concepts as well as how you would annotate analysis and design decisions. In our small system were examples of classes we could track. It also provided some suggestion of other items we might want to trace.

We'll use our earlier example as a framework for our examination of different object-oriented methodologies. You will see many similarities between them. Using the same example in the study of each methodology will provide continuity and a baseline for comparison. As we examine each methodology, you may see areas where you want to make changes or additions to suit your particular situation. This is perfectly acceptable. I encourage you to select a methodology that best suits your needs and then make whatever adaptations you need.

As we examine methodologies in the next several chapters, it is important to distinguish methodologies from the implementation of a system. This is not always easy to do. Those new to object-oriented technology often confuse object-oriented analysis and design with the details of a specific object-oriented language. Many books focus on methodology within the context of a single language and the reader ends up with a view of a methodology that is narrowed by the focus of a particular language. They miss much of the rich expressiveness and options available for use with other object-oriented languages.

At the analysis level, a methodology must be language independent. It is far too early to make implementation decisions during the analysis phase. The top level of an object-oriented design should also be language independent. You need to take a general approach as long as possible. Still, a methodology must be able to support the implementation decisions you make. This is one area where we will see the greatest differences between methodologies. If the methodology does not support the implementation detail you need, you will have to find a substitute or create your own.

You should delay implementation issues as long as possible. Some methodologies ignore them altogether. Solidify the higher levels of the design first. There are several ways you can accomplish this. Concentrate on modeling the problem—this focuses your attention at a higher level. Discover class and object interactions before deciding on the details of an interaction. Later in the book, we will discuss how to abstract these interactions into additional classes, which is one of the more powerful techniques in object-oriented systems design. This said, feel free to note implementation issues whenever they occur.

WHY A NEW NOTATION

Before we start our examination of the different methodologies, we ought to ask why we need new notations. The most important reason is that the old ones are inadequate for expressing the new ideas found in object-oriented methodology. Traditional SA/SD concepts don't work, and the notation that supports them doesn't provide the support needed for object-oriented concepts. If you can't express an idea, you can't communicate it. That leads us to the next reason for a new notation. A standard notation makes it possible for one person to communicate a design to another.

Standard notations are found in electrical and mechanical engineering. It is highly unlikely that we would see the progress that has occurred in these fields if they did not have a standard notation for conveying information. Schematics, with their standard symbols, let electrical engineers clearly communicate their designs to others. Standard dimensional and true position notation work the same way for mechanical engineers. Because these notations are standard, they have an additional advantage: they provide the basis for automated design systems.

Most electrical design systems, for example, have tools for automatically generating bills of materials, performing design testing and validation, and generating information needed in the production process. Once the engineer has laid out a schematic, he or she can run tests on the design that characterize its performance. The engineer can iteratively make changes until the design has the desired characteristics. At that point, he or she can automatically generate the net list and bill of materials needed for designing a circuit board. If changes are made to the design at the circuit board level, they can automatically be back-annotated into the schematic. This assures consistency between the original design and final product.

With a robust notation as a foundation, the same should be possible for software tools. You should be able to eliminate much of the tedium associated with validating a design and checking for correctness. A good set of tools should also provide a way to update a design based on changes at the implementation level. None of the tools that are currently available can do all this for the software engineer. Fortunately, that is changing. More sophisticated development tools are becoming available to support object-oriented development. A good notation will support their development.

There are two quotations worth considering as you learn a new notation. The philosopher Alfred Whitehead said in his 1911 book *An Introduction to Mathematics* "By relieving the brain of all unnecessary work, a good notation sets it free to concentrate on more advanced problems, and in effect increases . . . mental power." Grady Booch, in his book *Object Oriented Design with Applications* said that "designing is not the act of drawing a diagram; a diagram simply captures a design." To illustrate these ideas we need only look at electrical schematic notation. The symbols free the engineer from trying to find ways to express an idea and let him or her concentrate on the idea itself. Likewise, the schematic is not what the engineer has created, which is a design. The schematic and its notation simply capture that design in a form that can be understood by others. The same thing is true for a good notation in object oriented methodology.

Our simple example from the last chapter showed us a little of the process used to create an object-oriented system. We analyzed our problem using object-oriented concepts. We then created diagrams that annotated our analysis and design decisions. These diagrams showed us items we wanted to track during the development process. The class specifications captured the details of each class we needed to develop. The class diagram identified the relationships between the different classes. We also saw items outside the standard methodologies we might want to track. We added a requirements section to the class specification so we could verify that our design addresses all the requirements we have agreed to meet. We also added a testing section to understand what had to be in place for a class to be thoroughly tested and to help us develop a schedule that would ensure this to be the case.

Our example provides a context for comparing the different object oriented methodologies. We will show the example in the notation of each methodology. This will help us understand the similarities and differences between them. This comparison can help you determine if a particular methodology meets your needs. It will also be easier to see where you might want to make additions or changes. These notations have been used successfully in large and small projects. In that sense they are complete. However, sometimes your requirements or needs will not be addressed by a methodology. At that point you will need to supplement the methodology to fulfill your desideratum. This is not unusual. Many adapt an existing methodology to fit their particular situation.

THE BOOCH METHODOLOGY

The full details of Grady Booch's methodology are found in his book *Object Oriented Design with Applications*.[1] (This is the version used in the examples throughout the present book. The second edition of Booch's book, retitled *Object Oriented Analysis and Design with Applications*,[2] adds additional notation and concepts, particularly from James Rumbaugh's work. Fundamentally, the methodology remains the same and the additional notation adds expressiveness.) Our examination of his methodology will give us the first real look at the process of developing an object-oriented system. We will examine, at a high level, the basic steps of analysis and design. Later in the book we will explore the development of a real system and examine these steps in even more detail. In our examination of Booch's methodology, we show analysis as the first step in modeling the problem. The result of the analysis will be a description of the problem. In Booch's approach, we will see that design is a refinement of the work done in analysis. At this stage, you create the mechanisms that define the system's behavior.

These steps are really an iterative process. They are not accomplished in a lock-step approach. There is no mandated sequence of steps. You can revisit previous steps as needed or dip down into those that usually occur later. The movement from analysis to design is not accomplished at a single point—it is a process of refinement. You may start with some high-level analysis, move on to a designing part of the system, and then return for more analysis. Moving from one stage of the process to another is a matter of changing emphasis. In the earlier stages of analysis, you may dip into the design phase but not stay there for long. You know you are leaving the analysis stage when your major classes and key abstractions start to stabilize. You concentrate more on the details of each class and revisit the analysis stage only for brief periods. How do you know where you are in the design cycle or even know when you are done? We will look at several strategies for managing this process and understanding where you are in the cycle later in the book.

One thing is clear for all of the methodologies. There is no cookbook approach to designing object-oriented systems. All of the methodologies require thinking designers. For this reason, it is important to understand the why of a step as well as the what. If you want to adapt a step to your needs, you need to do so based on the knowledge of why something is being done. You don't want to simply mimic something someone else has done without understanding why they made the decisions they did.

The first step in Booch's methodology is to identify the classes and objects in the problem domain. These become the vocabulary for discussing the problem. They also provide the beginnings of a definition of the problem. These classes and objects are candidates for further analysis. The product of this stage is a list of classes that would be found in the system. You will find that this list changes quite a bit initially through iteration and discussion of the problem. We show such a list for our banking simulation example in Figure 3.1.

The second step is a refinement of the first. Here we identify the key abstractions and mechanisms in the system. A key abstraction is a class or object discovered in the first step. They define the boundaries of the problem. There are two ways to uncover them. The first is by discovery. You can talk to a domain expert and learn what is important. You can look at similar systems and see what they thought was fundamental. You can also do your own analysis of the

- Person
- ATM
- Account
- Savings
- Money

FIGURE 3.1. Candidate Class List

problem domain. The second way to uncover key abstractions is by invention. Look for what is missing in the analysis. This is difficult if you are unfamiliar with the problem, but as your expertise grows it is easier to see what is missing. At this point you can also see if any of your abstractions match ones that already exist. Reuse is a fundamental part of developing abstractions. We capture our key abstractions in our class diagrams. At this point we have not given much thought to the relationships between the classes. We can still capture the classes in the diagrams and add the details of the relationships later.

Within our example, we could think of a transaction as a key abstraction. A transaction might be the fundamental activity tracked by a bank. This abstraction can be broken down further. People think in terms of a deposit, withdrawal, or funds transfer. These are specific types of transactions. In our earlier diagrams, we did not include transaction as one of our classes, but if we fill out the design further, it and its components would be natural classes to add to the system. When we consider a transaction as a key abstraction, we are not considering it as a transforming process as would be found in a structured analysis. Instead, we are considering it an object in its own right that can be counted and changed.

The process of discovering or creating mechanisms is the process of adding behavior to our key abstractions. Mechanisms are the structure and interactions between classes that provide system behavior. Booch calls mechanisms "the soul of the design." He says that determining what mechanisms will exist in a system is a strategic decision in that it defines what behavior the system will have. There are two places where we can capture this information. The first is the class diagram, where we see the uses and contains relationships that define class interactions. The second place is in a new type of diagram—an object diagram. It is used to capture the details of object interaction. The details of a mechanism are refined in the design phase, but the decision that they should exist happens during the analysis phase.

In our banking example, the interaction of the Person, ATM, and Account classes is a key mechanism. This interaction lies at the heart of our original problem statement. If this mechanism did not exist, we would be unable to satisfy our original task. Another key mechanism is the interaction of the Account and Money classes. Without this interaction, it would be impossible to make deposits or withdrawals.

The next step in the Booch methodology is to identify the semantics of the classes and objects you uncovered earlier. The basic question you ask about each of these is, why does it exist? In answering this question, you establish the meaning of each class. In our example, we can ask why the ATM class exists. It exists to provide a way for a person to interact with his or her account. The account class exists as a repository of funds owned by the person and held by the bank. It also serves to track the status of those funds as a result of a person's interactions with the bank. The person class is the fundamental class in our example. The others exist because a person wishes to interact with the bank that holds his or her funds.

We next ask a question that is the flip side of understanding a class's meaning. What can be done with a class? Furthermore, we want to identify who can do what to a class. This is where you take a hard look at the interface to each class. As you identify the methods each class makes visible to others, you can begin to fill out the class template or specification. We saw this information captured in our class specification for the Person class. Such a specification is shown in Figure 3.2. The Booch methodology actually uses a template that is slightly different. We will see more of it later in the chapter.

Figuring out the interfaces for each class and determining who does what to whom is an iterative process. In the earliest stages of design, this is where you will see most of the changes. You will discover that classes come and go as capability gets moved around. One of the things that quickly becomes apparent is the amorphous nature of a design in its early stages. The design changes daily. It seems as if nothing remains fixed. You will have lots of debate at this point in the design process. There is always more than one way to do something and it usually takes several iterations to get the best result. Don't worry, this process can be tracked and controlled. Later in the book you will see how this is done in the context of a large system. Because of the fluid nature of the early design, you will find yourself reiterating to earlier steps. You will revisit earlier steps as classes change and others appear or disappear. When new classes are created, you need to understand how they fit in with your key abstractions and mechanisms. New classes may become new key abstractions, or they may supplement existing ones as part of a mechanism. You will also identify new objects in your problem domain that weren't obvious earlier.

The next step is to identify the relationships between the different classes. This is where you identify the Uses, Contains, and Inheritance relationships. The Contains relationship shows what class contains another to implement a capability identified earlier. The capabilities of the contained class become a fundamental part of the class that does the containing. The Uses relationship

Class Specification

   Class Person

   1. Purpose

This class will simulate a person interacting with an automatic teller machine in a banking simulation.

   2. Inheritance

None

   3. Requirement Reference

None

   4. Data

int PIN	// Personal Identification Number for account transactions
String Accnt	// The account number
Money Dollars	// The money used in the banking transaction

   5. Methods

   Public

// Constructor for the Person class

Person(PIN, Accnt, Dollars)

//Destructor for the Person class

~Person()

//The method for making a deposit to an accountvoid

  makeDeposit(Money, ATM, AccntType)

//The method for making a withdrawal from an account

  Money makeWithdrawal(Money)

//The method for writing a check on an account

  void writeCheck(Check#, Money)

   Private

None

   6. Testing Dependencies

ATM, Account

FIGURE 3.2. Person Class Specification

shows the interactions necessary to create a higher-level behavior. These interactions are the heart of the system, and it is this set of interactions that is the most difficult to pin down. The Inheritance relationship recognizes commonality in capability among classes, and it provides a way to effectively organize this commonality.

This step is an extension of the previous one. You begin by looking for patterns and mechanisms. As you identify and refine these relationships, you will see the system structure change. The earliest structures will be incomplete, but continual refinement leads to stability. Refinement happens as you iterate through all the steps. The cycle of iteration is not only between different steps such as analysis and design, it occurs at different levels of detail. Your initial work begins at a high level. You then dip down into the design of the system for a particular part. Rather than complete the entire detailed design at that point, you return to a higher level to work on another portion of the system. With each iteration, you add additional detail to the system until it is all captured.

Relationships are captured in class and object diagrams. We saw a class diagram in our discussion of the banking example. We will see the object diagram shortly. The purpose of these diagrams is to capture the details of the mechanisms and interactions that define the system. Everything in an object oriented system happens through these relationships. For this reason, these diagrams are often the most important in understanding how a system works.

The final step is to implement the classes and objects. At this point you make your final implementation decisions. You will define the details of your class's interfaces. Once this is done, if you are working in C++ you can create the class prototype in the class header file. You also need to design the algorithms needed to implement each method in each class. It is helpful at this point to group the classes together in ways that make sense for implementation. For example, if you have a set of classes that are related by inheritance, you might want to group them together in a common module. Module diagrams capture this view of the system.

As you review the implementation details for each class, you have the opportunity to revisit earlier steps. For example, with a deeper understanding of the system, you might find that requirements need to be clarified or changed. This may mean you iterate to the earliest steps. You may also find additional opportunities for code reuse through inheritance. You may want to reorganize classes you've designed, or you might find similarities to classes in existing libraries. Either one will help you maximize your effort by minimizing the amount of

```
#include <string.h>
#include "money.h"
#include "atm.h"


class Person
{
private:
            int PIN;
            String Accnt;
            Money Dollars;


public:
            Person(const int pinum, const String &accntnum,
      Money cash){
                  PIN = pinum;
                  Accnt(accntnum);
            }

            ~Person();

            void   makeDeposit(Money   cash,   ATM   machine,   String
&transtype);

            Money makeWithdrawal(Money cash);

            void writeCheck(int checknum, Money cash);

};
```

FIGURE 3.3. Person C++ Class Prototype

code you need to write. As you test your design against your requirements, you may find gaps. This is often the case for large projects. In this case you will iterate to earlier steps to fill in the missing pieces.

In our banking simulation, we can see the results of our decisions about implementation details in the class prototype for the Person class and the implementation of the makeDeposit method for the Person class. The class pro-

```
void Person::makeDeposit(
        Money cash,
        ATM machine,
        String &transtype){
    machine.enterCard(Accnt);
    machine.enterPIN(PIN);
    Account savings = machine.selectAccount(transtype);
    savings.deposit(cash);
}
```

FIGURE 3.4. Person makeDeposit Method

totype is shown in Figure 3.3, and the implementation of the makeDeposit method is shown in Figure 3.4.

DIAGRAMS

Our next step is to look at the diagrams we created and see how they relate to the steps of the analysis and design process. It is important to see how what we learn about a design is captured. Each diagram provides a useful view of the system, but no single diagram can tell us all we want to know about a system. It is the set of diagrams that provides the complete view of the system. Each shows a portion by itself. Together, we can see the system as a whole.

The Class Diagram

The first diagram we will look at, the class diagram, is one of the most important. It gives us a static view of a system. If we think of our system as a building, this diagram shows the skeleton or structure of the building. When you look at a class diagram, you see the logical structure of the system. The notation shows the existence of classes and their basic relationships. Figure 3.5 shows the class diagram for the banking example.

In the class diagram, we see three aspects of a system's class structure: classes, the relationships between those classes and (where appropriate) class utilities. The cloud shapes represent the system's classes. There is one for each class. In this illustration, we see the Person, ATM, Account, Savings, and

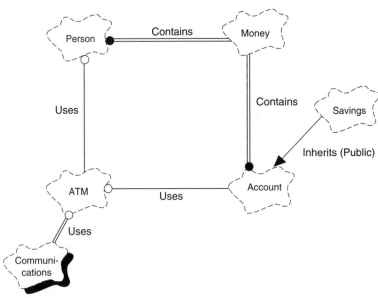

FIGURE 3.5. The Banking System

Money classes. The diagram also shows the three basic relationships that classes can have. The line with the open circle is the Uses relationship. We see that the Person class uses the ATM class. A line with a filled circle represents the Contains relationship. We see the Account class contains the Money class. The Inheritance relationship is noted by the arrow pointing from the child class to the ancestor class. In this diagram we see that the Savings class inherits its basic capabilities from the Account class.

A new item in the diagram is the class utility. A class utility may be a set of stand-alone subroutines or existing legacy software. Its notation is the same as that for a class, but part of the border is shaded. This is always a uses relationship. For this system, we can envision the ATM class using some existing communications software package. We show this relationship between our object-based system and the existing communications software as a uses relationship between the ATM class and the Communications class utility.

Closely related to the class diagram is the class category diagram shown in Figure 3.6. If you think of a class diagram as a detailed electrical schematic, the class category diagram is a high-level system block diagram. Each block represents a more detailed class diagram. To illustrate this, we step back from the example we specified and look at the problem from a higher level. We could imagine all of the classes needed to implement the ATM transaction system grouped into one category, and a central banking system in another. We might

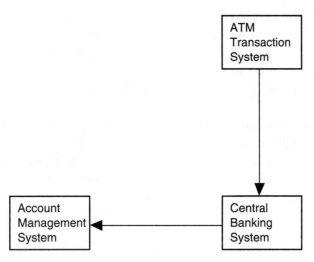

FIGURE 3.6. Class Category Diagram

then put an account management system in a third category. The arrows show categories interface. Notice that the ATM system does not talk directly to the account management system. All interaction is filtered through the central banking system.

Since his book was published, Booch has added to his notation. Most of these adornments were added to annotate specific design decisions in a particular language. Most of them support design decisions in C++. It is helpful to have them if you need them, but obviously they do not apply to all object-oriented languages. This does not mean the methodology is becoming appropriate only for work in C++. It's just that it now has support for decisions you make in the language but had no way to annotate previously.

There is one important change in relationships at the class diagram level. Booch now calls the contains relationship a "has" relationship. A set of adornments is available for this relationship. At the end of the line next to the class contained within the other, you can have a small solid or filled rectangle. The solid rectangle means one class has the other by value. This is called containment. An open rectangle means one class has the other by reference. This is an indirect relationship.

There are new adornments for classes as well. You may want to show the public methods or attributes of a class in a diagram. This makes it easier to understand what a class does without searching for its template. If you list these things, the cloud becomes known as a compartment. Each item noted in the compartment is a separate method or attribute. This is very similar to the notations used by Rumbaugh and Coad (see Chapters 4 and 7). If you have an abstract class (a class used only for inheritance purposes) you can add an inverted triangle with the letter A in it. This makes it easier to identify your base classes.

The relationships can be adorned by annotating them as public, protected, or private. This follows what C++ allows. Furthermore, you can show the relationships between classes as being friend (a C++-specific notation), virtual, or static. Virtual is used to show sharing with a multiply defined superclass. Static is used to indicate the difference between class and instance variables. These are annotated by using an inverted triangle with an F, V, or S.

THE CLASS TEMPLATE

Our class diagram shows the relationship between system classes but tells us nothing about their structure. This information is captured in a class template like that shown in Figure 3.7. Here we see a template for the Person class. The details of each class are captured in the template. In the template, we capture the semantics of our classes. Notice that it is a bit different from the class specification we introduced in the last chapter. Let's see how this one differs.

The first item in the template is the Name of the class—no surprise here. The next section is Documentation: you put your description of the class and its purpose in this section. The next section is Visibility: the options are exported, private, or imported. These refer to the visibility of the class from within its class category. Here you determine if other class categories will be able to see this class. The next item is Cardinality: the options are *0, 1,* and *n*. This tells us how many instances of this class we will have in the system. The next section is Hierarchy: here you note the classes and metaclasses that are inherited from. The Parameters section is next. This is the list of allowable parameters and their types that would be used in constructing an instance of the class.

The next three sections are the heart of information about the class. Here we define the internal structure of the class and what it can do. The three sections Uses, Fields and Operations can be repeated as necessary to capture those items that are public, private, or protected. The Uses section captures superclass and metaclass information. Fields lists the attributes of the class. Operations captures the methods of the class. As much or as little information as desired can be captured about each of these items.

The next section is Finite State Machine. This section refers to another type of diagram we will see shortly. It's enough to note that this section points us to another view of the system.

Class name:
> Person

Documentation:

This class will simulate a person interacting with an automatic teller machine in a banking simulation.

Visibility: Exported

Cardinality: 1

Hierarchy:
> Superclasses: none

Generic parameters: int PIN, String Accnt, Money Dollars Uses for Interface:
> ATM

Uses for Implementation:
> Money

Public Interface:
> Operations: Person
> ~Person
> makeDeposit
> makeWithdrawal
> writeCheck

Private Interface:
> Fields: PIN

int - Personal Identification Number for account transactions.
> Accnt
> > String - The account number.
> Dollars

Money - The money used in a banking transaction.

State machine: No

Concurrency: Sequential

Persistence: Transitory

FIGURE 3.7. Booch Class Template for Person

Concurrency is the next section. The options here are sequential, blocking, and active. The next section, if needed, is Space. In this section you can note any memory requirements the class has. The final section is Persistence: the options are persistent and transitory. This section tells us if an instance of the class will be able to exist beyond the running of the system.

The Booch notation supports many types of templates. These are generally used to capture the nitty gritty details of the system. For example, a class utility can have its own template. As you might expect, it is very similar to a class template. In fact it is a subset. It uses only the Name, Documentation, Visibility, Parameters, Uses, Fields, and Operations sections.

These templates capture quite a bit of information about a class, but more may still be needed. This is particularly true for the methods captured in the Operations section. The functions performed by a method may be quite complex, and it is important to clearly define the inputs as well as the outputs of a method. To support this, the Booch notation has Operation templates. These capture all of the expected items and may be associated with additional diagrams that capture the interaction of objects.

STATE TRANSITION DIAGRAMS

State Transition diagrams give us our first dynamic view of the system. They show what is happening within a class. The diagram shows us the different states a class can be in. It annotates the events that cause transitions from one state to the next. We can also see what actions a class will take as a result of a transition. These diagrams do not show us interactions between classes. That dynamic view is shown in timing diagrams, and we will get to them shortly. Previously, we noted that a class template may refer to a state diagram, which provides a dynamic view of the information a template captures statically. The actions shown in a state diagram may point to object diagrams. These diagrams detail the interaction between classes.

Let's look at the notation for the state diagrams. These diagrams use the Mealy model—they associate every state transition with an action. An example of this type of diagram is found in Figure 3.8. Each state in the diagram is noted by a circle and the name of the state. The name of the state matches the event that caused the transition. Event names must be unique within a diagram. A diagram can show two special states: a start state is a circle with an unfilled double line around it, and a terminal state has a filled double line. The

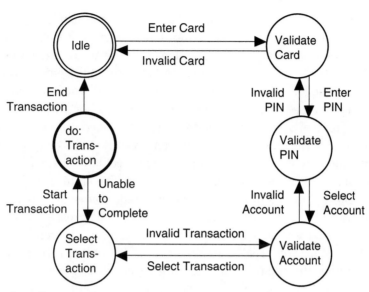

FIGURE 3.8. State Transition Diagram

labeled arrows show the actions in the diagram. The labels are the actions and the arrows are the transitions. Together, they tell the what and why of transitions. Each diagram may have an associated template, which can have three parts. The documentation section is for any explanatory text. There is an Events section where you list the events in the diagram. There is also an Action section where you describe what the actions are. This description can be in PDL or it can point to an object diagram that will provide more clarification.

Once again we use our banking example to illustrate how the diagrams work. Here we see the state transition diagram for the ATM class. The ATM has an Idle start state. This is where it waits for a person to begin a transaction. When a person begins a transaction, he starts by entering his card. This is noted by the Enter Card action. The arrow shows that when a person enters his card, the ATM moves to the Validate Card state. Note that the ATM can return to the Idle state if the card proves to be invalid. This is shown by the Invalid Card action. As we explain what is happening within the diagram, we see the need to refer to other classes. In the next section we will map these actions to an object diagram. This will provide another view showing which objects in a system make these actions occur.

There are two additional states in the validation process: Validate PIN and Validate Account. For each of these, success means you move to the next state;

failure means you return to the previous state. This is not mandatory in state diagrams, it simply reflects our own design of how we think the ATM class should behave. The actions that cause the transitions to these states are Enter PIN and Select Account. If the PIN and account are valid, the ATM object will move to the Select Transaction state. The person selects a transaction, and the ATM moves to a state where it tries to complete the transaction. If it is unable to do so, it returns to the Select Transaction state. If it successfully completes the transaction, it ends the transaction process and returns to its original Idle state.

Depending on how you look at it, the Idle state could be a starting state or a terminal state. Many state diagrams have neither. The state an object starts in depends on the conditions in which it was created. You could create an object and have it wait quietly in the background, or you could create the same object and immediately have it do some work. The starting state depends on why and where in the system you created it. When the ATM object returns to the Idle state, this signifies the end of a person's interaction with it. It waits in this state until another transaction begins.

Since Booch's book was published, there have been two additions to state diagrams. The first is that state diagrams may be nested within others. This makes diagrams much simpler to read. The second is the addition of connectors. It is difficult to draw complex diagrams without crossing transitions. A labeled rectangle serves as a connector. You have a transition go into the connector, then on another page, with a similarly labeled connector, you pick up the transition where you have more room to draw it. This is the equivalent of an off-page connector in an electrical schematic.

OBJECT DIAGRAMS

Object diagrams show what objects will exist when a system runs. It is a snapshot of the system frozen in time. You could even think of it as a detailed version of a class diagram for a specific moment in time. Remember that a class diagram only shows that there is a relationship between classes. The object diagram shows the details of that relationship. In this way, object diagrams reflect the logical design of the system. A single diagram may represent all or part of a system's object structure. The diagrams are not just a random collection of objects. Usually, they focus on particular mechanisms. They show the details of the interactions that make up a mechanism. Object diagrams are one of the best ways to annotate how a mechanism works.

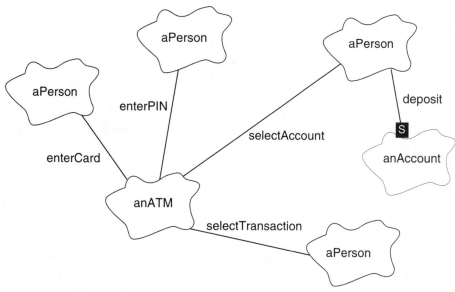

FIGURE 3.9. Object Diagram

Let's take a look at the notation. Figure 3.9 provides an example. Notice the similarity to the class diagram. Again we see the cloud shapes, only this time they are solid, not dashed. The solid shape means that they are individual objects, not classes. The notation for relationships is a simple labeled line. If the line is solid, it means the relationship is inside the system. If the line is gray, it is a relationship with something outside the system. The label is the name of the message between the two objects. A list of messages may also be used. Often, the tools supporting the notation do not support multiple messages per line. The compromise is to show the same objects many times—once for each message. Another allowed twist is that objects may be nested inside other objects. Again, most of the available tools do not support this part of the notation.

The diagrams can also show object visibility, or how one object knows about the other. You do not always need to show visibility. This notation is available for clarification and supports three ways an object can be visible to another. In the first case, objects may be in the same lexical scope, that is, they were created at the same level in the code being executed. An object can become visible to another if it is passed in as a parameter. This is one of the main ways an object learns about others. Finally, an object may be visible because it is a field (attribute) of another object. This is the contains relationship we have already discussed. The notation for visibility is the letter S, P, or F in a small square. The square may be a solid black or unfilled. If the square is filled, an object has unique access to the other object. An unfilled square indicates a structural sharing.

New adornments since the book was published are a blank rectangle for an unspecified scope, one with a G for global scope, and one with an L for local scope. Global means the object is in the enclosing lexical scope (the immediate universe that encloses an object). Local means it is local to a method.

How objects pass messages to one another can be complicated. Accordingly, the Booch notation supports ways of showing how the messages get back and forth (message synchronization). Five kinds of interaction are supported by the notation: simple, synchronous, balking, time-out, and asynchronous. Each of these types may be annotated with a list of message names. These different types of message passing support both single and multiple threads of control.

Objects may have their own templates. The items in an object template include name, documentation, class, and persistence. In later work, Booch added qualification to this list. Qualification indicates if the object represents the class, subclasses, or only an instance of a class. There are also templates for the messages. The items in these templates are operation (name), documentation (now called responsibilities), frequency, and synchronization. Synchronization matches the five choices listed earlier. The choice in frequency is aperiodic or periodic, indicating how often the message is invoked.

Let's take a closer look at our banking example. Earlier we stated that a state diagram could be related to an object diagram to give more information about what was happening in a system. This example provides some additional details for the state diagram shown in Figure 3.8. In the object diagram, we see the actions from the state diagram. These include enterCard, enterPin, select-Account, and selectTransaction. Notice that our startTransaction action has changed—it is now deposit. In the diagram, there is the object anATM, the object anAccount, and several instances of the object aPerson. For aPerson, these are not really different objects with the same name. The common name means that they are really only one object. Our diagram shows only one aPerson object, but it is shown in several places. This is a limitation of the design tool. I mention it here to show the difference between the ideal defined in the book and the real world of the tools you use. Also note that the deposit message has an adornment that says anAccount is in the same lexical scope as aPerson. This is not really true. The object anAccount is local within the deposit method. Unfortunately, the original Booch notation and tools did not support showing local scope.

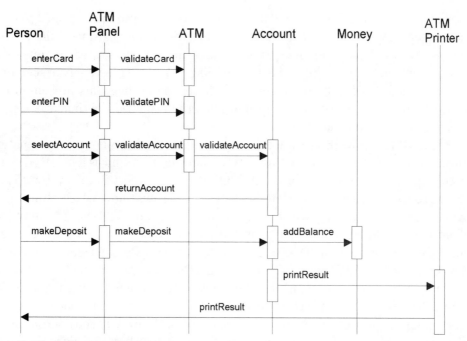

FIGURE 3.10. Interaction Diagram

TIMING DIAGRAMS

Timing diagrams answer the question, How does information flow through the system? Our previous diagrams gave us a static view of the system. State diagrams showed what happened within a class, but not in the system itself. Timing diagrams give us a dynamic view of a system in two ways: they show us the behavior of mechanisms, and they give us an ordering of events in the system. This is very valuable. When you look at a class diagram, you get a good sense of how the system is structured, but you can't tell where the action starts or stops. Timing diagrams break the system into bite-sized chunks and let us view dynamic interactions in a meaningful way.

Originally, there were three ways to create timing diagrams in the Booch notation. Which one to use depended on your personal tastes. The first approach was to number each message in the object diagrams. This worked for the simple cases, but it was difficult to show conditional flow in this manner. The second approach was to add PDL to the object diagrams. PDL lets you describe in more detail what is happening. Since PDL is a language of sorts, it can easily annotate conditional flow. This was the approach taken by most developers. The third approach had its roots in electronic hardware timing diagrams. If you have ever seen timing diagrams for integrated circuits, you would immediately recognize this type of diagram. If you have never seen one, you may find it difficult to understand. These timing diagrams presented the dynamic view of the system as a graph. The graph showed the time ordering of messages passed among objects.

Figure 3.10 shows Booch's latest representation of the flow of information through a system. It is called an interaction diagram and is borrowed from Jacobson's methodology. Each vertical line shows an object in the system. Time flows from top to bottom and left to right. The arrows show which object calls which other object using which method. It is a dynamic version of the object diagrams. In this case, we've elaborated on the object diagram a bit to show more system interaction. The interaction begins with Person calling the enter-Card method of ATMPanel. This in turn calls the validateCard method of ATM. When this interaction is complete, Person calls the enterPIN method of ATM-Panel. The interaction proceeds from left to right and top to bottom in this fashion for the rest of the diagram. Later in the book, we will see a variation on Booch's original second method, which works as well or better. This is the event flow diagram and language shown briefly in Chapter 2. The reason for the variation is that Booch's current diagrams do not provide algorithmic information.

MODULE DIAGRAMS

Module diagrams are the first place we annotate the physical design of the system. The first step is the organization of classes into modules. Modules can be basic modules, something more sophisticated (ADA packages), or tasks. The organization depends on your own particular implementation. Modules can have visibility, which can be a compilation dependency like you have with include files in C or C++. This type of diagram helps you organize the way in which you will build your system.

Figure 3.11 shows a new view of our banking system. Here we step back from our earlier level of detail. We look at the banking system from a higher level and view the system as a whole. We have created three possible groupings for our classes: ATM, ATM Bank, and Account Bank modules. The ATM module contains those classes necessary to operate an ATM. There is a dependency between this set of classes and the classes in the ATM Bank

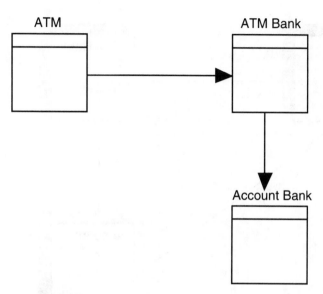

FIGURE 3.11. Module Diagram

module. The ATM Bank module has those classes needed to operate a network of ATMs and communicate with other banks. Since this software must access accounts for transactions, there is a dependency between this module and Account Bank module. Since the ATM Bank must communicate with the Account Bank, the Account Bank must be visible to it. The Account Bank module has the classes required for non-ATM bank account administration. It controls all access to accounts.

Simple templates can be associated with module diagrams. A module template would have the name of the module, documentation about it, and any declarations it needs. The declarations could be the defines and include statements needed in a C or C++ header file.

PROCESS DIAGRAMS

Process diagrams show us the second part of the physical design of a system. They show us how processes are divided up between processors and devices. Not every system needs this type of diagram. They are used when you have a multiple process configuration. Figure 3-12 gives us a high level process view of our banking example. The notation is fairly simple. Cubes with shading are

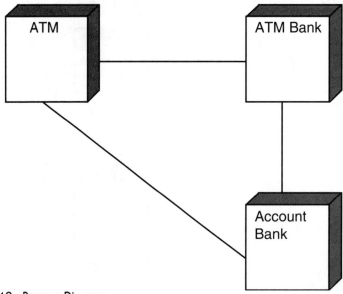

IGURE 3.12. Process Diagram

processes. Cubes without shading are devices. Lines are connections between processes or devices. These lines can be labeled.

Notice the similarity to the previous module diagram. Here we show we are running three processes on three processors: ATM, ATM Bank, and Account Bank. They all need to communicate with one another. Process diagrams can have templates. If you are annotating a process, all you need is name, documentation, and priority information. If you are annotating a device or connection, then you need the name, documentation, and characteristics of the connection or device. Annotating a processor is a little more complicated. The first items you need are the name, documentation, and characteristics of the processor. Next, you can add a list of the processes to be run. Finally, you can have scheduling information. The types of scheduling supported are preemptive, nonpreemptive, cyclic, executive, and manual.

SUMMARY

The Booch methodology includes numerous diagrams and templates to capture the complexities of system design. The most important of these is the class diagram, which shows the static structure of the system—the classes, class utilities, and class categories. All of these are supported by their own templates, which provide additional documentation. A class may also have an operations template that documents how the methods of a class work. The class diagrams are supported in turn by state diagrams. A class template may refer to one or more of the state diagrams. State diagrams provide a dynamic view of what happens within a class. The template for a state diagram may refer to additional PDL for clarification or may point to object diagrams that provide more information about state transitions. Many systems do not make use of state diagrams.

Another important system diagram is the object diagram. This diagram shows the details of interactions between different objects in the system. Many implementation details are captured at this level. Object diagrams are supported by two types of templates. Object templates give us more information about what the object actually represents in the system. Message templates provide details about how messaging works between objects. They support single and multiple threads of control. The object diagrams are in turn supported by timing diagrams. These diagrams provide a time ordering to the messages shown in the object diagrams. There are three different types of timing diagrams: numbered messages in an object diagram, object diagrams with PDL, and the equivalent of hardware timing diagrams. The most popular approach is to annotate the object diagrams with PDL to describe what is happening.

Module diagrams give us our first look at the physical system. They show us the compilation dependency and visibility needed between different parts of the system. There are module templates that help capture the details. The final type of diagram also covers the physical design of the system—this is the process diagram. This diagram shows what process will run on what processors and devices. There are templates for processes, processors, and devices. These diagrams are used in multiprocess configurations. They are not needed for other applications.

There are a number of benefits to using the Booch methodology. It supports an evolutionary approach to development. The process is one of refinement and not discrete steps. The methodology provides a consistent set of diagrams and tools from analysis to implementation. Recent changes in the methodology provide even more support for implementation issues, in fact, it has more support for these than any of the other methodologies. This is particularly true for C++. There are similarities in the diagrams and templates that make them easy to remember and consistent to use. Moving from one tool to the next is usually a refinement of earlier work, not something completely different.

The Booch methodology has a good general approach to analysis. The analysis stage is independent of language choice, as it should be. The design step is a refinement of the analysis phase. Details can be captured in a language-independent fashion. You do not need to use the language-specific adornments if you don't want to. Most developers leave their use to the very latest stages of development.

We used the Booch notation in our earliest object-oriented example, and we will use it later to show how a more complex system was designed. Does this mean the methodology is perfect? No. One problem is that there is no way in the methodology to annotate how your design fulfills the requirements it was tasked to meet. If you don't know what requirements you are meeting, how do you know what you should be designing and what problems you should be solving? Another feature that is missing is testing information. You need to annotate how to test classes, subsystems, and the system as a whole. Without this information, you will not be certain that your testing procedures are adequate. Metrics are another part of the methodology that is missing. How do you know your design is any good? Object-oriented metrics are a hotly debated issue, and there is no clear agreement on what the best metrics might be. Still, there are some that might provide guidance, and it seems inappropriate to ignore them altogether.

There are also some notational difficulties. With the current set of tools, it is difficult to show multiple message passing between objects. Currently, you need to show the same object multiple times. This can make the order and direction of messages unclear. There is also difficulty in showing the flow of information through the system. What is needed is a more compact method of showing flow and annotating the action. This is why we created event flow diagrams. The current approach seems inadequate or in pieces too disjoint to provide a meaningful dynamic view. One final nit is the need for off-page connectors. This convention would allow you to create diagrams that span multiple pages. This approach is used successfully with electrical schematics, and it would be beneficial here as well. It is often very difficult to capture a large class diagram without them.

The Booch methodology has proven to be a very powerful and thorough methodology. It has been used successfully on large and small projects. It supports the evolutionary approach to development favored for object-oriented technologies. It provides a consistent set of tools from analysis to implementation. It is the most complete of the available object-oriented methodologies. We will see more of this methodology when examine the large project later in the book.

REFERENCES

1. Booch, Grady. *Object Oriented Design with Applications.* Redwood City, CA: Benjamin/Cummings Publishing, 1991.
2. ———. *Object Oriented Analysis and Design with Applications.* 2d ed. Redwood City, CA: Benjamin/Cummings Publishing, 1994.

CHAPTER 4
Choices in Methodology: OMT

The Object-Modeling Technique (OMT) by Rumbaugh et al. is the second major methodology we will look at. The original details of this methodology can be found in the book *Object-Oriented Modeling And Design*.[1] Subsequent information can be found in the *Journal of Object-Oriented Programming* (JOOP). This is one of the more popular methodologies. Its use of modified E-R diagrams and standard data flow diagrams makes it more comfortable for those already familiar with structured analysis techniques. This doesn't mean it is simply structured analysis and design in sheep's clothing—the emphasis is still on objects and their relationships. The OMT uses these tools to illuminate and define the nature of objects and their relationships. This turns out to be a very powerful use of existing tools.

OMT BASICS

There are four major steps in the OMT. The first is analysis. In this step we create an abstract model of what the system must do. We don't define how to do it. At this stage, we begin creating a series of diagrams that define the basic structure of the system. The next step is system design. In this phase, we make specific architectural decisions about the system. We break the system into subsystems and deal with issues of resource allocation. This is done in conjunction with the analysis phase. The third step is object design. In this step, we define the implementation details for each step. We use the same diagrams started in the analysis phase, but we simply add more detail as we continue through the process. The final step is the implementation itself. These are not discrete steps that only happen in a sequential order. As with the Booch methodology, the steps are iterative and incremental. Each visit to a later step may require you to revisit an earlier step.

There are three basic kinds of models created in the OMT. The first is the object model, which provides us with a static view of the system's structure. The notation used in the object model is a modified version of an E-R diagram. Its function is similar to Booch's class diagram. The second model is the dynamic model. The dynamic model can have several diagrams. The first of these is the state diagram, which provides us a dynamic view of what happens within a class. It is identical to Booch's state diagrams. The dynamic model may also have event trace and event flow diagrams, which give us a dynamic view of the system. They show the flow of events and methods between classes. Although they are treated as secondary diagrams, they are very useful in their own right. The final model is the functional model, which shows the transformation of values in the system. It uses traditional data flow diagrams from structured analysis and design for its notation. The functions it annotates should be operations in the object model or actions in the dynamic model. Later steps in the development process add detail to these diagrams, which are started in the analysis phase.

OMT ANALYSIS—THE OBJECT MODEL

We want to begin our examination of the OMT by looking at the analysis phase and understanding how and why the different kinds of models are created. As we will see, later steps are not something separate from the analysis phase. They reflect a change of emphasis as we add details to the existing analysis models. As with all of the methodologies we will examine, the place to begin is with a definition of the problem. You must know what the problem is before you can create a system to solve it. Your problem statement may be a complete set of requirements, or it may be a simple statement. Rumbaugh suggests that even if you have a complete set of requirements, you write a simple statement anyway. This statement should clearly express the goal of this system. If you cannot write the statement, perhaps you need to give more thought to the problem you are trying to solve.

Once your statement and requirements are in place, the next step is to create an object model. The first step in this process is to identify classes needed in the system. In the last chapter, we saw various ways of identifying these classes. The same approach works here. One point that Rumbaugh clearly makes is that your initial list of classes will contain unnecessary classes. It is just as important to know what to throw away as it is to know what to keep. There are several characteristics that you can look for to identify unnecessary classes. The first of these is redundancy. You may find that you have more than one class modeling the same thing. If they are identical, keep the best one and get rid of the other. If their functionality overlaps, you may have identified the need for a common ancestor and inheritance.

Another category of unnecessary classes is irrelevant classes. You may come up with classes that deal with issues outside the scope of the problem. Eliminate them. Vague classes are also unnecessary. These tend to be "kitchen sink" classes that have no specific function. They just do a little of this and a little of that. Classes need to have a clearly defined purpose. Break such classes into others that have specific purposes, or move the functionality to more appropriate classes. You may also have created classes that should really be attributes. Unless a class has a specific purpose that requires its own methods, it may be best to make it an attribute of an existing class. Likewise, you may have created classes that should really be operations or methods of a class. If a class is applied to others and is not used in its own right, it should be a method in another class or classes. Do not confuse the intrinsic nature of a class with the role it plays in a relationship to another class. If you were modeling a family, a person may be a mother, wife, or daughter, depending on which relationship you choose to emphasize. The best approach is not to create these as separate classes. You will find many redundancies between them. It is better to create a person class and let it assume the roles it needs in the appropriate context. Finally, you may create classes that are implementation specific. The analysis phase is too early for these. Eliminate them at this stage. They will color your analysis and design and make it less flexible. Wait until the final stages of detailed design to create these if necessary. You may find that they are not as necessary as you thought.

Once you have come up with your initial list of classes, create a data dictionary to capture the details about each class. The data dictionary captures more than data. It serves the same function as the class templates in the Booch methodology. In the data dictionary, you not only want to know what the classes are, you want to track the attributes each has and what operations they perform. This concept of data dictionary is similar to that used in structured analysis and design, but with an object-oriented twist. One way to start your data dictionary is to write a simple paragraph about each class. In the paragraph, describe each class's purpose and the essentials of its structure.

After you have identified your initial classes and captured some information about them in your data dictionary, the next step is to identify the associations between them. *Associations* is the term Rumbaugh uses for relationships between classes. These go beyond the inherits, uses, and contains relationships defined in the Booch methodology. They allow for the capture of much more information about the nature of the relationship. Basically, associations are a dependency between two or more classes. These dependencies do not need to be just one way. They may be bi-directional. Another important related concept is that of the link. A link is an instance of an association—a physical or conceptual connection between object instances.

THE BANKING OBJECT MODEL

The easiest way to understand a methodology is to apply it to a specific problem. Let's use the OMT with our earlier banking problem and see how this approach differs from our earlier design. The object model for our banking example is shown in Figure 4.1. It looks similar to the class diagram we created using the Booch methodology. This is to be expected, since the problem is the same, and our list of candidate objects is identical. There are, however, some notable differences. Lets examine the notation we see in the object model. We no longer see the clouds of the class diagram. Instead, we see that each class is represented by a rectangle. At a minimum, the rectangle will contain the name of the class. This is not too different from Booch's approach. However, we do see something different with the Person class. The rectangle for the Person class is divided into three sections. The top section contains the class name—in this case, PERSON. The second section contains the attributes of the class. In the Booch notation, these were tracked in the template. In the OMT notation, they can be made visible in the class-level object diagram.

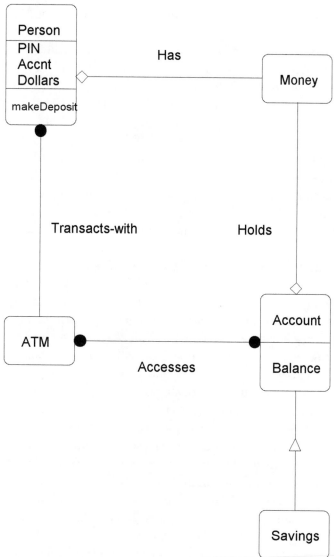

FIGURE 4.1. Object Model Diagram

This can be an aid in remembering what has been decided about a class and its functions. The attributes listed here are PIN, Accnt, and Dollars. The third section of the rectangle lists the operations of the class. In the OMT methodology, operations mean the same thing methods do in the Booch methodology. In the OMT, methods are the implementation of operations. In this example, we are only showing one of the operations of the Person class—make Deposit.

In OMT notation, you can choose what you want to show in the object model. For example, the Account class only shows its attribute Balance and no operations. If you attempt to show all attributes and all operations for each class, your diagram will quickly become very confusing. It is difficult to show many associations between objects and the details of those objects simultaneously. The diagram becomes cluttered. There are limits to what you can show on a single sheet of paper. Instead, it is best to capture all of the information in the data dictionary and only show those parts that help illuminate the object model. In the Booch methodology, this information was captured in the class template, but not shown in the class diagram. Recent changes in the Booch methodology allow you to show information with the same class notation used in the OMT object model.

The next notational change is for the class relationships or associations in the diagram. It is not simply a matter of new symbols meaning the same thing. You can see more information about the associations. Associations expand on the concepts of inherits, uses, and contains. These concepts still exist, and are still worthwhile as general categories. The first difference we see in notation is that most associations are named. The name tells us something about the relationship between the classes and should provide some information beyond the general Booch categorization of relationships. In fact, these associations may become classes in their own right. We will explore this possibility shortly. The basic categories of relationships still exist. The triangle shown in the relationship between the Account and Savings classes indicates inheritance. This is identical to the inheritance relationship we saw in the Booch class diagram.

The next kind of association is aggregation. We see an example of aggregation between the Account and Money classes. The diamond shape is the notation for this relationship. This is identical to Booch's contains relationship. In this diagram we see that the Account Class contains the Money class. The nature of this relationship is defined by its name—Holds. The Account holds Money. The name serves to tell us why the aggregation association exists. We see the same thing in the Person—Money aggregation association. The Person has Money. Again, the name helps us understand why the relationship exists.

The next type of association is equivalent to the Booch "uses" relationship, but can take many forms. The difference lies in how the notation shows the multiplicity or number of the association. For example, a straight line between two classes indicates that the relationship is exactly one to one. A solid circle at one end indicates a many-to-one relationship. In our example there is a many-to-one relationship between the Person and ATM classes. By annotating the diagram in this way, we are saying that many Persons can use a single ATM. This association has the name Transaction.

There are other options for this relationship. We can just as easily show a many-to-many association between classes. We see this notation between the ATM and Account classes. With a solid circle at each end of the association, we are saying that many ATMs can access many Accounts. This also explains why the association is named Accesses. A variation on this type of association is shown with an empty circle. An empty circle indicates an optional zero-to-one association. The multiplicity notation can be used in conjunction with an aggregation association. For example, we could say a car contains wheels. The diamond in the association would be next to the car class because it does the containing. We would show a solid circle by the wheel class, because more than one wheel was contained by the car.

This notation covers the relationships that are the equivalent of Booch's. However, the OMT supports an expansion on these concepts that is very powerful. There are ways of looking at associations that may uncover additional classes or mechanisms. This is a very powerful tool for object-oriented analysis. Let's revisit the association between the Person and ATM classes. We named the association Transaction, and in fact, there is additional information we can capture about this association. This information is not yet modeled elsewhere in the system. In this case, a transaction between a person and an ATM happens at a specific point in time. We could capture this information as the date-time of the transaction. But where do we put it? Using the OMT notation, we can show this as a link attribute. The notation for a link attribute is shown in Figure 4.2a. When we actually go to implement our system, we would put this in the most suitable class—in this application, the ATM class. The value of link attributes is that they provide more information about associations and help uncover information that might otherwise be missed. Link attributes help show the importance of an association and may become classes in their own right.

Why would a link attribute become a class? Enough information about the association may be uncovered that it takes on a meaningful life of its own. We see an example of this in Figure 4.2b. Here our Transaction association has evolved into a class. The first thing you see in the notation is that the association is no longer just between two classes—it is ternary. The diamond in the relationship

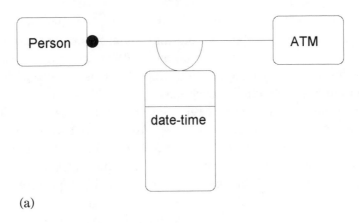

(a)

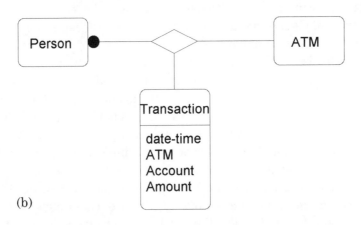

(b)

FIGURE 4.2. A Link Attribute (a), and a Ternary Association (b)

between the classes is the notation for this. The name of the association has become the name of the new class. The link attributes that were uncovered become the attributes of the classes. We would add methods to the operations section of the Transaction class as needed. This is a very powerful technique, because it provides an explicit method of uncovering new classes. It is a significant step beyond the traditional noun-verb approach to class discovery. Ternary relationships are also important because they may uncover and define mechanisms. It may be that the interaction between the classes provides important system functionality. This way of looking at associations is a valuable technique regardless of the method you ultimately use for implementing your system.

We can summarize our creation of the object model by noting that it is composed of two parts: the object model diagram and the data dictionary. The data dictionary holds the details about the attributes and operations of each class. The object model diagram shows a static view of the system's structure. This structure is composed of classes and their associations. Associations can capture information about a relationship between classes and may even become classes themselves.

THE DYNAMIC MODEL

Creation of the dynamic model is the next step in analysis. The dynamic model shows us the flow of events and actions at different levels in the system. It does this by using three types of diagrams: the state diagram, the event trace diagram, and the event flow diagram. The emphasis in the dynamic model is on the state diagram. The keys to the dynamic model are events and states. States are attribute values or links held by an object. An event is an external stimulus to an object. The response to an event may be a change of state, called a transition. When an object moves from one state to another, the transition is said to fire. This emphasis on events and states make the state diagram central to the dynamic model. State diagrams, however, only show us what is happening within an object. As we shall see, the other diagrams provide a higher-level system view. Quite frankly, these other views are often more valuable than the state diagrams.

How do you begin creating a dynamic model? Rumbaugh suggests starting with scenarios of typical interactions with the system. This is a common theme in many methodologies. In later chapters, we will see there are methodologies where this activity is the central activity of analysis. If the system has a user interface, the scenarios should reflect how a user interacts with the system. It's important to ensure that your scenarios cover the entire range of interaction and requirements. You may miss key mechanisms if your scenarios are not comprehensive. This is a very difficult thing to accomplish, because you may need many scenarios.

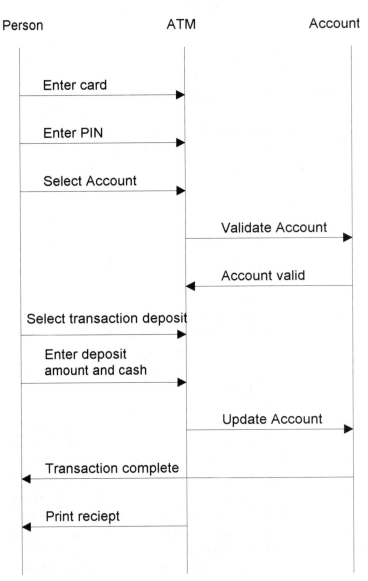

FIGURE 4.3. Event Trace Diagram

Once you have created your scenarios, you need to identify the events that occur between objects. One way to do this is to prepare an event trace diagram for each scenario. An example of this type of diagram is shown in Figure 4.3. The event trace diagram shows the transfer of information from one object to another. The events are time ordered from top to bottom. This diagram is the closest equivalent of the event flow diagram we introduced in Chapter 2. In this figure, we show the interaction between three classes: Person, ATM, and Account. The vertical lines indicate the object, and the labeled arrows show the event. The arrow shows with whom the event originates and with whom it terminates. As the analysis process iterates back to the object model, you should map events to operations in the object model. In this example we see several events going from the Person object to the ATM object. The first three are enter card, enter PIN, and select account. These events are the external occurrences that will drive the initial state changes in the ATM object. We will see this activity when we get to the state diagram.

We can summarize these diagrams by creating an event flow diagram for the scenarios. Event flow diagrams in the OMT methodology are used to show a higher-level view of events. In these diagrams, we show the flow of events between groups of classes or subsystems. This is different from the event flow diagrams shown earlier in the book, which were a closer match to the OMT event trace diagrams. Although they have the same name, their functions are different. The event trace diagrams and event flow diagrams of the OMT do not have a supporting language to describe what the diagrams illustrate.

We see an example of an OMT event flow diagram in Figure 4.4. Notice that the time ordering or sequence of events is not evident in these diagrams; the events are simply grouped together. Events in the OMT event flow diagram should show events from all scenarios. It is the dynamic counterpart to the object diagram. In the object diagram, paths show possible information and control flows. In the event flow diagram, paths show only the possible flow of control. In our example, you can see the group of events that flow from the Person object to the ATM object and vice versa. We also see the groups of events between the ATM object and the Account object.

The final type of diagram we create for the dynamic model is the state diagram. The state diagram shows the flow of events and the changes of state that occur within an object. It does not show events external to the object. Figure 4.5 shows an example of a state diagram. Does it look familiar? It should. It is identical to the state diagram created in the Booch methodology. In this example, we see the changes of state within the ATM class. This provides a view of what is happening within an ATM object in relation to the events found in the event trace diagram. The event trace diagram shows the events happening to the ATM object. The state diagram shows how the ATM

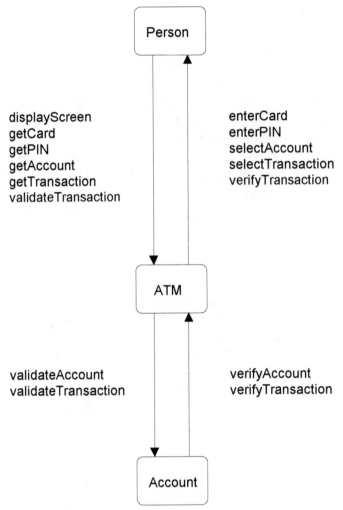

FIGURE 4.4. Event Flow Diagram

object responds internally to these events. It takes both to give us this dynamic view.

A state diagram is created by starting with an event trace diagram and mapping the events to state changes in each object they effect. It is important to check for consistency and completeness between the events and states. You only need to create state diagrams for the classes that need it. This state diagram is rather simple and other features can be included. For example, it is

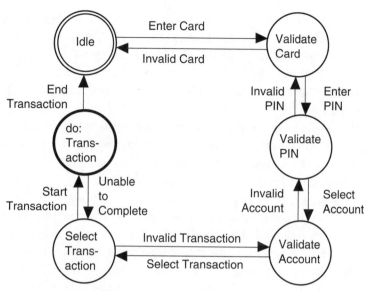

FIGURE 4.5. State Transition Diagram

possible—and often desirable—to nest states. This keeps the diagrams from becoming unwieldy. You can also add conditions to events that show what is required to make a state change occur. Subdiagrams can be used to show concurrent sub-states within an object. You can also use them to show the synchronization of concurrent activities. Events and states can be organized into inheritance trees. Transitions are inherited by the descendent states.

Combine these three types of diagrams to create the dynamic view of the system. At a minimum, the dynamic model is equal to the state diagrams plus a global event flow diagram. It is important to understand the relationship between the object model and the dynamic model. The object model provides the system's structure and constrains the dynamic model. The dynamic model shows how the object model supports all allowed scenarios by providing additional information on the states of attributes and link values.

THE FUNCTIONAL MODEL

The third and final model in OMT analysis is the functional model, the purpose of which is to describe the computations performed within the system. In this model we see the flow of information rather than the flow of events we saw in the dynamic model. The object model shows us what does the work. The dynamic model shows us when the work is done. The functional model shows us how the work gets done. In so doing, the functional model adds meaning to the operations in the object model and the actions in the dynamic model. It also serves to define the boundaries of the system. Specifying what work can be done limits the scope of the system.

The functional model is composed of three parts: processes, data flows, and constraints. These elements are combined in a single diagram, which is a traditional data flow diagram as created for structured analysis and design. It serves a similar purpose here, but as we shall see, the emphasis is different. In the structured design methodologies, data flow diagrams drive the design. In the OMT, they serve to illuminate the object and dynamic models. I stated earlier in the book that both an object view and algorithmic view of a system were needed to provide a complete picture of a design. I also stated that you will get very different results depending on which one you start with. We see this in the OMT methodology. Here we start with an object-oriented view of the system and use this as a framework upon which to build the algorithmic view. A structured analysis and design approach would start at the opposite end and give us a very different result.

The first step in creating a functional model is to define the system boundaries. In this step, you'll need to revisit your requirements and make sure you have a clear understanding of what is to be done and what items you have to work with in the system. It is important to identify your input and output values for events between the outside world and the system early in the process. You can use your event trace diagrams and event flow diagrams to identify which events are meaningful in this respect. You may also want to identify any obvious constraints for the values.

The next step is to create the data flow diagrams, which show the functional dependencies in the system. It's important to remember that this is done in the context of the object and dynamic models. The result is not the same as if you began with the functional model. The difference lies in the fact that the other models identify items that should become the data flows and functions in the diagram. They provide a context for constructing the functional model. For example, the data flows in the diagram will usually correspond to objects or attribute values in the object model. If they don't, you've found something you need to add back into the object model.

We follow this step by describing each process in the diagram. This is usually a natural language description of what the function is to accomplish. Processes should map to action verbs in the problem statement or operations in the object model. These usually correspond to low-level processes. You next identify functional constraints, which should map to conditions in the dynamic model. The main goal of this step is to identify constraints between objects. If you uncover any new constraints, you will want to incorporate them into both the functional and dynamic models. Next specify optimization criteria. Identify which values should be minimized or maximized in the system. In creating the data flow diagrams, you may uncover additional operations that are needed to transform data flows. Be sure to map these back to events and operations in the other diagrams. Finally, compare the functional model to the object and dynamic models for completeness and consistency. If you find that one model has uncovered items needed in another model, make the adjustments needed to keep the diagrams consistent. The functional model can be summarized as consisting of the data flow diagrams plus constraints.

A DATA FLOW DIAGRAM

The functional model, and the use of Data Flow Diagrams (DFD) in particular, is the most controversial part of the methodology. We see an example of a functional model in Figure 4.6. This is a view of our system unlike any we have seen previously. This particular diagram covers only a small part of our original problem statement. The notation corresponds to what we would expect in a standard data flow diagram—the circles represent processes. Processes transform the data flows. They may combine flows, create new flows, or modify existing flows. Labels with a line above and below are data stores. In traditional DFDs, these are repositories of the data; here, they are thought of as passive objects storing data. This diagram tells us nothing about the structure of these repositories. In a structured methodology, you would find that information in an E-R diagram. In the OMT you find that information in the object model and the data dictionary descriptions of class structure. A labeled box may be either a data source or sink. It is external to the system. These are also known as actors. In a structured methodology, we may not retain much information about data sources outside the system. With an object-oriented approach, they are an integral part of our system design, and are found in the object model. The lines with arrows are data flows. Data flows can be in more than one direction. You may find arrows on either end or both ends of the line. In the notation, these lines are called arcs.

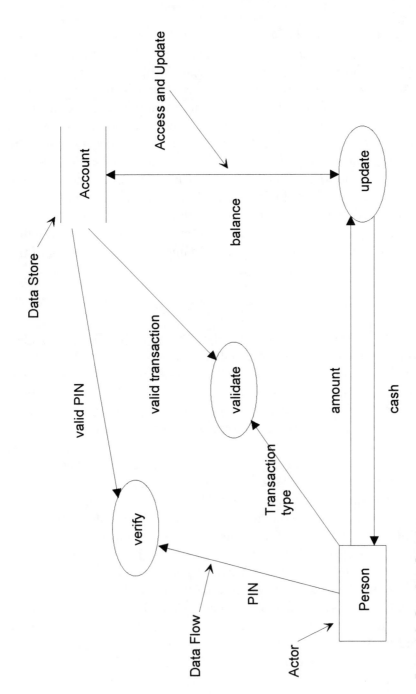

Figure 4.6. Dataflow Diagram

We can see how a functional model can help us by looking at our example. Our functional model shows one data source—Person—from which we see several outward data flows. These are for PIN, transaction type, and amount. Each of these is transformed by a separate process. The PIN data flow is transformed by the verify process, which verifies the PIN. The validate process validates the transaction type. The update process transforms the amount data flow into balance data flow stored in the Account data store. The balance data flow goes in both directions. It is known as an access and update data flow and it is appropriate for use with a data store such as Account, since Account holds information that needs to be updated and retrieved. Access and update data flows have arrows on both ends.

We can see how the functional model relates to the object and dynamic models. The functional model describes what is going on in the system. What is not clear is how this is happening. The dynamic model clearly shows us how the ATM object changes state and moves the process along when the data flows change. These data flows map to the events that are driving the ATM object in the dynamic model. If the functional model shows us what is happening, the dynamic model shows us when it happens. Still, there is more going on than is contained solely within the ATM object. The object model shows us how the different objects that actually do the work are connected to one another. The processes are found in the operations categorized for each object in the object model. Also, the data flows correspond to the attributes listed in the object model. If the functional model tells us what is happening and the dynamic model tells us when, the object model tells us who is doing the work. It is important that the models be consistent. For example, it is easy for the functional model to capture actions overlooked in the dynamic model or attributes missed in the object model. By providing complementary views, these three models provide a complete view of a system. The difficulty lies in keeping all of the models up to date and consistent.

One area that can be confusing to the beginner is the use of different terms to mean very similar things. For example, operations, activities, events, actions, and processes are terms used in the three models, but they are used almost interchangeably. Keeping all of this straight can be difficult.

SYSTEM DESIGN

Rumbaugh describes two levels of design: system design and object design. The difference between the two is reminiscent of the difference between strategy and tactics. They both serve the same end, but make their contribution in different ways. We will examine both. System design is an exercise in strategy. It is here that you make high-level decisions about the architecture of your system. Tradition would say that this step occurs after analysis. This is not entirely true. For example, suppose you know that your application will have to support a client-server form of interaction. This part of the architecture will appear in your object model. In fact, there may be numerous architectural restrictions in your requirements. From a practical point of view, system design starts while you are collecting requirements and continues after analysis. You need to iterate through this step as much as any of the others.

One of the first things you need to do for system design is to determine which requirements will affect your approach to implementation and which will not. You also need to decide how to distribute operations between software, databases, hardware, and operations. Next, you need to decide how you will break the system down into subsystems. This is done based on your analysis and architectural decisions. It is important to look for a cohesive purpose when creating subsystems. Otherwise, they tend to become kitchen sinks, with a little bit of everything thrown in. Think of subsystems in the same way you do classes. A subsystem may be created as a class with other classes encapsulated within it. The subsystem class will provide the external world with the necessary interfaces. Obviously, if the internal classes are cohesive and their interaction serves a cohesive purpose, then the subsystem can present a clean and useful interface to the rest of the system. If a subsystem is a "kitchen sink," then the interfaces will be cluttered and the subsystem will not be cohesive.

The next step in system design is to identify concurrency in the problem. This may aid you in creating subsystems by grouping in different systems processes that are concurrent. You must also choose how you will manage your data stores. You have to identify the resources that will use them and the mechanisms for controlling access to them. This leads you to the next issue, which is choosing how to implement software controls, that is, classes whose main purpose is to control the interaction and flow of information between other classes. You must also decide how to handle system boundary conditions. Naturally, many of your system's needs may be at cross purposes. You should establish what your system priorities are and determine your trade-offs accordingly. We can summarize system design as being equal to the basic system architecture plus high-level strategy decisions.

OBJECT DESIGN

If system design is a strategic exercise, then object design is a tactical exercise. It is here that we finish off the details of the design and prepare for implementation. In object design, we will specify more details of the system architecture and refine the analysis models. Analysis and design are iterative steps. Design is a detailed refinement of the analysis steps. In design, what you have is a shift of emphasis, not an entirely different activity. Another way to think of the process is this: analysis determines what a system must do. System design determines the plan of attack. Object design determines the full details of the system. Once object design is complete, you will be ready to implement your system.

In many ways, object design is an integration step. One of the first steps in object design is to combine the analysis models and see what is missing in each. For example, processes in the functional model that do not exist elsewhere indicate the need for additional operations in the object model. On the other hand, it may be that a process that is really outside the scope of the system should be removed from the functional model. Viewing each model within the context of the others clarifies what is missing in the system and what is unnecessary. During this process, you should feel free to add new classes and operations as necessary. While viewing the interaction of several classes, you may uncover a mechanism or framework that requires additional support classes to function correctly. Similarly, you will need to assign responsibility for operations and attributes not associated with a single class. For example, you will need to move link attributes into a class if they do not evolve into one of their own.

At some point in the object design, you will need to design algorithms for each of the operations. Accessor operations, which set or return attribute values in an object, need little or no algorithm design. The details of these are implementation issues. The work on algorithms should focus on ones whose implementation is not so obvious. Related to this is the need to flesh out the mechanisms that implement control in the system. Control mechanisms within operations can be fairly straightforward. Control implemented by the interaction of several objects can be far more complex. You need information found in all three models to describe and detail these types of mechanisms. You should also spend some time optimizing access paths to your data. One thing to avoid is creating a chain of message passing just to return a value from an object lower in the chain to a higher one. This is often referred to as an explosion of message passing. Optimizing such paths can improve performance. You can uncover potential problem areas by comparing data flows and processes in the functional model to the objects that implement the processes in the object model. If there is a long chain of objects between the origin and end of a data flow, you may have uncovered a path worth optimizing.

Once you believe that the structure of your objects and their operations is in place, you should adjust the class structure to optimize inheritance. This increases code reuse within the system and minimizes the amount of work you have to do to implement the system. It also serves to isolate functionality in single sites. This minimizes the ramifications of changes. You will also need to design how to implement associations. You must decide if you want to treat an association as a class or simply add attributes to existing classes. Finally, you will need to determine the exact representation of all of the attributes and objects in the system. Once this work is complete, you can package classes into meaningful modules. These may correspond to your subsystems or they may form another level of granularity. Modules are valuable because they provide support for development and project-management issues. We can summarize object design by saying that it is equal to a detailed object model plus a detailed dynamic model plus a detailed functional model.

OMT METHODOLOGY SUMMARY

The OMT methodology provides an iterative approach to object-oriented system analysis and design. In the analysis portion of the OMT, you create three models: the object model, the dynamic model, and the functional model. You begin the process by creating an object model. The object model shows the static structure of the system. It shows us who does the work in the system. It is equivalent to the class diagrams in the Booch methodology. There are three basic parts to the object model. First there are the objects, each of which has a name, attributes, and operations. Next comes the associations between objects, which come in various flavors. Regardless of type, associations are named in a way to provide meaning. The three basic types of relationships are inheritance, aggregation, and those that show the multiplicity of a basic relationship. The meaning of inheritance is the same as in Booch methodology. Aggregation is the same as Booch's contains relationship. A basic relationship with multiplicity is the same as Booch's uses relationship. This last relationship can evolve in interesting ways. An association may have attributes associated with it, which become link attributes. The link attributes may become complex enough to evolve into classes in their own right. When this happens, you create a ternary relationship. Support for this is one of the more powerful tools in the methodology. The final part of the object model is the data dictionary. Here, each object and its function is described in natural English.

The next step in the methodology is to create the dynamic model. The dynamic model gives us a dynamic view of our system. It shows us when work happens in the system. There are three types of diagrams in the dynamic model: state diagrams, event trace diagrams, and event flow diagrams. The state diagrams are just like those in the Booch methodology. They consist of events that are an external stimulus to a class and states that are the set of attribute values of an object. State diagrams only show what is happening dynamically within an object as the object transitions from one state to the next. Event trace diagrams show the transfer of information from one object to another in a time-ordered fashion. It is the closest to our own event flow diagram described earlier in the book. The OMT event flow diagram completes the triad of the dynamic model. This diagram shows the events that occur between groupings of objects or subsystems. There is no time ordering of these events, which gives us a system view of information transfer.

The final step in analysis is to create the functional model. This model shows us what work is being done by the system using the data flow diagrams of structured methodologies. The data flow diagrams show data flows, processes that transform the data flows, data sources and sinks that provide or consume data flows, data stores that are repositories for data, and finally constraints that determine which processes are executed. This view of a system is not found in other methodologies. The models are not created in sequential steps. Their creation is an iterative process where information uncovered in one model may require changes to the other models.

System design starts early in the process, but the bulk of it occurs after the three analysis models are almost complete. In system design you make strategic decisions about system architecture and other high-level issues. Object design is a detailed iteration through the three analysis models. Object design is a matter of ensuring consistency and completeness between the diagrams and fleshing out all of the details required to implement the system. No new types of diagrams or documentation are created at this point. The final step in the methodology is to implement the system.

There are a number of benefits to using the OMT methodology. The clearest is the concept of associations and the mechanism for turning associations into classes. This is a very powerful tool for uncovering system-level mechanisms. In most other methodologies, you have to recognize mechanisms without help from the methodology. Another benefit is the similarity of the object model to E-R diagrams. Those already familiar with the notation from the structured methodologies find it comfortable to work with. The main differences are the primacy of the object model in OMT and the enhancements to the notation to support object-oriented concepts. The OMT methodology also provides additional ways of viewing the flow of information and events in the system. In the dynamic model, we see the addition of event trace and event flow diagrams. The functional model itself, which is created with data flow diagrams, is not used in other methodologies. Certainly, those acquainted with structured techniques find the use of data flow diagrams familiar.

With the similarity of OMT diagrams and structured techniques, you might think that there is not much difference between them, but that is not the case. The fundamental difference is a very important change of emphasis. In the OMT, the object model is first and foremost. It provides the structure for the rest of the system. The data flow diagrams of the functional model serve to illuminate the object model, not define it. In structured analysis, their roles would be reversed and you would end up with a very different design.

There are some weaknesses in the methodology. It can be a difficult process tying the three models together. There is not always a clear mapping from one to the others. For example, an association may map to multiple methods or data flows. It takes a trained eye to uncover some of these relationships. There are also inconsistencies in the use of terminology. The system also lacks support for design detail. The emphasis of the methodology is on analysis. Also, implementation support is missing. There is no specific way to annotate implementation decisions. This focus of OMT may be more by choice than oversight. Rumbaugh has said that capturing implementation details is more a tool than a methodology issue.[2] Other weakness include missing information for testing. Testing may not be part of a design, but it is important as part of the development cycle. It is particularly important in large systems. How systems are tested is a significant development issue. Finally, there is no tie back to requirements. There is no explicit method to ensure that your system actually satisfies the requirements you signed up to deliver.

The use of the functional model to show information flows and the transformation of information may be viewed by some as a drawback, and it certainly is controversial. Other methodologies have found little need for this. The functional model is also the most difficult to map to the other models because a transformation may or may not happen within a single object. The functional model does not provide a clear view of how a transformation relates to the complex relationships of objects that perform it. It also doesn't tell us who affects or is effected by a transformation. What is clear is that the functional model is an attempt to help understand these issues, but it is not a perfect answer. Additional tools might be useful to model and measure system complexity and help the designer understand the ramifications of information transformation within a system.

The OMT methodology provides a strong analysis tool with powerful techniques for examining relationships between objects. It has been used successfully on projects of all sizes. Its use of familiar tools and techniques have helped make it popular. We see, however, that the influence of conventional techniques does not dominate. The object model has preeminence. Objects still prevail.

REFERENCES

1. Rumbaugh, James et al. *Object-Oriented Modeling and Design.* Englewood Cliffs, NJ: 1991.
2. This is based on a phone conversation in June 1993.

CHAPTER 5

Choices in Methodology: Use Cases

Most of the methodologies currently used in object-oriented projects originated in the United States. They are certainly the best known. However, they are not the only ones in use. One that is becoming much better known in the United States is the use case methodology of the Swede Ivar Jacobson. The details of his methodology can be found in his book *Object-Oriented Software Engineering.*[1] It is actually the oldest method. Development started on it in the mid-1960s as an object-based approach to development. The current version of the methodology was formalized by 1987. The book, which was published in 1992, brought about a surge of interest in the methodology. A tool called Objectory was created to implement the methodology. The processes described in the documentation for the tool are even more complete than those described in the book. I'll not draw too fine a line between them. The differences are more a matter of depth and details.

The use case methodology is very complete. It provides traceability through all models from front to back. There are ties from requirements through testing. Other methodologists are finding value in some of the things Jacobson has to say. The concept of use cases is creating interest among many doing object-oriented development and is being adopted to some degree by certain methodologists. Along with completeness comes complexity. Fortunately, it is not necessary to use all of the models in the methodology. Various subsets are available, depending on our goals and resources. The documentation for Objectory defines these as Lite, Average, and Complete.[2,3,4,5] We'll look at all phases of the process. You can then select whatever subset is useful to you.

THE USE CASE PROCESS

One general process that Jacobson advocates is more philosophical than detailed. It describes a general approach to object-oriented development. The first step in the process is requirements analysis. This is a much more thorough process than merely collecting requirements. This step lays the foundation for all that follows. One of the main differences between this and other methodologies is the fundamental importance of this step to the completion of all others. The next step is the design of the system architecture. Jacobson's methodology provides its own underlying architecture as a framework. The next step begins the development of major components. Jacobson recommends that you start with the system's user interface. After that portion is complete, you design, implement, and test the rest of the system in stages. Finally, you need to test the complete system. This is an interesting outline for development, but it's more useful to see how he has broken the development process into specific phases.

There are five specific phases in the development process. Each of these phases creates one or more specific models of the system. Although we will go through the phases sequentially, it is important to remember that Jacobson's outline for the development process is iterative and not linear. The phases are requirements analysis and robustness analysis, followed by the design, implementation, and testing phases. The requirements model captures the functional requirements that the system must implement. The robustness or analysis model defines the ideal, robust object model. The design model refines the ideal structure so that it can be created in the current implementation environment. The implementation model is the implementation of the system. The test model verifies the system. Many kinds of documentation can be created for each model.

REQUIREMENTS ANALYSIS

Requirements analysis is the heart of the use case process. It sets the stage for the rest of the models used to create a system. The main goal of this phase is to create a use case model, which will drive the rest of the system's development.

What is a use case, and what makes it so important? The functionality of the system is defined by a number of use cases. Each use case represents a different flow of events through the system. A description of a use case defines what happens in the system when a use case is performed. Another way to look at use cases is to think of them as the set of scenarios that completely define a system's functionality from the actor's viewpoint. Why this emphasis on use cases? With other approaches, Jacobson found it difficult to see how a system accomplished the things it was supposed to do. This is the same rationale we used when we introduced the event flow diagrams and language early in the book. Here it is the starting place for the methodology. Since the emphasis is on uncovering and capturing the functional requirements, does this make it the same as a structured analysis and design approach? Not at all. As we shall see, it still retains its object-oriented orientation. The use cases provide a way to uncover the objects needed in a system. They are more useful than a list of nouns and verbs because they are focused on what the system is trying to accomplish.

The use case model has three components. The first component is made up of those things that exist outside the system, called *actors*. The second component captures what a system is supposed to do, called a *use case*. Several of these are usually needed to capture a system's functionality. The third component shows the interaction between a system and its users. The purpose of the model is to help the developers agree on what the system will do and create a model to capture this. The first step in this process is to define potential actors. This shows who the system is built for. You should also begin to look for and make note of objects and use cases you will need in later steps. The next step is to find use cases based on requirements and actors' needs. You can use information you noted earlier to describe each use case. As you proceed through this process, feel free to create new actors and use cases as needed.

Once you've found the basic components of your use cases, you should begin structuring them with associations, which are directed relationships between two object or other items. Being directed means that an associating object knows about and depends on the associated object. Use cases are related to one another through extends and uses associations. The uses association means that use case A can do its function for use case B. This is very similar to the uses relationship between classes that we discussed in the Booch methodology. In this case we are saying that one use case may provide its functionality for another use case. The extends association, when extending from use case B to A, says a class may stop obeying use case A and start obeying B. You can think of this association as a way of adding new functionality when that defined for one use case is not enough for a system. Imagine in our old banking example that we have a use case defined for a person's normal transaction with the bank. What happens when through some system failure we need to abort the transaction and reset our system? We switch from one use case to the next, which covers the changed events. We have extended the original use case by providing another, which can take control should events require it.

You can also structure your actors by looking for common roles that can be used in an inheritance association. This is for actors only, not use cases. You can also relate actors to use cases through a communication association. This simply says that an actor interacts with a use case. When the use case model seems stable, you should describe each use case in detail. We can see an example of a use case model for our banking example in Figure 5.1. This is a slightly different view of our banking system than we've seen before. We originally defined our banking system as a simulation and the users as the people who run the simulation. Here we treat our system as if it were the actual banking system. We have an actor named Person communicating with the makeWithdrawl and makeDeposit use cases. They in turn use the accessAccount use case. Again, we treat this as a

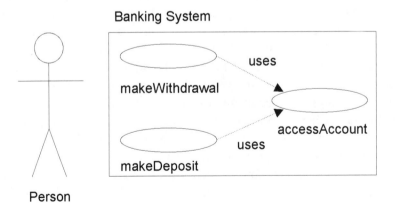

FIGURE 5.1. Use Case Model

sample of a system. Obviously, not all possible use cases are presented here.

The use case model is one model you create in the requirements analysis phase. The other model you create in parallel is the domain object model. This model captures the objects and subsystems that will be part of the system. The first step in this model is to capture the "real" world objects in the system. These are the objects that participate in the different use cases. The usual approach is to create the model as you go through each use case. Identify, as best you can, the objects that make the use case work. You also want to model interacting objects. One of the interactions you can capture is inheritance. You can also create an acquaintance association between objects to show a relationship between them. An acquaintance association says one object holds a reference to another. You can also capture the consistsOf association. This is our old friend aggregation. It is a special type of acquaintance association. You can also create communication association between objects to show that they interact. Figure 5.2 shows a domain object model for the new version of our banking system. We see one inheritance association between the Savings and Account objects—Savings inherits from Account. We also see a consistsOf association between Account and Money. This shows aggregation. Money is a part of

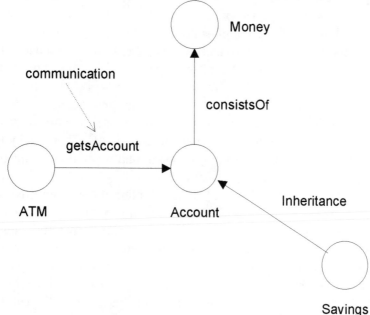

FIGURE 5.2. Domain Object Model

Account. Finally, there is a communications association between our ATM object and the Account object. We have labeled this association getAccount. The ATM object communicates with the Account object to get a specific type of Account object returned to it.

Where are we after this phase? We have captured a lot of information already. We have a good idea of the system's functionality, which is defined by the use cases. We also have an idea of how these use cases relate to one another. These relationships are captured in the associations of the use case model. We have also started to discover the objects we will need to construct our system. We have captured them and some information about their relationships in our domain object model.

ROBUSTNESS ANALYSIS

The purpose of robustness analysis is to describe the ideal structure of the system without regard to implementation details. The actual design will change from this model, but this step helps create a robust system structure. In discussing this phase, Jacobson talks about moving from a naive view of what objects are in a system to a robust selection and structuring of objects. Just coming up with a list of objects doesn't mean you have the best set of objects for your system. This step provides a way of creating a robust selection of objects and system structure. It is often bypassed when only some of the phases are used, which is regrettable. Robustness analysis gives the system an ideal goal and provides a solid foundation for the design phase. The weakness of this step lies in the fact it does not tie itself down with implementation issues, therefore it is often not simple to implement this model. That is why there is a separate design phase. However, in the design phase you don't want to deviate from the ideal any more than necessary.

The first step in robustness analysis is to define the system architecture in terms of subsystems. This provides a high-level structuring of the system. It also provides a context for the objects that may move from one subsystem to another before the system stabilizes. The next step is to create static views of the basic analysis objects. This is another process of uncovering objects. We are not yet ready to define their interactions. Often you will see a need for objects beyond those uncovered in the requirements analysis phase. We can focus this work by looking for additional objects that are needed by the use cases. As you

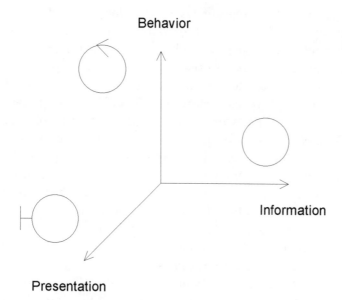

Behavior

Information

Presentation

FIGURE 5.3. OOSE Architectural Framework

uncover objects, you should outline their behavior. You then take these objects and create views of all of the objects that participate in each use case. These views offer a more detailed look at the system and are created for each use case. They show how work is done in the system.

The methodology provides a framework for interaction in these views. The framework defines the interaction space of the objects, which is defined by three components or dimensions: behavior, information, and presentation. If you think of these components as defining the axis of a three-dimensional (3D) space, you can envision how an object's position in the space reflects its purpose. Figure 5.3 shows this framework. The three axes are the three components we mentioned earlier. The figure also shows three basic types of objects. All objects in the diagram fit into one of these three categories. The control object is represented by a circle with an arrow on it and resides closest to the Behavior axis. The interface object is a circle with the sideways "T" attached to it. An interface object lies closest to the Presentation axis. The third type of object, an entity object, is a plain circle. An entity object lies closest to the Information axis and models the data or informational aspects of a system. Some objects may contain aspects of all three axes. You could imagine these positioned in 3D space according to how much of each axis' properties they contain.

The methodology's use of a framework is a particularly powerful addition. It provides a fundamental architecture for the system. It is the major reason that this step moves beyond naive objects to a robust structure. Most methodologies provide no underlying architecture. In the use case approach, one is provided for you. If you are familiar with the Smalltalk language, you will notice the similarity between this architecture and Smalltalk's Model-View-Controller (MVC) structure. The MVC is the framework or mechanism that controls the user's interaction with a Smalltalk system. In the MVC, what the user sees is the View. The underlying system and data is in the Model. The Controller looks for user interaction and supports communication between the user, Model, and View. This is a powerful structure for creating systems that need a user interface. However, the structure is of limited value if you don't have a user interface component. The same is true for Jacobson's Information-Presentation-Behavior structure. It is somewhat more general than the MVC, but is of limited value if you have no user interface in your system.

We see an example of this static view of a use case in Figure 5.4. This is a view of the makeDeposit use case. It shows us more of the interactions necessary for makeDeposit to work. Notice that we have created some new objects: ATM Panel and ATM Printer. These are interface objects. They model the interfaces to the actor that uses this use case. We also made a change to one of our earlier objects. Here we see the ATM object as a control object. It provides the control interaction between a person and his account. We also have three entity objects: Account, Savings, and Money. These form the core data or model in our system. Contrast this figure with Figure 5.2. The domain object model was a very limited static view of objects and their relationships. It doesn't really tell us anything about how the objects will function in the system.

The objects ATM Panel and ATM Printer handle interaction with the system's user. Their interaction with the ATM control object are modeled with communications and acquaintance associations. Often acquaintance associations are used with interface objects. In this case a named acquaintance association is shown between ATM and ATM Printer. There is no dynamic interaction between them, so a communications association is not needed. Acquaintance associations can be named. This one is named "print summary." A communications association is shown between ATM Panel and ATM. There is a great deal of interaction, which is initiated by ATM Panel. Dynamic communications associations are not named, because a single name would not accurately reflect the full nature of the relationship. We see another communications association

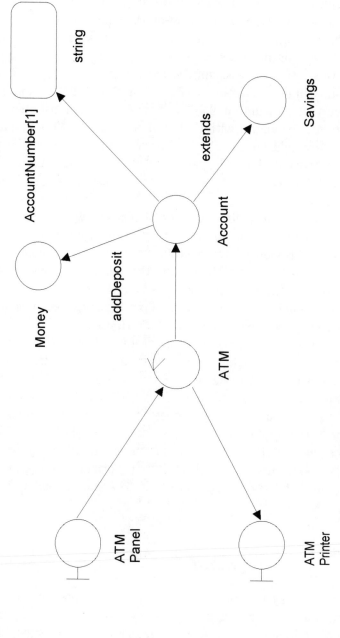

FIGURE 5.4. The Banking System in the OOSE Framework

between ATM and Account. Here the ATM object is getting the appropriate account. There is a consistsOf association between Account and Money, since Money is a part of the account. We show the relationship between Account and Savings as an extends relationship, since Savings is extending the functionality of Account. Finally, we see that the Account class has an attribute. In this case, the attribute is AccountNumber. There is only one instance of this attribute in Account. We also see that AccountNumber is of type String. Attributes are shown as round-cornered rectangles with their type information listed underneath. The name and cardinality of the attribute appears on an arrow pointing from the object to the attribute box. The cardinality tells us how many of the attributes are needed. You can annotate all the non–consistsOf association attributes in this fashion.

The next step in robustness analysis is to unify all of the views you have created into a whole. You should look at this view as a system version of the diagrams. The goal is to use this view to create a robust model. Create connections between individual views for use cases. Reevaluate the individual views in light of this overall view. Work to distribute the system's behavior for use cases. The purpose of this step is to minimize the tendency to put too much behavior into too small a set of objects. When behavior is well distributed, you will have a more robust system. Once you've distributed the system's behavior, you need to look closely at what each object does. Collect the demands made on each object and describe its behavior. This will help you uncover the attributes each object needs. You can also use this information to find inheritance, acquaintance, and consistsOf associations between objects. Once you have completed the associations, try to evenly distribute the associations in the model. This does the same thing as distributing behavior in the system. By distributing the system's functionality, you create a more robust system. As a final step, you can group your objects into what Jacobson calls packages. These are a module level of grouping.

DESIGN

The design step moves the system model from its ideal structure to the real world of the implementation environment. This step is necessary because it is usually not clear how to implement the ideal robustness analysis model. The result of the design model should be a design that is straightforward to implement. This model reflects the design of the system that will be maintained over the system's life cycle. You want to leave as much of the analysis model untouched as you can because the analysis model reflects the most idealized robust design. The first steps in the design process are the same as those for the robustness analysis process. The reason for the overlap is that robustness analysis is not always done. The first steps of the process are still needed. If you have completed a robustness analysis, you will be able to move quickly to the later steps of the design process. Again, the process starts by defining the system architecture in terms of subsystems. Next proceed to uncover your basic objects. You model all of the objects needed by each use case. Once you have reached this point, the process changes. You merge your different views into a whole, but once this is complete, you start to adjust the whole model to the implementation environment. This is where you make compromises with the real world. If either the language you have chosen or your computer environment has constraints, you must account for them here. For example, since you are now considering real world constraints, there is no use in creating structures that require multiple inheritance if your language only supports single inheritance.

Once you have accounted for your implementation environment, you work to distribute use case behavior among the system's objects. This is similar to what was done in robustness analysis, but with an important difference. You create a new diagram at the design level that provides a better view of the interaction between objects. Both the domain object model and the analysis model gave us static views of the system. The analysis model provided more detail about the interactions, but it was still a static view. There was no information to tell us about the order in which interactions occurred. In the design phase, we will create interaction diagrams to show the flow of events through the system. Interaction diagrams are created for each use case. By modeling the flow of events, they show how the system supports the behavior required in each use case.

We can show how an interaction diagram works by modeling our makeDeposit use case as in Figure 5.5. At the top are the objects that participate in the use case. They are the objects from the analysis model in Figure 5.4: ATM Panel, ATM, Account, Money, and ATM Printer. At the far left of the model is the actor who starts the interaction with the use case. In this case, the actor Person is the initiator of event flows for the makeDeposit use case. Time flows from the top and moves to the bottom. The direction of each event is from initiator to receiver. Individual interactions are labeled arrows.

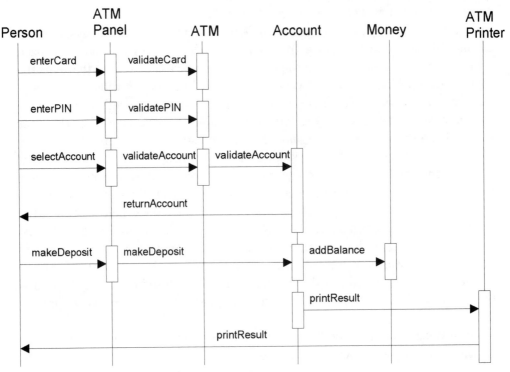

FIGURE 5.5. Interaction Diagrams

In earlier chapters we uncovered some of the operations needed to make a deposit. The initial one was enterCard. Since we have added new objects, we will need additional operations. An example would be the last event—print-Result. This is a new method required by the ATM Printer object. Notice the similarity between this diagram and the event flow diagrams we originally created. The picture is different, but the information is the same. There is no event flow language, but by labeling the arrows, almost the same information is captured. The nice thing about the language was that it captured flows in a form very close to what you needed to implement. Here, you have to do a little more work to get to that point. We were not the only ones to recognize the value of this type of diagram. Booch has adopted them as part of his methodology. This is now the preferred diagram for showing a dynamic view of a system. This implies that you will want to create something like use cases when you use the Booch methodology. You may not need the use case diagrams, but you should have use cases or scenarios that encompass the system's functionality. You can then create an interaction diagram for each scenario.

The process of creating interaction diagrams is iterative. You begin by creating a diagram. You study it, decide what operations an object should have, and finally name the operations in the diagram. You may change the flow of the system as you distribute operations among objects. Remember that the purpose of these diagrams is to help you distribute behavior around the system. This means that objects will change what they do and you may even find the need for additional objects. Once you have completed your diagrams, all of the objects in the system should be defined. Your final step is to take these objects and distribute them to the subsystems originally created for your system architecture. Once you have completed this, your design should be complete and you should be ready for implementation.

IMPLEMENTATION AND TESTING

The implementation model is the implementation process itself. There are no new diagrams created at this stage. Here you create your code. Jacobson views design, implementation, and testing as an iterative process. You should design, code, and test small pieces at a time. This harks back to the original development philosophy we discussed. You could begin with the user interface. Design, code, and test important portions of it. Then begin to add additional functionality to your system by designing, coding, and testing other objects. Integrate these objects together and test their interactions.

We've mentioned testing already—as you can see, it is difficult to separate from implementation. The test model is the documentation for what testing needs to be done. Methods of testing can be tied directly back to use cases and operations defined in various diagrams. We can also use the earlier diagrams to define different levels of testing. We can define test procedures for individual objects, subsystems, or the whole system. This approach provides a way of capturing all the testing that needs to be done. By using the use cases as a basis for system testing, you can ensure that your system has been tested for accepted requirements and functionality.

SUMMARY

There are a number of benefits to Jacobson's use case–driven methodology. The models are integrated from front to back. Jacobson has recognized the difference between a naive design and a robust one. He created robustness analysis as a specific step in creating a robust design. His methodology is one of the most complete, as demonstrated by the inclusion of a testing phase. His concept of use cases is recognized by many as a valuable concept. Other methodologists are adopting the concept, if not the diagrams. Other portions of the methodology are also being accepted by others. Most notably, Booch has adopted the interaction diagrams for the latest version of his methodology. Jacobson's approach is also the oldest methodology and has been used successfully on numerous projects.

There are also some weaknesses in his method. The most obvious of these is the method's complexity. Many steps must be followed to complete a project. This means you spend much of your time trying to capture and integrate large amounts of information. The process is so complex that you really need the support of a tool to provide the front-to-back connectivity the methodology supports. A tool called Objectory is available, but some consider it expensive. The requirement for tool support means that this methodology is not really for the pencil-and-paper crowd.

Another problem with the complexity is that it is difficult to have a unified view of the system. You must mentally patch together the different diagrams. There is no clear comprehensive view of the whole. This can be compounded when a single object is defined for multiple use cases. It is difficult to ensure that the same object is not multiply developed in different versions, leading to redundant code and other problems. Some may also find the distinction between the different types of associations unclear. It can be difficult to know which one should be used.

Finally, in the analysis model the methodology enforces an architecture with its use of control, entity, and interface objects. This is a strength if you have a user interface as part of the design, but a weakness if another framework is needed. The methodology does not appear flexible in accommodating other frameworks. Additionally, you may find that functions masquerade as control objects if you do not take care in how you define your objects. However, the incorporation of an enforced architecture should bring home the message that it is important to have an architecture and not just a jumbled collection of objects.

Jacobson's methodology contains some powerful concepts, of which use cases is the one most adopted by others. Jacobson provides an underlying framework for systems, and this is a positive step in creating robust systems. The methodology has been used successfully on numerous projects, but is quite complex and requires tool support to be used to its fullest.

REFERENCES

1. Jacobson, Ivar et al. *Object-Oriented Software Engineering: A Use Case Driven Approach.* New York: Addison-Wesley, 1992.
2. Objectory. Objectory Guide. Krista, Sweden: Objective Systems SF AB 1993.
3. ———. Objectory Process. Krista, Sweden: Objective Systems SF AB. 1993.
4. ———. Objectory Overview. Krista, Sweden: Objective Systems SF AB 1993.
5. ———. Objectory Tool. Krista, Sweden: Objective Systems SF AB 1993.

CHAPTER 6

Choices in Methodology: CRC and Responsibility-Driven Design

Some techniques are often used in conjunction with other methodologies. The best known of these involve the use of CRC note cards. The CRC technique was created by Kent Beck and Ward Cunningham.[1] CRC is not a complete methodology by itself. Its use has been enhanced and extended through the use of responsibility-driven design (RDD). The most definitive text on RDD is *Designing Object-Oriented Software* by Rebecca Wirfs-Brock et al.[2] This text shows how to use the CRC approach and expands the technique beyond the use of note cards.

When developers are introduced to an object-oriented methodology in the popular computer press, this is the one they encounter. The popular summaries often fail to do justice to this technique. While it is not as comprehensive as the Booch or OMT methodology, it does provide additional insights into how object-oriented systems can be developed. The behavioral approach taken by the CRC technique is useful enough to be adopted to some degree by other methodologies. Because it is so frequently encountered, it is worthwhile understanding something of CRC technique and the RDD methodology.

CRC AND THE RDD METHODOLOGY

CRC stands for Class-Responsibility-Collaborator. These three words define the essence of this technique. The CRC approach provides a behavioral approach to system design. It is behavioral, because the emphasis is on the interaction of objects. There are some notable differences from other methodologies. When combined with RDD, it is really more sophisticated than the emphasis on note cards implies. Still, the combined approach is not as complete as the other methodologies. There are a number of issues that RDD does not address. In spite of its emphasis on object interactions, it has no method for capturing a dynamic view of the system. There are no state diagrams to show what happens within classes. As we review the methodology, you will notice other areas where it differs from the other methodologies. Because CRC is an integral part of RDD, we will discuss it in the context of the methodology.

RDD has three phases: the exploratory phase, the analysis phase, and the design phase. There are three goals in the exploratory phase: find the classes, determine their responsibilities, and find their collaborators. You begin by searching for possible classes. This is where finding nouns in the problem statement or requirements comes in, which will provide you with some, but not all, basic system classes. You then begin to explore the responsibilities of these classes by looking for the verbs in the same documents. These verbs tell what a class must do and indicate its purpose. They become the operations a class is responsible for. They may also indicate what knowledge a class must maintain. Finally, you will discover collaborators when you find a class needs to interact with others to fulfill its responsibilities. Determining which responsibilities need collaborators completes the exploratory phase. The results of this phase are a list of classes, a description of their responsibilities, and a description of each class's collaborators. The process sounds fairly simple, but it is actually much more involved. Let's go exploring.

CRC—THE EXPLORATORY PHASE

We begin this phase by exploring our problem statement or requirements for nouns and noun phrases. These are our candidates for classes. This is one of the most well-known parts of the methodology. From our ATM problem statement, Person is a noun that would be an obvious candidate for a class. You can also look for hidden nouns. Often requirements are written in the passive voice.

Verbs that are in the passive voice are simply nouns in disguise. You can add them to your list of class candidates. As you examine your requirements, there are several types of nouns that are good candidates for classes. The most obvious are physical objects. In our case, ATM is a class representing physical objects, which are machines used by the Person. Conceptual entities are also good candidates. For example, we might think about all the ways a person can interact with a bank and his account. We can conceive of this interaction as a Transaction. We've mentioned Transaction before as a possible class, although for our simple example we chose not to use it. Categories are also candidates for classes. In our example, Account may be thought of as a category of relationship between a person and a bank. Establishing an account and the management of it is one reason a person may have established a relationship with a bank. Accounts can come in many versions. The top of a category may become the ancestor of an inheritance tree.

We see in Figure 6.1 the list that comes from the extraction of nouns from our problem statement. We should record each class on individual index cards. Each card should have a statement of purpose for the class, which should tell us why this class exists. This statement is an addition to the original Beck/Cunningham approach. We should also identify candidates for abstraction. These classes will be used later in our inheritance diagrams. Figure 6.2 shows an example of an index card for the Person class. We will add to this card as we proceed through the methodology. Note that this is not a comprehensive list of classes—it is just a starting place. Throughout the process, many classes will be added and others removed. Later steps in the process will help organize this set of classes. Additional steps will refine it.

Our next step in the exploratory process is to identify the responsibilities of our classes. These define the purpose of the class. There are two key items you need to capture when looking for responsibilities, the most obvious of which is the actions a class can perform. This is what most developers think of. The second

```
Person
ATM
Transaction
Account
```

FIGURE 6.1. Candidate Class List

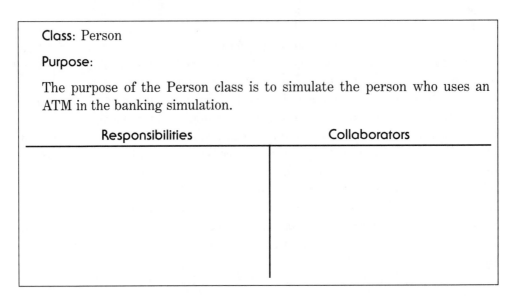

FIGURE 6.2. The Basic Person CRC Card

is understanding what knowledge an object must maintain to carry out its actions. This knowledge becomes the class's attributes. There are three ways you can identify responsibilities. You can start with the purpose you wrote on the index card. The second place to look is in the requirements or problem statement. Instead of looking for nouns, this time you look for verb phrases. This is the flip side of the noun coin. In our ATM example, "make deposit" is a responsibility identified for the Person class. The third way to discover responsibilities is by examining the relationships between classes. You identify the relationships by walking through scenarios that describe how a system will be used. In tracing the interactions through the system, you identify what functions each class needs to perform and simultaneously identify who it needs to work with to accomplish its goals.

The typical approach to walking through scenarios is to use a role-playing method. In this approach, team members play the roles of different objects. By interactively emulating the system, developers can quickly identify both responsibilities and collaborators for each class. It is best to use several scenarios, as multiple scenarios help you cover a system's full functionality. The more complete the scenarios are, the better. Scenarios give shape and scope to the requirements. They serve as a guide to much of the discovery process. Walking through scenarios in detail is a powerful technique. It quickly uncovers missing classes and poor design choices. We used scenarios earlier in the book to create event flow diagrams and language. Others are also adopting this behavioral approach.

There are three kinds of relationship to look for while examining relationships between classes. The first is the "is-kind-of" relationship, which indicates inherited characteristics. The "is-part-of" relationship is also important. It shows us aggregation. This is the same as the Booch "contains" relationship. It helps identify information required to fulfill responsibilities. Finally, there is the "is-analogous-to" relationship, which says that a class belongs to an as-yet-unidentified superclass. It is a class that will belong in some inheritance tree.

Once you've uncovered responsibilities, you need to assign them to classes. There are several guidelines for doing this. First of all, try to distribute intelligence throughout the system. Wirfs-Brock recommends that you distribute it evenly in the system. Sometimes developers take this too far. You need to distinguish between base and support classes. Base classes will contain more functionality than support classes. A better approach is to distribute intelligence among base classes. You should also state responsibilities in general terms. This is an exploratory phase, not the final design. It is too early to commit to specifics at this point. Later steps will bring additional changes. Another important guideline is to keep behavior with related information. This will help you create well-encapsulated classes. This guideline may conflict with the first. Distributing intelligence does not mean distributing a single function. Keep information about a function in a single place. Another step along the same line is to share responsibilities among related objects, which will help you form good subsystems. Figure 6.3 shows the additions we've made to the Person note card as a result of this step. Here we see the responsibilities (methods) for the Person class identified earlier in the book.

The final step in the exploratory phase is to identify the collaborators needed by each of the classes to carry out its responsibilities. The basic question answered at this stage is: Does a class fulfill its responsibilities by itself or in collaboration with others? What specifically is a collaboration? A collaboration is a client-server relationship between classes. A client requests a service and a server provides a service. A collaboration is a request from a client of a server. It is important to note that the only reason a collaboration exists is to fulfill a responsibility. There are several questions you can ask in your search for collaborators. (This sounds like something done by the French underground in an old World War II movie.) Does a class fulfill a responsibility by itself? If so, no

Class: Person

Purpose:

The purpose of the Person class is to simulate the person who uses an ATM in the banking simulation.

Responsibilities	Collaborators
makeDeposit	
makeWithdrawal	
writeCheck	

FIGURE 6.3. Responsibilities Added to Person

collaboration is necessary. If not, what is needed? By this we mean what is needed from itself, and what support from others is required. Once you've identified what is needed, the next question is: Who can it get it from? This is the collaboration. You can also ask who uses this class. This is the flip side of the previous question.

You can also look at relationships to discover collaborations. The "is-part-of" relationship is a good place to start. As mentioned earlier, this is the contains or aggregation relationship. From our ATM example, we could say that Money is a part of the Person class. You can also look for a "has-knowledge-of" relationship. This means the same thing as "which-gets-it-from." These are key relationships for collaborators. For our example, we could say that a Person has knowledge of his Account. Another important relationship is "depends-on." This can be thought of as the same thing as "changes-with." This relationship indicates that classes are attached in multiple ways. In our example we can say a Person "depends on" the ATM to access his account. Figure 6.4 shows our enhanced Person index card updated to show collaborators for responsibilities. It is clear that Person cannot make a deposit in isolation. Different relationships and interactions are needed to create system-level behavior. Conversely, if you have classes that collaborate with no one at this stage, you should discard them. It is unlikely that classes that don't interact with others serve any useful purpose.

Class: Person

Purpose:

The purpose of the Person class is to simulate the person who uses an ATM in the banking simulation.

Responsibilities	Collaborators
makeDeposit	ATM, Account, Money
makeWithdrawal	ATM, Account, Money
writeCheck	Account, Money

FIGURE 6.4. Collaborators Added to Person

The result of our exploratory phase is essentially a preliminary design. This is not a finished design, because we are still exploring. Later phases will flesh out what we discovered in this phase. There are some problems with the results of this phase. It is difficult to make the connection between a client card call for a server and the server's responsibility because it is only on cards and not clearly shown anywhere. Also, all we have at this point is a disconnected view of the system—a handful of bits and pieces. The task of integrating them into a coherent whole still remains.

RDD—THE ANALYSIS PHASE

In the exploratory phase, we ended up with index cards, which are the equivalent of building blocks for our system. In the analysis phase, we take those building blocks and connect them in meaningful ways. The cards will continue to be enhanced, but new diagrams that show the structure of the system will emerge from this stage. The end result will be diagrams that give us a static view of our system.

The first step in this phase is to create hierarchy graphs. These provide the first integrated look at inheritance within the system. This is the only type of

FIGURE 6.5. Hierarchy Graph

relationship shown on this diagram. Figure 6.5 is an example of inheritance from our banking example. Superclasses or ancestors are shown above or to the left in such diagrams. Subclasses or children are shown below or to the right. The only thing shown here is Savings inheriting from Account. Because Account is above Savings in the diagram, it is considered the ancestor. More complex systems have more complex inheritance trees. The first thing you need to do in creating an inheritance graph is identify super- and subclasses. One technique uses Venn diagrams. If the name sounds familiar, it should. Think back to your first class in algebra and the earliest explanations of set theory. This is exactly the same type of diagram. In math they are used to show what sets have in common. In this methodology, they are used to show common responsibilities between classes. If a diagram shows that classes have common responsibilities, then these responsibilities are candidates to become part of a superclass or ancestor. Figure 6.6 shows a Venn diagram used this way.

This is a variation on our banking example. Here we see that classes CheckingTransaction and SavingsTransaction have some overlapping responsibilities, which could be thought of as common responsibilities for both types of transactions. This indicates that we should move these responsibilities to a superclass we could name Transaction. If we choose to do this, we would then create another hierarchy graph to show this relationship. Such a graph is shown in Figure 6.7. Here we see SavingsTransaction and CheckingTransaction inheriting from

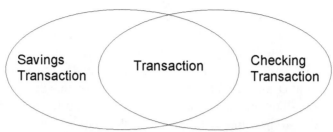

FIGURE 6.6. Using a Venn Diagram to Show Overlapping Responsibilities

Transaction. The regular rectangular shapes around the SavingsTransaction and CheckingTransaction classes indicate that they are concrete classes, meaning there are actual instances of these classes in the running system. The common responsibilities of these classes are in the Transaction class. The darkened corner indicates that Transaction is an abstract class. That means Transaction only exists to provide a common level of functionality needed in children classes. No instances of this class will be found in the running system.

The next step in the analysis process is to look at each class we have created and put related responsibilities into common groups within the class. The term used for this is creating contracts for each class. A contract defines a set of requests that a client can make of a server. Let's try to understand this within

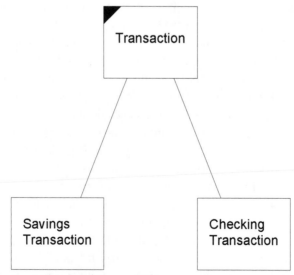

FIGURE 6.7. Hierarchy Graph with Abstract Class

the context of a full-blown Person class. We might have a group of responsibilities that are accessor methods. We could use these methods to ask questions about the Person. For example, we could ask the Person its name or how much money it had. We could group these kinds of methods into a contract called Accessor. We could create a contract called Motion. In this category, we would group all of the methods we could use to tell the Person to run, jump, or walk. Some Smalltalk systems support a concept called categories, which serves the same function. It is a convenient way to group related methods or responsibilities.

Contracts provide another layer of abstraction to our classes. These contracts will be used as we identify relationships between classes and subsystems. In uncovering and creating contracts, it is important to define them as cohesive sets of responsibilities. You do not want contracts that are catchalls. Cohesive contracts indicate we have properly structured and encapsulated classes. If the contracts are not cohesive, then the classes may not be properly designed. We may need to break them into additional classes or distribute the functionality to more appropriate classes. Contracts also help us define "a-kind-of" relationships. They help us put the right level of responsibility at the correct level in an inheritance tree.

There are several techniques we can use to create contracts. Each of these focuses on helping us maximize the cohesiveness of our classes. The first step is to group responsibilities used by the same clients. If a client uses more than one responsibility of a class, it may be important to group them together. These responsibilities may need to work together, which would tell us something about the cohesiveness of the class. The more tightly coupled our responsibilities are, the more cohesive the class is. It is easier to create inheritance hierarchies if classes are cohesive. Classes with many diffuse contracts are difficult to place properly in a hierarchy. They carry along a lot of baggage that is not needed by the child classes. Cohesive classes have clearly defined sets of responsibilities that make them better candidates for inheritance. Inheriting classes are easier to create when the set of responsibilities they inherit is clear and focused.

The next step in creating contracts is a natural extension of the work you've done to maximize cohesiveness—you need to minimize the number of contracts in each class. One way to do this is to generalize similar responsibilities. If you do this, it is often possible to move those responsibilities up higher in the hierarchy. Generalization of responsibilities also supports code reuse by creating classes that provide a more generic functionality. Responsibilities that are narrowly focused are often application specific. Providing more general approaches to functionality increases the potential for reuse.

Once you have done these things, you need to update and enhance your existing diagrams with the contracts you've just created. Then you need to make additional changes to reflect the contracts you've discovered. Start at the top of your inheritance hierarchies and define each contract. Then give the contract a number and brief description. Do this for each contract in each class. Then number each responsibility according to the contract to which it belongs. Finally determine to which contract each collaboration belongs.

The next step in the analysis phase is to create a view of the system that shows the relationships between the classes you've uncovered. This view is provided by a collaborations graph. The graph shows the classes, contracts, and collaborations that exist in a system. Figure 6.8 provides an example of a simple collaborations graph for our banking system. It is the equivalent of the Booch class diagram or

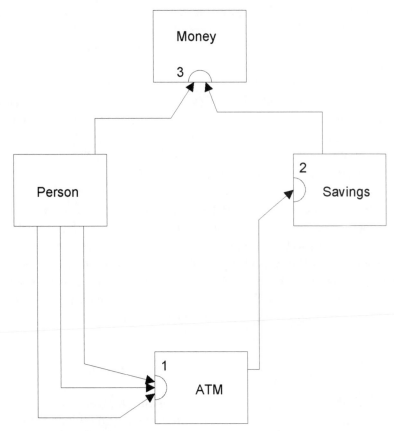

FIGURE 6.8. Collaborations Graph

the Rumbaugh object model. The boxes in the illustration are classes. The diagram shows one arrow for each collaboration. The arcs at the edges of the boxes represent the contracts. The number corresponds to the number you assigned to the contract in the previous step. In this illustration, we see that the Person class has three collaborations with the ATM class—all through one contract. The ATM contract would be one that encompasses all user interaction with the machine. We could call this contract Interaction and so note it on the card created for the ATM class. The three collaborations are calls the Person class is making of the ATM object's responsibilities or methods. These could correspond to the enterCard, enterPIN, and selectAccount responsibilities we discovered in our earliest exploration of this system. Likewise, we see the interactions with the Savings and Money Classes. The collaborations graph shows all paths along which information flows. In this respect, it is much like Booch's object diagrams.

If we were creating a larger system, we would use the diagrams to show subsystems as well as classes. The process of creating subsystems is very similar to the analysis work we have just completed. The first step is to look at our collaborations graph and identify candidate subsystems. You will need to create a card for each subsystem. Determine the contracts that are appropriate for each subsystem. These contracts are the cohesive set of responsibilities that the classes within the subsystem work together to support. You annotate the collaborations between subsystems in the same manner you did with classes. The only diagrammatic difference is that subsystems are boxes with rounded corners. You can show the internal class collaborations within each subsystem box. Add the subsystem to your graphs and then work to minimize the number of contracts supported by each subsystem. The strategy for this is identical to the same operation for classes.

The final step in the analysis phase is to create protocols for each class. The protocol contains the specific signature for each method or responsibility a class has. This is identical to the prototype specification for a method in C++ or American National Standards Institute (ANSI) C. It is important to make each method as generally useful as possible. You should also provide default parameters if possible. At this point you could create a set of C++ header files for each of your classes.

RDD—THE DESIGN PHASE

The design phase is the process of refining the analysis work. It is still iterative. It is a matter of filling in the missing details. You may find the need to create new classes or to reorganize or discard others. This process is complete when you can satisfy your scenarios and you feel you have enough information to begin implementation. The results of the design process are hierarchy graphs showing the inheritance structure of the system, collaborations graphs showing the communication paths in the system, a set of formal contract specifications listing all client-server collaborations and the services each provides, a specification of each class and subsystem, and a set of protocols for each method in each class.

SUMMARY OF CRC AND RDD

There are a number of benefits to using the CRC and RDD. First of all, this approach can be used to show the tie back from design to requirements. This was a problem in other methodologies. Also, the behavioral approach is a very powerful tool. This part of the methodology has caught the attention of other methodologists. One technique for analyzing system behavior is to do role playing. This is a very physical and hands-on approach, which encourages the developers to look at a design from an object's perspective. One of the better publicized aspects of the methodology is the use of index cards for organizing and capturing information. The use of cards is simple and nonthreatening. It is also inexpensive and highly portable.

There are some weaknesses in the methodology. It is not as comprehensive as the others we have looked at. In fairness, we note that it is not as simplistic as it is often portrayed. It really is more than just index cards. One of the features missing is a formal mechanism for capturing many of the details about a class. Index cards are fine as far as they go, but they don't capture any of the algorithmic information you need to implement a method. They also miss other general information about collaborations. For example, a collaboration may need to be synchronous or asynchronous, blocking or nonblocking, etc. To see what is missing, contrast the index cards with the type of information captured in the Booch templates or the OMT data dictionary. Also peculiar is that this methodology lacks a formal dynamic system view. The dynamics are implicit in the process. Role playing and the use of scenarios ensure that. However, there is no real mechanism for capturing those dynamics explicitly on paper. The current diagrams are similar to the Booch class and object diagrams or the OMT object model. The methodology lacks state diagrams or system-level event flow or dynamic model diagrams, so it is not easy to see the flow of events in the system. Finally, there is a bit too much emphasis on the noun/verb approach to discovering classes. Reliance on this approach alone makes it difficult to discover abstract mechanisms or classes.

Many people have used CRC and the RDD methodology successfully. The behavioral approach is the key advantage. It offers a view not explicitly found in other methodologies. The noun/verb and index card aspects of the methodology are perhaps the most well known, but we have seen that there is more to it. The CRC method offers an interesting place to start for an object-oriented project, but the methodology is inadequate in many ways. Although it may be fine for small systems, you will probably want to use a methodology that helps you capture more information if you are developing a large system.

REFERENCES

1. Beck, Kent and Cunningham, Ward. "A Laboratory For Teaching Object-Oriented Thinking." *OOPSLA '89 Proceedings*, 1989.
2. Wirfs-Brock, Rebecca et al. *Designing Object-Oriented Software*. Englewood Cliffs, NJ: Prentice-Hall, 1990.

CHAPTER 7
Choices in Methodology: Coad–Yourdon

There are many methodologies you can choose from. Fortunately, to educate you in object technology, it is not necessary to review them all. In this chapter, we will examine our final popular methodology—the Coad–Yourdon methodology. The details of Coad–Yourdon methodology are covered in three books: *Object-Oriented Analysis* by Peter Coad and Ed Yourdon,[1] *Object-Oriented Design* by Coad and Yourdon,[2] and *Object-Oriented Programming* by Coad and Jill Nicola.[3] The last book provides a summary of the first two and shows applications of the methodology in both C++ and Smalltalk.

Why are we examining this methodology? Peter Coad has done a good job of making his methodology accessible to developers, and its notation is often used in magazine articles. Learning the methodology from Peter Coad himself can be an unforgettable experience. If you've ever watched him teach a class, you would have to describe the experience as lively. He uses music, sound, and participation to engage all the senses in the learning process. Coad believes software development should be fun. If you don't have an opportunity to attend one of his classes, you can buy "The Object Game," which consists of a videotape of him teaching a class along with all the cards and noise-making accouterments he uses in his classes. If you know nothing about object-oriented technology, it provides a gentle introduction. Unfortunately, it doesn't go beyond that. Coad's method is perhaps the best documented, with the three books listed earlier covering all phases of the process.

THE COAD–YOURDON METHODOLOGY

The fundamental concept in Coad's methodology is the single underlying model for all phases of the process. Coad took this approach because of the perceived difficulty in unifying different models in other methodologies. The different views that are needed at different points in the process are provided through a multi-layer approach. Different layers hold different information about the design. Needed views are created by turning on and off the appropriate combination of layers. This eliminates the need to unify models, because there is only one. This approach is similar to that used in electrical and mechanical CAD systems. A single underlying model holds all information. Different views are provided by layers that let you look at different parts of the model. In Coad's methodology, you simply use the layers that are meaningful at a given point in time.

The principles that are the heart of Coad's process are based upon requirements for managing complexity.[4] The first of these is methods of organization. The first step in organizing a problem domain is to separate experience into objects and attributes. By doing this, you distinguish between objects and their parts. You can use this same approach to form different classes of objects. For example, there may be a user interface class of objects or database access class of objects. We are not talking about a single class in these cases. What we are referring to is a group of classes related to one another by the similarity of their functions.

The second principle of managing complexity Coad uses is to categorize behavior. You begin by trying to uncover the immediate causes of behavior in a system. In our banking example, a person entering his bank card into an automatic teller machine starts the behavior of the ATM class. The next step in categorizing behavior is to find what causes changes in behavior over time. You might think of this as the history of a system's behavior. If we went back far enough in time for our banking example, we would find a person interacting with a human teller. Automation changed the behavior of the system by making

ATMs possible. Such a change has implications for the architecture of the system. Understanding this kind of change can help us create systems that are robust over time.

The final principle Coad uses is personification. He uses it to unify the other principles. By personification, he does indeed mean giving human characteristics to objects. It provides a key method of discovering objects. One of the questions he believes each object must answer is, What do I know and what can I do? Can an object know and do? This is personification in action. Personification provides a context for applying the other principles. Behavior is thought of in human terms. Organization is viewed from a human perspective.

THE COAD–YOURDON NOTATION

Coad's notation for his methodology has evolved over the last few years. Unlike others, his has become cleaner, less complex. This makes it simple to use but denies it the richness needed to capture design details. His notation for a class is the rectangle. Figure 7.1 provides an example for the Person class. There are several parts to this notation. The simple rectangle is an abstract class, a class for which no objects are created in a system. It serves as an ancestor from which others can inherit behavior. A lighter or dashed rectangle around the first means that the class is a concrete class, which will have instances of itself

FIGURE 7.1. Class Notation

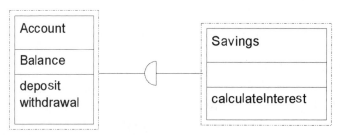

FIGURE 7.2. Generalization-Specialization Relationship

in the running system. Our Person class shows both rectangles since a Person object will be needed in our simulation system. The main or inner rectangle is divided into three sections. The top section is the class label, where you put the name of the class. The center section is where you list a class's attributes. The bottom section is where you list a class's services. Service is Coad's term for method. This structure is very similar to that seen in Rumbaugh's OMT notation.

Coad provides a notation for what he calls a generalization-specialization structure—what everyone else thinks of as the proper use of inheritance. Strictly speaking, you might not choose to call it inheritance. If you are implementing in a language that doesn't support inheritance, you may find another mechanism for creating this structure. This, however, is stretching the point. Inheritance is a fundamental part of object-oriented technology, and this is the notation for that relationship. In Figure 7.2, we see the generalization-specialization structure for the Account and Savings classes. The half-circle shape on the connection between the two classes indicates generalization-specialization.

Coad also provides a notation for what he calls the whole-part structure. This is the same as aggregation in the OMT methodology or the contains relationship in the Booch methodology. In Figure 7.3, we see an example of the whole-part structure with our Account and Money classes. The triangle on the connection between classes indicates the whole-part structure. The top of the triangle points to the class that is the whole portion of the structure. The flat portion of the triangle is on the side of the "part" portion of the structure. You can also use range or limit marking to indicate the number of the relationship, which is the number of a particular class known to the other class. This is the same use of number we have seen in the other methodologies.

Coad provides notation for other object relationships. The first of these is the object connection, which is the same as the Booch uses relationship. The nota-

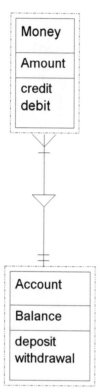

FIGURE 7.3. The Whole-Part Relationship

tion is a simple line between objects. You may include number information on this relationship, but nothing else. The object connection tells us there is an association between objects. Figure 7.4 shows us the complete banking system in Coad's notation. We see an example of the object connection relationship between the ATM and Account classes. As an example of number, we see that an ATM object may know about 0 to m Account objects.

Another type of relationship is found in the notation for a Message. This is used to show an interaction of objects and is similar to the type of information you find in a Booch object diagram. The notation is an arrow pointing from one object to another, indicating that one object sends a message to another object. In Figure 7.4 we see an example of a message where Person is sending the enterCard message to ATM. Instead of stating the actual message, you can label each message connection with the name of a scenario and the number of that message in the scenario. Our banking example in the figure shows only a portion

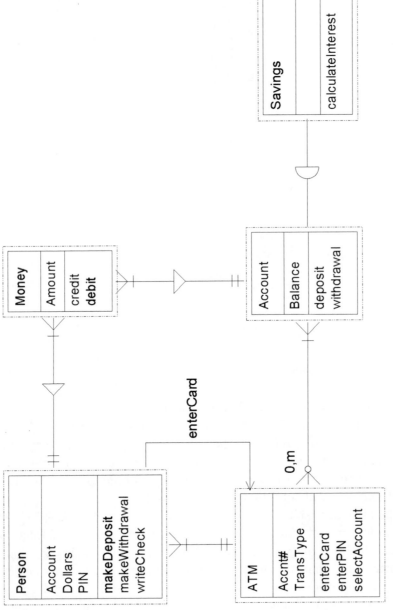

FIGURE 7.4. The Banking System

of what we could illustrate with the notation. It would be easy for us to add additional message connections between objects. This would make the diagram rather cluttered. This view resembles a combination of the class and object diagrams from the Booch methodology. For any reasonably sized system, this diagram could become difficult to read. That's the reason for using multiple layers—by separating information into different layers, we can be selective in what we see.

Another approach to minimizing diagram complexity is to use what Coad calls a subject. This is the same as a subsystem. The notation used for this is a shaded box. Shaded boxes indicate major portions of a system. Another use of the shaded box is for components. All systems are divided into four components, which provide the underlying architecture of the system. The four components are the Human Interaction component, Problem Domain component, Data Management component, and Task Management component. These are loosely coupled with one another using a broadcast/receiver model. One domain broadcasts "I've changed." The others receive the broadcast and know what to do about it. It is this interaction that provides the architectural mechanism for system behavior. There is a bit of additional notation not shown on our diagram. If you took an object connection and put three dots (ellipsis) on it, it would indicate that you collapsed part of the diagram. It's a way to indicate that not all of the diagram is visible.

We've mentioned that in the underlying model, information may be kept in different layers. Coad uses five layers, the first of which is the Subject layer. This is used to identify the major groupings of classes in the system. The second layer is the classes and objects layer. This is where you put the classes and objects, but not the relationships between them. The third layer is the structure layer. Here you put the generalization-specialization and whole-part structures. The fourth layer is the attribute layer, where you put each class's attributes and the object connections with other objects. The final layer is the service layer, where you put each class's services and the messages sent to other objects.

THE COAD–YOURDON PROCESS

Coad does not talk about the steps in his process. Instead, he talks about activities. He does this because steps imply a sequence like the waterfall approach to development. Coad's activities are very iterative. He uses what he calls the baseball model, which is similar to the whirlpool approach. You start with some object-oriented analysis, followed by object-oriented design to capture some details about the system. This is followed with a bit of object-oriented programming to build and test what you have designed. Keep repeating that process until you are done. The activities Coad uses begin with discovering the classes and objects the system needs. The next activity is to uncover the generalization-specialization and whole-part structures that relate objects. Once this activity is complete, you identify system subjects (subsystems). The next step is to identify an object's attributes. These say what an object knows. Finally, you identify each object's services, which define what an object can do. These activities taken together define Coad's version of object-oriented analysis and object-oriented design.

It is not clear how well this particular approach scales up for implementing large systems. You usually need an architecture to provide a framework early in the process of developing large systems. This is more important than worrying about generalization-specialization. Without an underlying architecture or identification of major subsystems, the other activities will only lead you to a hodgepodge of classes that will not work well together.

It is useful to take a closer look at these activities and see how they affect the development process. Looking for classes and objects is part of the analysis process. Coad suggests you begin by look for persons, places, or things in your problem statement.[5] You should be thinking in the first person when looking for objects. It is part of personification. He then recommends you take a "breadth-then-depth" approach to looking for classes. Make a list first, then create hierarchies from that list. You can also look for analogs to help identify candidate classes. You can often find them if there are similar systems that already exist. Finally, Coad says to act it out. Take the behavioral approach and act out your scenarios. This approach is used extensively in the CRC methodology and is often quite useful.

The next activity in the analysis process is to identify structures in the system. The first one to look for is the generalization-specialization structure. The key to finding this structure is to look for classes that have similar behavior, of which some may appear to be specializations of a more general version. This is also where you can ask, "Is A a kind of B?" Once you've identified the inheritance in your system, you should look for the whole-part structures. There are three key questions you can ask about a class to uncover this relationship. "Is it an assembly?" "Is it a container?" "Is it a collection?" Identifying this structure is also your first step in uncovering the attributes a class will need.

The third activity in the analysis process is to identify subjects or subsystems in the system. To do this, you should look for classes that might be naturally grouped together. You might discover candidates from your understanding of the problem domain and the natural groupings it may provide. You should also look for groupings that simplify the interfaces between subjects. Always look for good partitioning in your subjects. This promotes reuse not at the class level, but at a more beneficial subsystem level.

The activities in the design process are similar to those in the analysis phase. You are simply refining the details. One of the design activities is to define the attributes your classes need. Here you determine what an object can know. You can discover some of these by understanding how a class supports the scenarios it participates in. You might also find attributes in the problem domain. Be sure to define and constrain each attribute. By this I mean define its limitations and characteristics. You also want to capture the services for each class in the design phase. You use the services to define what each class can do. One way to come up with a list of potential services is to look at the behavior an object is supposed to have. Describe the class's basic capabilities and ask how these capabilities add value to the system. You can also look for state-dependent behavior. Is there behavior that changes over time? In our banking example, the ATM class may not respond as expected to a request for withdrawal if the machine is out of money—its behavior can change. Identify these changes to put constraints on a class's services. You can also look for event-response behavior. This type of behavior is best uncovered through play-acting and scenarios. The basic idea is to use events as stimulus to behavior. Finally, you can capture miscellaneous details as text.

The third main activity in Coad's baseball model of development is object-oriented programming. Coad believes there is a systematic mapping from the results of object-oriented analysis and design to an object-oriented language. Attributes become variables. Services become methods. The generalization-specialization structure becomes inheritance. The whole-part structure defines connection variables or attributes. In making this mapping, you will have to answer questions about the visibility of parts and the dependency of the whole on the parts. Another part of object-oriented programming is the creation of helper objects. These are support classes for your application classes. You often do not discover them until you are implementing the system. Coad defines a process for programming. The first step is to build your core classes. Next add in your whole-part structures and object connections. Third, add in messages and method basics. Follow this by implementing your threads of execution. Finally, use this approach to demonstrate frequent and tangible results.

COAD–YOURDON SUMMARY

There are a number of advantages to the Coad–Yourdon methodology. The most important may be the use of the single underlying model. There is no problem integrating models, because there are no models to integrate. The use of layers to control the visibility of information has a long history in CAD systems. It is just as useful for software development. The notation is simple and it's not difficult to learn. Coad also supports an iterative evolutionary approach to development. This is particularly noticeable in the way he integrates the programming process as part of the overall analysis and design process. He makes good use of scenarios and the behavioral approach to uncovering a system's structure. Finally, as Coad would tell you, his method is "fun."

There are some weaknesses in Coad's approach. There is no clear tie back to requirements. You need to document the tie back outside the methodology. If you use scenarios to define your system's functionality, there is no way to document or integrate them with the rest of the model. As with other methodologies, testing information is missing. The notation is easy to use because it is simple, but the drawback is that it is not rich enough for capturing many design and implementation details. It is also difficult to use the multilayer approach without extensive tool support. Finally, the approach seems to ignore the issue of uncovering abstractions that might make useful classes or using architectures other than Coad's components in a system.

The single-model approach is perhaps the most important philosophical difference from the other methodologies. Indeed, Coad's classes offer a gentle interdiction to object technology. Unfortunately, it lacks some of the richness needed to capture design details, and it is also weak in its support for uncovering complex interactions and abstract classes. Still, it has been used successfully on numerous projects. Its best use may be for small or medium-sized projects.

REFERENCES

1. Coad, Peter and Yourdon, Edward. *Object-Oriented Analysis*. 2nd Ed. Englewood Cliffs, NJ: Prentice-Hall, 1991.

2. Coad, Peter and Yourdon, Edward. *Object-Oriented Analysis.*Englewood Cliffs, NJ: Prentice-Hall, 1991.

3. Coad, Peter and Nicola, Jill. Object-Oriented Programming. Englewood Cliffs, New Jersey: Prentice-Hall 1993.

4. Coad, Peter and Mayfield Mark. *OOA & OOD to OOP: A Practitioner's Guide.* Austin, Texas: Object International, 1993, pp. 3–4.

5. Coad, Peter and Mayfield Mark. *OOA & OOD to OOP: A Practitioner's Guide.* Austin, Texas: Object International, 1993, pp. 12–13.

CHAPTER 8

Making the Choice: Comparing Methodologies

So far we've taken a look at the five most commonly used methodologies for object-oriented projects. Our review shows that they are not identical. Since this is the case, we might ask if one methodology is the "right" one. Is there one methodology that is superior to all others? No. No one methodology has all of the answers. Each makes a unique contribution and has its own strengths and weaknesses. All are incomplete in some respect. We begin this chapter by noting the similarities and clearly showing the differences between them. In comparing these methodologies, we will take a practical view of what is actually needed from a methodology to complete a design. This examination will raise a number of issues that anyone selecting a methodology must address. We will see that there are no cookbook approaches to object-oriented development. By understanding these issues, you will be able to choose a basic methodology and blend in the best techniques from the others. Finally, no discussion of methodologies is complete without trying to understand what constraints language choice places on your design. We will look at C++, Smalltalk, and CLOS as the most common and

155

widely used representatives of object-oriented languages. Each imposes different constraints on the developer. We will also examine how you might use an object-oriented methodology with a procedural language such as C, COBOL, Fortran, or Pascal.

A COMPARISON OF METHODS

There are many similarities among methodologies. Several of them seem interchangeable at the analysis level. These similarities allow you to mix and match techniques. We see several common themes in analysis. The first is in how to find objects. The simplest approach is to use nouns from the requirements or problem statement. Every methodology can use this approach to come up with an initial list of objects. Some of the methodologies may use scenarios as well as the problem statement for this approach. Once you've found the obvious objects, the next step is to find the "hidden" and abstract objects. Rumbaugh provides an approach to uncovering hidden objects by turning associations into objects. This is a powerful technique. Booch takes a different approach by understanding how multiple objects work together to provide higher-level behavior. He calls this interaction of objects mechanisms. The interaction between objects may reveal the need for additional objects. Booch additionally supports this approach by looking for metaobjects, or a society of objects. Again, it is interaction that uncovers the need for additional objects.

There are strong similarities between these approaches and the behavioral approach preferred by Jacobson and Wirfs-Brock. Jacobson's use cases provide a framework for uncovering objects. The CRC methodology uses role playing and acting out for the same purpose. The dynamics of moving through a scenario or use case uncovers objects. Interactions reveal missing components. This behavioral approach is being adopted by other methodologists as an additional technique. It integrates easily with methodologies that had not earlier provided support for it.

The next step that all methodologies address is determining what relationships exist between objects. Booch has the clearest view of relationships. His class diagrams show only three types of relationships: inherits, contains, and uses. This set provides a useful categorization of relationships. It is clean and simple, and it provides useful categories for metrics as you analyze your design. This set of categories is often called "Booch Lite." This is because his expanded methodology allows for other types of relationships in his diagrams. In the latest version of Booch's methodology, he has adopted the concept of associations from Rumbaugh's OMT methodology. This does not minimize the usefulness of his main categories. Most other methodologies simply expand on these. The basic difference is in the uses relationship, which becomes many different things in other methodologies. All additional types of relationships are simply a variation on the "uses" theme, created to provide additional information about the uses relationship.

In Rumbaugh's OMT methodology, the uses relationship becomes an association. To each association, you can add detail about the relationship. This step is most useful when an association turns into a class in its own right. In our banking example, we mentioned how the interaction between the Person class and the ATM class could become a Transaction class. Jacobson uses extends, acquaintance, and communication associations to model the uses relationship. Each provides its own unique flavor in explaining the uses relationship. The CRC methodology turns uses relationships into responsibilities and contracts. Coad turns them all into services. All provide more detail about the uses relationship. However, none of them seems to have the power of Rumbaugh's associations.

Most methodologies begin uncovering relationships by looking for the verbs in the problem statement. Every methodology can use this step. The differences lie in how the methodologies categorize relationships. A more difficult question is, How do you uncover complex relationships? A complex relationship is usually one where the interaction of several objects defines a key aspect of a system's architecture. Decisions about complex relationships are important, because they are decisions about your fundamental system architecture. Some methodologies force an architecture on you, others do not. In any case, these are a vital area in system design. Decisions about complex relationships determine the robustness of your system. The Model-View controller (MVC) mechanism, mentioned earlier in the book, is an example of a complex relationship. The interaction of these three components controls the user interface behavior. This mechanism can be a key architecture for any user interface system.

Booch uses mechanisms to model complex relationships. Mechanisms are defined to be interactions of objects that provide behavior to satisfy a requirement. Booch notes that the selection of mechanisms is a strategic decision, because they form the underlying system architecture. Mechanisms are not predetermined in Booch's methodology. Rumbaugh does not specifically address mechanisms. You might consider the OMT associations as a weak form of mechanism. Jacobson provides a fixed architecture or mechanism in his analysis model. He defines the space of an application using a Behavior-Presentation-Information framework. All objects are placed within this framework. All objects must also be categorized as control, interface, or entity objects. These two sets of constraints provide a framework that is similar to the MVC, but more general. Coad provides a more generalized framework. He insists that all classes fall into one of four components. These components are the problem domain, task management, data management, and human interaction. The relationships between these components are not formally defined. The architecture of the relationships is the result of the analysis process.

There are some notable differences between the methodologies. While they may look similar at the analysis level, there is great variation at the design level. For most of the methodologies, design is a refinement of the analysis process. This is a bit different for Jacobson, because he adds interaction diagrams in the design phase. Many different levels of design detail can be expressed by the methodologies. Most of them lack explicit notation for capturing implementation details. Booch's methodology is the most complete for capturing implementation details using a specific notation. A lack of detail can make implementation difficult. In other methodologies, the developer is often left to his or her own devices to adequately capture or invent this information.

All of the methodologies are lacking in some aspect. The inability to tie the design back to the original requirements is a failure most of them share. Jacobson is a notable exception in this case. His use cases are fundamental to the design process and are directly tied to requirements. It is important to note that all of these methodologies are evolving. They have been used successfully in projects and continue to grow as they are put to the test with new systems.

It might be interesting to consider what we would like to see in an ideal methodology. Such a methodology would be simple to use and understand. Techniques and notation to handle complex issues would be optional, but available. Methodologies that are too complex for the value they bring to a project would not be used. An ideal methodology would provide diagrams that give a static view of a system's architecture. It would also provide diagrams that clearly show the flow of events through a system. These diagrams should explain how a system accomplishes its desired functionality and provide explicit support for creating different architectures. Using an architecture is fundamentally important to creating a robust system. However, it should not force an architecture on a system. It should use the power of the behavioral approach to uncover new objects and provide a tie back to requirements. Something like use cases would be fine. It should also support concepts such as OMT's associations. The ability to turn relationships into additional objects is a powerful technique. The methodology should also have explicit support for capturing implementation details. We want to make implementation as easy as possible and not stumble over missing or incompatible pieces. Finally, it should support the testing process at class, subsystem, and system levels. Since none of the existing methodologies is ideal, we need to create one that is ideally suited to our own needs.

METHODOLOGY ISSUES

One of the main reasons this book exists is to help you understand how to use a methodology successfully. A little later in the book, we'll look at a real system that was created with a methodology modified to meet our needs. Before we get to that point, it is important to understand the choices involved in selecting a methodology and the ramifications of making changes to it. As we have seen from our examination of different methodologies, it appears that none is complete. How then do you choose a methodology for a project? All of the methodologies have been used successfully, as they exist, on object-oriented projects. Surely that implies that they are complete in some sense. It is really a matter of viewpoint. Different people have different needs. Outside forces may impose constraints or requirements that a methodology simply does not address. For example, the issues involved in developing real-time systems are often completely ignored by methodologies. (This is changing with the introduction of Don Firesmith's ADM methodology, which focuses on concurrency and real-time issues.[1]) What help is methodology in your work with memory and timing budgets? There may be other areas where, to respond to reporting requirements, you have to create documents that the methodology does not support. It is simply a fact that most methodologies will not accommodate all your needs.

What do you do when you need something extra or different from a methodology? Should you modify it, or is the methodology so strict that any change will subvert the entire development process? We can look to the methodologists for an answer to this. We have seen how different methodologies provide techniques that give useful insights into the design of a system. The methodologists have seen the same thing and are adapting ideas from other methodologies. Booch is now making use of associations from the OMT methodology and interaction diagrams from Jacobson's approach. Both he and Rumbaugh appreciate the value of use cases and have noted where they may fit into their methodologies. The fact is that few people use a methodology without some adaptation. No single methodology can hope to address every issue for every developer. What they do is provide a well-developed framework in which development can take place. These frameworks are well enough developed that the modifications made to them are usually minor in nature. Our creation of event flow diagrams was a deviation from Booch's methodology. Although his methodology supported the concept of a dynamic view, his existing diagrams didn't work well for us, so we created our own. Since then Booch has added interaction diagrams that we could have used instead of event flow diagrams.

One of the mistakes developers make is to forget that a methodology is flexible. I've usually seen this in the context of groups required to adhere to a structured methodology. They keep doing the same things over and over, regardless of their problems, in the belief that all things will turn out bright and beautiful in the end. They are usually disappointed. There are no magic bullets or cookbook approaches to development. This is true of both object-oriented and structured methodologies. Many believe that inflexibility equals a consistent and successful process. Inflexibility does not guarantee success. CASE tools, for example, have not turned out to be the magic solution people wanted. They are rigid in structure and often require you to do many things that are irrelevant to the task you are trying to complete. Many people have bought them and abandoned them. They were simply too much work for too little benefit. If they remained in use, it was often because a small portion of the tool was found useful. It is important for developers and tool makers to realize that there is no one answer to everyone's needs. Both developers and tools need to be flexible and adaptable to individual requirements.

We can extend our question a bit further. If it is OK to modify a methodology, is it OK not to use all of a methodology? Both Booch and Rumbaugh strongly suggest that you use their methodologies with an appreciation of your own goals in mind. Not all views and diagrams are needed for every project. For example, why create Booch process diagrams if you have a single process system? Likewise, if you are going to use a certain type of diagram, you do not necessarily need to generate them for every part of the system. Diagrams that do not provide you with additional information or insight are of little value. Usually, the most important diagrams are those that show the static structure of the entire system, for example, the class diagrams for Booch or the object model diagrams for Rumbaugh. You will want to be thorough with these diagrams. Only use things like state diagrams where they provide useful information.

There is no complete set of simple—or even complex—steps that guarantees a desired result at the end of the process. All methodologies prescribe steps after a fashion. They are guidelines. You must understand the purpose of the steps if you want to get the most from them. You must also understand your own needs to see where you need to supplement existing methodologies. Select only those parts of a methodology that are appropriate to your needs. This requires planning. There are no mindless answers. This is why development is still very much a human activity. Tools can support human activity, but they cannot, at this time, replace human activity. Having said all this, I don't want to imply that selecting a methodology is like selecting from a Chinese menu. You cannot simply pick one part from method A and the next part from method B and hope to end up with a coherent approach to development. The methodologies were designed to be used as a whole. Their steps are integrated. While they are amenable to change, they are not amenable to being ripped apart and then sown together in a patchwork process. Select the methodology that is closest to your needs, then make the modifications or additions you need. By selecting one methodology as your basis, you provide a consistent framework for the development process.

Object-oriented methodologies require a change in the normal development cycle. All of the methodologies are iterative and incremental. None of them uses or recommends the waterfall approach. This is very different from what many organizations are used to. Large programming shops are often organized on the basis of the waterfall approach to development. The analysts are grouped together and rarely talk to anyone else. Once they have completed their part of the project, they toss their analysis over the wall to the designers, who in turn toss the results of their work over the wall to the implementors. None of the groups talks to each other, and once they have completed their part of the project, they never see it again. This kind of approach to organization and development makes object-oriented development an important management issue. Managers can create organizations that thwart the communication needed for iteration to work.

Iteration is not unique to object-oriented development. Programming on a small scale is often iterative. Developing small systems in small groups often closely resembles iterative prototyping. Even for large projects, many firms use a more iterative approach than is usually envisioned for them. In practice, the waterfall approach is not as arbitrary as some would think. Iteration is often needed to accommodate change. It is ignored at the risk of building a system that doesn't serve the user. We will look at these issues later in the context of a real project. Also, in the next chapter we will examine object-oriented development and object-oriented life cycle. Our emphasis will be on the practical, not the theoretical.

LANGUAGE ISSUES

Before we leave our study of methodologies behind, we need to look at how the choice of language affects our use of a methodology and the development process. C++, Smalltalk, CLOS, Eiffel, and Objective C are the best known object-oriented languages. There are other object-oriented languages on the horizon. Almost everyone has heard of Ada. Ada83 is only class based, but a proposed set of extensions, known as 9X, would give it several object-oriented characteristics. In this section we will look at the most common languages: C++, Smalltalk, and CLOS. We are not going to try to teach C++ or any of the other languages. Instead, we will highlight their features and the issues that arise in using them. We will also examine the issue of using non–object-oriented languages with an object-oriented methodology.

C++

C++ is currently the hands-down leader in the object-oriented language market. It is portable and found on many platforms. C++ is more than just a better C, although it is very often used that way with the strong typing C++ provides. However, if you limit yourself to that use, you will miss most of the power it provides. C++ added several new features to C, including encapsulation through classes, multiple inheritance, polymorphism through virtual functions, operator overloading, templates, and strong typing. The class is the key concept in C++. It is the way encapsulation is done. C++ provides several methods to control accessibility and visibility. These methods provide C++'s data-hiding capability. In C++, attributes and methods can be declared public, private, or protected. Declaring a method or attribute public means it is accessible from outside the class. Declaring part of a class protected means it is accessible by the children that inherit from the class, but inaccessible to those outside the class. Declaring an attribute or method private makes it inaccessible from outside the class. By convention, attributes are made private. This improves the encapsulation of the class. C++ provides a mechanism to get around encapsulation. By declaring one class a friend of another, you provide accessibility to a class's internals no matter how they were declared.

C++ provides no high-level data types or primitives. This may change. The ANSI standards committee is being pushed to provide a standard library of classes. This library would serve much the same function STDIO does for C. Classes being considered for the library include Strings, Stacks, Lists, Arrays, etc. Currently, you either buy a commercial library that has these or you reinvent the wheel. Reinvention is one of the things most C++ developers would like to avoid. A rich body of classes would benefit all.

Lack of performance was one of the early criticisms of C++. Many felt the virtual function mechanism would make C++ very slow. This has turned out not to be the case. Optimization makes C++ as fast as C, and a single pointer dereference is all that is needed for virtual functions. The only time there may be a problem is when you get an explosion of message passing. Here, one object calls another class, which calls another, and so on until finally the object you were trying to get a message to is reached. This type of problem is usually the result of a poor design and not an inherent fault of C++.

C++ is a subtle language. The nuances of its semantics and usage take time to learn and recognize. This is partly because C++ is still evolving. There is no definitive standard yet. As a result, some things are not clearly defined, and you will see different compilers do different things. A clear example in this area is the lifetime of temporary objects a compiler creates. As the language stands, a compiler could destroy the temporary right after it is used or it could live until the end of the block. If you are not careful about the creation of temporaries in your code, you can get different results from different compilers. The standards committee has decided that temporaries may live until the end of a statement, but it may be a while before these decisions are implemented. Issues like this do not mean that C++ is in such a state of flux as to be unusable. It is very usable, but you must be aware of the subtleties.

Another way in which C++ is subtle is that it allows so many options. Some think it allows more than it should. The use of references, pointers, pointers to member functions, and the need to do your own storage management all add complexity and potential pitfalls. Figure 8.1 shows an example of a class definition. It is our old friend the Person class. We show it here to give you a flavor of what the language looks like. Development environments for C++ are

```
#include <string.h>
#include "money.h"
#include "atm.h"

class Person
{
private:
      int PIN;
      String Accnt;
      Money Dollars;

public:
      Person(const int pinum, const String &accntnum){
            PIN = pinum;
            Accnt(accntnum);
      }
      makeDeposit(Money Dollars, ATM machine, String &transtype);
      makeWithdrawal(Money Dollars);
      writeCheck(String Accnt, int checknum, Money Dollars);
};
```

FIGURE 8.1. Sample C++ Code

increasing in sophistication. They provide a much easier approach to development than just using stand-alone tools. This leads to shorter development times. All in all, C++ is a language that provides powerful mechanisms for creating robust object-oriented systems.

Smalltalk

Smalltalk is a pure object-oriented language. In C++, you can mix the object-oriented paradigm with procedural code. In Smalltalk, everything is an object. All work is accomplished by objects sending messages to other objects. It is impossible not to do object-oriented development in Smalltalk. It's also difficult to talk about the language without talking about its environment. The Smalltalk environment comes with all the language development tools you need and a library of hundreds of classes. The tools are a part of the library of classes. You can modify the tools to suit your own needs. As you create new classes, they are added to the system. They are as much a part of the system as the classes that came with it. The nice thing about having so many classes available is that it is often possible to develop complete applications by simply extending or changing existing classes. The Smalltalk developer is not concerned about reinventing the wheel just to achieve basic functionality.

The dynamic nature of Smalltalk results in a very interactive development environment. This is one reason Smalltalk is used for rapid prototyping. An interactive environment combined with hundreds of classes greatly reduces development time. One of the initial problems with Smalltalk was that to run an application, you needed the environment. This is no longer true. Current systems essentially strip out what is needed from the original environment, add your classes, and let you deliver a stand-alone application. Since you can now deliver stand-alone applications, Smalltalk is rapidly moving beyond its use as a prototyping-only language. One of its major uses is now in business applications. Smalltalk's tight integration with a Graphical User Interface (GUI) makes it easy to quickly deliver end-user applications. It is often the language of choice, rather than C++, in this type of application. Smalltalk also has a strong presence in MIS applications. It has also been used in real-time process control and embedded system applications.

Smalltalk is a dynamic language, which means that binding to the correct objects occurs at run time, not compile time. It can be contrasted with C++, which is a static language. Saying that C++ is static means that binding is done at compile time. Smalltalk's dynamic nature gives it tremendous flexibility. This flexibility is aided by the fact that Smalltalk is a typeless language, whereas C++ is strongly typed. Another way to think about this is that the type of objects passed to other objects is not checked by the language in Smalltalk. In C++, type checking is enforced at compile time. This gives the Smalltalk developer great freedom. On the other hand, if you believe that strong type checking contributes to the robustness of a system, you might find Smalltalk risky. While both Smalltalk and C++ are object-oriented languages, there are several differences between them. For example, Smalltalk only supports single inheritance, while C++ supports multiple inheritance. Single inheritance means that a class can have one and only one immediate ancestor. Here is an area where language capabilities impose on methodology. If your language only supports single inheritance, it makes little sense to design a system that requires multiple inheritance. You must use the methodology in a way that your design is implementable.

Storage management is another area where Smalltalk differs from C++. In C++, you must provide your own. Smalltalk provides a garbage-collection mechanism, which is built into the system. You can turn it off if you need to for an application. However, built-in storage management simplifies coding. You do not need to worry about memory leaks the way you do in C++. Smalltalk does not provide as many options to control accessibility as C++. In Smalltalk, attributes are protected and all methods are public. If you want methods to be private, you would categorize them as private, and then by convention no other classes should use them. The language does not enforce this. In C++ classes do not need to inherit from anyone. They can be completely stand-alone. This approach tends to create forests of inheritance trees that are broader than they are deep. In Smalltalk, every class inherits from the class Object. Object provides the basic functionality all classes need to operate in the Smalltalk environment. With this exception, classes can be stand-alone. Some people think that Smalltalk's enforced inheritance makes inheritance trees deeper than they are wide, but this is not the case. Excluding the relationship to Object, Smalltalk inheritance trees are generally no wider or deeper that those created for C++. If a tree is deeper, it is because there is more opportunity for reuse in the Smalltalk tree.

Some claim that since Smalltalk is an interpreted language, it must be slower than a compiled one. Some versions are compiled to machine code. What is true is that Smalltalk is not optimized for numerical computation. Even with interpreted versions, Smalltalk performance is relative. If you use Smalltalk as a tool for creating GUIs, you will find that the underlying architecture, such as X or Windows, has more to do with performance. In these applications, Smalltalk will work as well as any other language, but is faster to develop with. However, for computationally intensive applications, it is slower than C++— how much slower depends on the application. Smalltalk does provide a foreign function interface so that you can implement speed critical portions in another language. Businesses also often find it easier to convert COBOL programmers to Smalltalk rather than C++. These differences between C++ and Smalltalk may account for the fact that businesses seem more inclined to adopt Smalltalk, while technical organizations opt for C++. For many organizations, Smalltalk has proven to be suitable for a wide variety of applications.

Smalltalk also turns out to be quite portable. There are implementations for most major platforms. It really depends on what flavor of Smalltalk you use. Smalltalk is not standardized. There are three major variants: VisualWorks from Parc Place, Smalltalk/V from Digitalk, and IBM Smalltalk from IBM. VisualWorks is even more portable than C++ because the GUI is included as part of Smalltalk. This means that an identical set of classes can be used to provide functionality with different external windowing systems. In C++ you have to adapt classes, since there is no one set of classes that works for all windowing systems. Some companies are developing such tools for C++, but they have their own limitations. There is a new version of Smalltalk called Smalltalk-X, which compiles to C code, and can then be compiled on numerous platforms. Figure 8.2 shows an example of Smalltalk code. This is a small piece of a demonstration

```
Object subclass: #Atest
instanceVariableNames:
        'replyPane inputString inputPane replyStream drawPane ' classVari-
ableNames: "
        poolDictionaries: " !
!Atest class methods ! !
!Atest methods !
graph: aRect
"Initialize graph pane area to aRect."
                | aForm |
                aForm := Form
                        width: aRect width
                        height: aRect height.
                aForm white; offset: aRect origin.
                ^aForm!
inputMenu
                "Answer a Menu for exercising the test program."
        ^(Menu
        labels: 'Who are you?\Name?\Contents\Selected\Draw'
        breakLinesAtBackSlashes selectors: #(message1 message3 message4
        message6 message5))
        title: 'Test'!
```

FIGURE 8.2. Sample Smalltalk Code

program. You generally read Smalltalk code from right to left. In the example, the line "aForm white; offset: aRect origin." means send the origin message to the aRect object. Return its origin. This becomes a parameter to the offset: message aForm understands. The aForm object first receives the message white and then receives the message offset: with the rectangle's origin as a parameter. Although you see the code in this file form, that is not how the developer usually ly sees it. The code appears in a browser organized by class and method and is stored in this form when the system writes the code to disk.

CLOS

CLOS is the Common Lisp Object System. CLOS uses the metaobject protocol to extend standard Common Lisp. This protocol adds object-oriented features to Common Lisp. The purpose of this approach was to allow the developer to extend the language as well as construct on top of it in order to create a language with the expressiveness of Lisp and the efficiency of industrial strength languages such as C or C++. The developers of CLOS realized that no one language was perfect for all uses, which is why they chose to let CLOS allow alternatives through the metaobject protocol.

CLOS supports object-oriented concepts, but it does so in a way quite different from C++. Classes are still the fundamental unit for object-oriented development. However, they are organized differently than we saw in C++. One of the basic differences is that there is no requirement to organize the structure of a class with its methods. Many CLOS developers organize the structure of a class in one file and the methods in another. The attributes that make up the structure of a class are called slots. Each slot may have a number of options associated with it. These usually include several initialization parameters, accessors, readers, and writers. The developer has complete control over the visibility of each slot. By default, everything is visible. New classes, known as subclasses, can be created through inheritance. CLOS supports multiple inheritance. The inheritance of slots or attributes is a bit different in CLOS. Each slot must have a unique name. If an ancestor class and a child class have a slot by the same name, CLOS creates a union between them, that is, CLOS joins the different aspects of the two slots into one whole whose sum contains all the aspects of both. Although CLOS supports multiple inheritance, developers tend to use what are known as mixin classes instead of multiple inheritance. Mixin classes provide some fragment of functionality. That func-

inheritance. Mixin classes provide some fragment of functionality. That functionality is included in another class through aggregation. This is the CLOS version of the contains relationship.

Methods are a different animal in CLOS. Methods are often defined separately from their classes. At the heart of a method lies a generic function. A generic function is the basis of a method with no information that would relate it to a specific class. It provides a common name for a function. A specific method is a version of a generic function for a specific class. Which version of a function is called for which class is determined by its parameters. One of these parameters is its class. Using a class as a parameter makes the method specific to it. A parameter used this way is called a specializer. An example of this organization would be to create a generic function called draw that would receive a shape as a parameter. You would then write versions of this generic function for each class you wanted to draw. This approach tends to group methods by function, not by class. In the context of Lisp there is a valid reason for this. When you call a method in Lisp, there is no way to distinguish it from any other Lisp function. By grouping methods together by function, it is easier to figure out what the options are when a function is called. CLOS has a variant for using a single specializer parameter, known as multiple argument dispatch, to figure out what class a method belongs to. In this case more than one argument has a specializer. This breaks with the intuition that a method belongs to one class. The method must be applicable to all specializers. For example, let's reconsider our draw method. We could create one that works for a rectangle and a bit mapped display. We could create another that worked with a rectangle and a vector display. The functions that get executed vary based on both parameters. It also requires that both classes understand the draw method. Multimethods are very useful constructs. CLOS provides explicit support for them while C++ and Smalltalk do not. An additional wrinkle is the combination method. In combination methods, you can specify before and after steps to occur on either side of the method itself. This is used when you might want some special set up done before the method and some cleanup done afterwards.

CLOS works under most Common Lisp implementations. This makes it highly portable. Common Lisp is available on most machines. We see an example of a class definition in Figure 8.3, where we define a class named generic-attribute. It has five slots. One of those slots is named descriptive-label. It has two options. One is its initial argument, which is of type descriptive-label. It also has the accessor option defined. The methods for this class are done in another file and

```
(defclass generic-attribute (er-object)
((descriptive-label          ; for use by interface
 :initarg :descriptive-label
 :accessor descriptive-label)
 (cardinality                ; can specify multivalued attributes
 :initarg :cardinality
 :initform '(1 1)
 :accessor cardinaltiy)
 (relation-schema            ; for multivalued attributes
 :initarg :relation-schema
 :initform nil
 :accessor relation-schema)
 (parent-attribute
 :initarg :parent
 :initarg :parent-attribute
 :initform nil
 :accessor parent
 :accessor parent-attribute)
 (er-owner                   ; ER object containing attribute
 :initarg :er-owner
 :accessor er-owner)))
```

FIGURE 8.3. Sample CLOS Code

It is in use in numerous operational systems. Because it is a variant of Lisp, it still has an AI flavor, however, there is no need to limit it to AI. Many use CLOS because its flexibility and extensibility are very important to them. It provides an excellent environment for rapid development. The performance of CLOS is good. The issues with it are the same as those with Smalltalk.

USING NON–OBJECT-ORIENTED LANGUAGES

Many developers ask about using an object-oriented methodology with a procedural language such as C, COBOL, Fortran, or Pascal. I have heard some developers say "of course you can implement an object-oriented system in any language." I don't really believe it. The further a language is from the object-oriented paradigm, the more difficult it is to use it in an object-oriented fashion.

It's like pounding nails with a screwdriver. You may succeed, but why bother?

There are several issues involved in using a procedural language. It is not easy to support the same level of abstraction. One of the strengths of the object-oriented approach is its ability to model the problem domain. In these languages, only procedural abstraction is supported. Since objects encapsulate both data and the methods that work on them, procedures are an inadequate level of abstraction for modeling classes. There are ways you can try to add data abstraction and encapsulation. The first of these is to use a style guide, which provides an external definition of encapsulation. In an object-oriented language, this is something the language enforces. You must provide another mechanism for enforcement with a procedural language. In this case this is accomplished by using cooperation through acceptance of certain agreed-upon standards. You can also use programmer discipline as another form of enforcement. Here you are relying on the programmer for internal enforcement of standards. Finally, you can use team inspections. The peer review process provides a strong form of external enforcement. It also has the benefit of uncovering bugs in the code more quickly.

Inheritance is not something that can be explicitly implemented. The one thing you can do is try to factor commonality into individual routines. You might even be able to factor it in at the module level. In reality, there are very limited possibilities for code reuse. Again, you lose one of the benefits of object-oriented language by using a procedural language. This type of language has no explicit support for object-oriented organization in a system. Everything is a force fit. What does it mean to turn an association into an object in a procedural language? The best you can hope for is to create something that is object based, not truly object-oriented. The advantage you gain by doing this is the ability to create a more robust architecture than you would using the structured analysis and design approach. It will take a lot of extra work, because there is no explicit support for object-oriented architecture in the language.

Examine the total costs over the system's entire life cycle. The life cycle economics may indicate that the total costs are less when you use an object-oriented language. The use of procedural languages is often considered when developers think of reengineering a system. There are difficulties in applying an object-oriented model on top of an existing structured design. It is basically an issue of deciding if you can usefully encapsulate existing functions in classes or if you should start from scratch. We'll discuss this more in the next chapter when we examine the object-oriented life cycle.

CHOOSING A LANGUAGE

Your choice of object-oriented language will affect your design and implementation details. Not all languages support the same degree of inheritance, encapsulation, or polymorphism. You might also be tempted to choose an object-based language such as Ada. Ada is thought of as object based and not object-oriented because it does not support inheritance. However, encapsulation is supported, therefore it is considered object based. A new standard proposed, known as Ada 9X, would bring additional object-oriented capabilities to Ada. As we have seen, the less support a language has for the object-oriented paradigm, the more difficult it is to use object-oriented analysis and design techniques in a meaningful way. When you choose a language, you need to determine its ability to support the object-oriented paradigm. Does it support abstraction, encapsulation, inheritance, and polymorphism? It is possible to use object-oriented techniques with procedural languages. Unfortunately, if you choose this approach, implementation issues will intrude from the start. The less support the language offers, the more difficult it will be to implement an object-oriented design. Regardless of the language chosen, specific efforts should be made to ignore language issues until after the analysis is complete.

There is another issue we should at least acknowledge. Because of the close relationship between object-oriented methodologies and languages, the line between the two often becomes blurred. This is most evident in the difficulty encountered in distinguishing a methodology's capabilities from that of C++. As we have seen, other languages have a different view of the paradigm. It is important to separate the issues of methodology and language. Many developers fail to do this, and they often mistake C++ limitations as paradigm or methodology limitations. Different languages have different ways of implementing the paradigm. It is most important to make this distinction while doing analysis. Otherwise language issues play too great a role in the design. You want to postpone as long as possible the choice of language.

REFERENCES

1. Firesmith, Donald. *Object-Oriented Requirements Analysis and Logical Design: A Software Engineering Approach*. New York, New York. Wiley, 1993.

PART III
Running Deep: An In-Depth Look at a Real Project

CHAPTER 9

A Pragmatic Look at the Development Process

We begin this chapter with two questions. How do you develop an object-oriented software system? Is the process by which object-oriented software is developed independent of the specific techniques used to create it? For example, we know that certain things must be done to create any software system. You need to gather requirements and analyze them. You also need to design, implement, and deploy your system. Should the sequence of these processes be independent of the techniques used to accomplish each process? Another way to look at this is to ask, knowing that we will do analysis and design, can we use anyone's techniques for these processes?

Many developers believe that the sequence of processes is independent of the techniques used in the processes. This is not true for object-oriented development. The interaction of process sequences and techniques used for development is important. This interaction will affect the overall robustness of a system and the effectiveness of individual techniques and has broad implications for the development process. Businesses are often organized around process flow. This is often reflected in who reports to whom and the activities of individual groups. What happens when the process changes radically? Must the organization and the nature of its interactions also change? As we will see, the process of object-oriented development and its implications are not what many organizations expect.

WHAT WE DO NOW

For the development process, most organizations follow what is known as the waterfall model. The version of this model that is most used defines the process as a fixed sequence of steps. When the waterfall approach was originally proposed, it was not meant to be the strictly sequential version that many companies now use; it allowed some iteration to earlier steps. Unfortunately, it became more widely used in its rigid personification. This is the version that we will address.

We can see the steps of the waterfall process in Figure 9.1. The process begins with requirements analysis, the purpose of which is to define the scope of the problem. The next step is preliminary design. Here we decide the basic architecture of the system. The third step is detailed design, in which we flesh out the implementation details. This step is followed by coding, where we create the software. Coding is followed by unit testing, in which each module is tested on its own. The integration step is the cosmic big bang of software development, where the individual pieces come together as a whole for the first time. This is followed by system testing, the purpose of which is to answer the question: Does the system do what it is supposed to do? This is the point where most development efforts start to unravel. It can be a Herculean task to get all of the modules talking to one another. It is made more difficult by the fact that the integration of all the components happens at once. It is difficult to track down the source of problems when much of the system has not been tested. The final step is the delivery of the system, at which point you would make the system operational.

This approach has been used for so long in so many places that to many it seems to be the development approach ordained by nature. They can't envision another approach. This attitude is reflected in their organizational structures. Some businesses have organized their software-development organizations around these steps. In one corner, you have a group of analysts. They are separate from the designers, who are also separate from the coders who actually implement the system. Each of these groups can have a separate reporting structure. Often there is little or no communication between them. With this

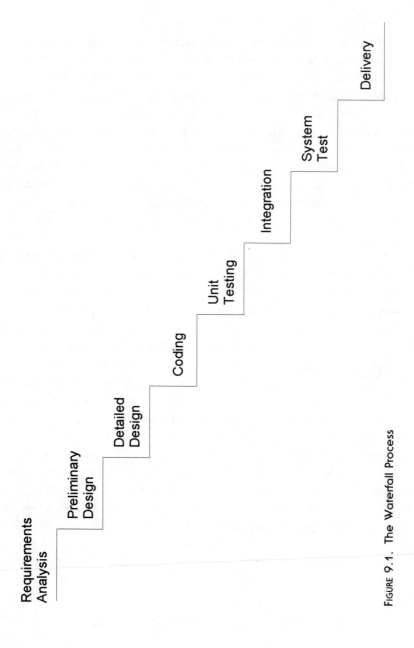

FIGURE 9.1. The Waterfall Process

structure, the organization reinforces the fixed steps of the waterfall process. It is a feedback mechanism where the process defines the organization and the organization discourages any deviation from the fixed process. This is probably why the inflexible form of the waterfall took hold in many organizations. Iteration blurs organizational distinctions. Each little kingdom found it easier to justify its own existence by promoting a rigidity that reinforced its own uniqueness. Interestingly enough, we see organizations using this fixed structure with different methodologies. This structure closely mirrors what happens using SA/SD. There are many variations of SA/SD, but the individual techniques do not seem to matter. The rigid structure produces the same result. This approach has also been tried with object-oriented development, but the attempt to impose the same rigidity on object-oriented development often results in failure.

Having said so many negative things about the waterfall approach and the structure of organizations that follow it, we should ask if it ever works. Certainly, projects have succeeded using this approach. The problem is how you define success. For many, it is fulfilling the original requirements. This is the crux of the problem. In almost every case, while development proceeds, requirements change. This is especially true for long or large projects. Every developer has seen this. What do you do? How late in the process can you accept changes? The stopping point comes early in the waterfall approach. The result is that a delivered system does not do what is currently needed. To solve this problem, you have to stop accepting new requirements for a given release at some point. The goal is to delay the stopping point as long as possible. The system must meet current needs as closely as possible. There will always be some difference in needs and the system's capabilities. What developers need is more control over the difference and a process that is more flexible. They want an approach that will let them do a better job of meeting user needs as well as help build more robust systems with better quality. This leads us to the iterative and incremental approach recommended for object-oriented development. Let's see how this approach can help us overcome some of the limitations of the waterfall approach and attain our goals.

THE WHIRLPOOL DEVELOPMENT CYCLE

An object-oriented methodology is not just a set of techniques for decomposing a system. The process in which those techniques are used is an integral part of how an object-oriented system is developed. Many developers find the object-oriented process a real change from how they usually work. Existing organizational structures may even impede the process. As we will see, communication is a fundamental part of object-oriented development. Organizational structures that don't encourage communication or that actively restrict it can doom an object-oriented project to failure. Let's look at the development process and see why communication is so important.

All object-oriented methodologies use iteration as part of the development process. Most of them use the whirlpool approach to development, which is fundamentally different from the waterfall approach. In the waterfall approach, we see planned construction. You determine the components you need, construct them, and then assemble them into a whole. You then test the whole to see if it meets your original specifications. This seems to be a reasonable manufacturing approach, but why do so many software development projects fail when done this way? It's true that developers have completed many projects this way. A manufacturing approach is one way to manage complexity. Still, there is a high percentage of failure. We need to ask why.

There is another model for building complex systems that we should consider—an evolutionary engineering approach. Evolution is a useful analogy, because software more closely resembles an organism than a mechanism. It's rare that software is simply manufactured and then used as is forever. Software needs to adapt to an ever-changing set of requirements, just as a living organism adapts to its changing environment. This is just as true during development as it is during the rest of a system's life cycle. The development environment changes because the software is changing. The parts you can integrate and test change from day to day. This fluidity is the changing environment into which new components are introduced and tested. With a construction approach, you try to work out all the details ahead of time. The problem is that the details will change. Since integration and testing are left to the end, adaptation becomes more difficult and more costly. An evolutionary approach to software development adapts to changes as they occur. You still want to know as much as you can ahead of time, but it becomes easier and less costly to adapt to changes because adaptation happens early in the process. This approach recognizes that you don't know all of the details ahead of time and that existing conditions may change.

The whirlpool model is an example of the adaptive approach. It is not unique to object-oriented development. Barry Boehm wrote about it in 1986[1] in the context

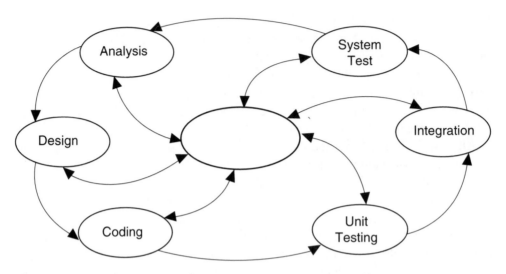

FIGURE 9.2. The Whirlpool Process

of structured analysis and design. We find, however, that object-oriented development is particularly suited to the whirlpool approach. Most methodologists have
variations on this approach to which they have given different names. Still, their
approaches are iterative and reflect the underlying whirlpool approach. We see an
example of the whirlpool in Figure 9.2.

Notice that the whirlpool encompasses the same activities that are in the
waterfall approach. What is different is how they work together. You still start
at analysis and move through design to coding. In the whirlpool approach, there
is no clear break from one type of activity to the next. Using the whirlpool
approach, you may do some analysis, some design, prototype code, and then
return for more analysis. These are not separate, unrelated steps. What you do
in each step may be distinct, but the order in which they are done is not fixed.
This approach recognizes that changes may be caused by decisions at different
levels in the process. Decisions made at the design or even implementation
level can mean changes to decisions made at an earlier level.

In the whirlpool process you may start with analysis and move to design and
coding, but you can return at any point to any earlier step. In practice, most of
this iteration is between the analysis and design steps. Many find it valuable to
iterate through additional steps. The usual process is to iterate as needed to
create a robust system. This approach supports rapid prototyping by letting

you implement and test ideas before committing to them. Because the approach is flexible, you have a greater ability to adapt to changing requirements later in the process. This does not mean you can accept changes at any time until delivery. It is simply an approach that lets you be more flexible about when you can accept changes. Whether or not you actually accept changes depends on where you are in the development cycle.

The whirlpool process as used for object-oriented development has additional characteristics. It supports incremental development. There is no big bang integration step at the end of the cycle. Instead, you can see the system evolve as it gains functionality. This lets you provide early feedback to users and respond more quickly to their requests. Furthermore, the whirlpool approach supports parallel development. Prototypes of design alternatives can be developed concurrently with the analysis and design processes. If multiple teams are involved in project development, they can simultaneously work through their own issues while team leaders keep work in sync at a system level.

3DB SOFTWARE ENGINEERING

All this talk about an iterative process sounds all well and good, but there are serious questions that anyone managing the process must ask. If the process is iterative, how do you know where you are in the development cycle? How do you know if you are making progress? With the waterfall approach, there is a clear transition from step to step. It is easy to see where you are. This is one reason that many managers feel uncomfortable with the iterative process. They see no way to tell if they are making progress. Others take an even more negative view of the iterative process. Instead of characterizing it as a whirlpool, they believe it closely resembles a rat hole that sucks down resources at a prodigious rate. They see no way out of iteration to a finished product. They are quite right to feel such disquiet. Most methodologists seem to assume that managers will automatically understand the implications of the whirlpool approach and understand how to make it work, but this is not always the case.

Developing an answer to the above questions is the motivation for the technique I call 3db software engineering. This technique is the direct result of answering management's question: How do you know where you are? The technique takes the form of a diagram, an example of which is shown in Figure 9.3. This diagram, drawn in response to a manager's question, shows a way of looking

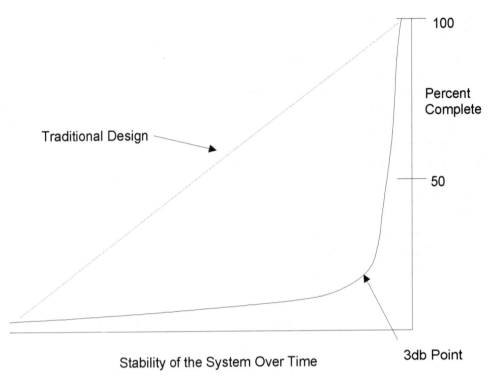

FIGURE 9.3. 3db Software Engineering

at the iterative analysis and design process. It provides a more linear view of the whirlpool process and shows how over time you can tell how close you are to completing your design. In a later chapter, I'll show you how to track the process through implementation.

Let's look at the graph. The dashed line represents the traditional waterfall process. The actual shape is more like stair steps, but the line is a reasonable approximation. Essentially, as you move from one step to the next, you move in a straight line from beginning to end. The curve represents the completeness of an iterative design. In the beginning of the process, everything is amorphous. Things are changing rapidly every day. Nothing is solid. Progress towards completion seems slow or nonexistent.

At the beginning of the process, you try to come up with an initial list of classes and define some of the relationships between them. That list of classes changes every day. As the classes change, so do the relationships between them. What is important to note at this point is the amorphous nature of early development. It is useless to try and solidify things at this stage. There would be nothing gained by imposing a fixed structure. Instead, it is best to generate lots of ideas and throw many away. Iterate freely, and let the classes and their relationships change each day. The value in this approach is that the best design often emerges from the consideration of many possibilities.

As the process continues, the design will start to solidify. The list of which classes exist changes less often. The relationships between the classes also start to solidify. The architecture of the system begins to appear less chaotic. It takes on the first indications of a stable shape and form. Soon a key set of classes begins to emerge. These classes remain fairly constant, while those around them change more frequently. These central classes become your key abstractions, and their interactions determine the overall system architecture. It is important to get these key abstractions correct. One way of doing this is to play the "what-if game" with them. Change a key abstraction and see how the system structure changes. Look for the more general solutions that support your goals. Before long, you will notice that the structure of your system is changing less. You find you are spending more of your time on the details of how a class works and the exact nature of relationships between classes than you do on discovering classes or relationships themselves. Once you reach this point, progress towards completing the design accelerates rapidly.

Notice the knee in the graph labeled as the 3db point. This is where your work changes in emphasis from analysis to design. This is not a distinct step from one process to the next. It is a shift in the focus of work being done. It is the point where you focus more on the details of the structure than on the creation of the structure itself. Before you reach the 3db point you will do some design, but most of the work will be analysis, where you create the underlying structure of the system. You begin to do more design as the structure stabilizes. After the 3db point, the emphasis changes to paying more attention to the details of the classes and their interactions. You can still make architectural changes, but this activity will not be your main focus. When you reach the 3db point, it is an excellent time for an informal design review. The review serves as a sanity check for the architecture. It is vitally important to get the architecture correct. You don't want to go too far down the design road without a real sense that your underlying structure is sound. Once the emphasis shifts to design, progress is much more rapid. It becomes more a matter of making sure you've covered all the functionality and details for each class.

With the 3db curve, you can see how the emphasis shifts from analysis to design, but how do you know when you are done? The curve does not meet the edge of the graph at the completion point. The graph is drawn this way for a reason. It represents the potential for never-ending iteration and endless refinement. It is the rat hole that many managers fear. Even though the curve does not meet the edge of the graph, there is a clear way to know when to end. Test your design against the scenarios you've developed for your application. This implies that the scenarios are comprehensive and cover all appropriate requirements. When the design supports all scenarios, the design is complete. This is one of the reasons scenarios or use cases are so valuable. Successfully supporting them in your design is the milestone for the design's completion. If you recall our first banking example, we created event flow diagrams and language specifically to accomplish this task. These diagrams served to illustrate exactly how the design supported the scenarios. They uncovered the details of the algorithms that were needed to implement the various methods. They detailed exactly what parameters were needed for each method and how they would be used by the method. There is no need to continue working on the design once you can document how the design supports the requirements.

There will be changes as you get into implementation. You'll notice ways to reorganize classes for even greater code reuse. Addressing some of the implementation details may mean revisiting the design or analysis steps. That's all right in the whirlpool approach. You will find that iteration at this stage is more a matter of refinement than one of creating major changes. Rapid prototyping can be part of this process. It is often helpful to quickly prototype a piece of code after you've designed it. This prototype can serve as a proof of concept for that part of the design. That doesn't mean that the prototype becomes production code. It is simply used to explore the design issues in more detail. Iteration can be used throughout the entire process. When you iterate, you see the emphasis of the work change as you proceed from step to step. In one sense, it is similar to the waterfall in that the same steps still exist. What is different is that there are no clear-cut changes from one step to the next.

You might be wondering where the name 3db software engineering came from. I was explaining how to use the graph in Figure 9.3 to Joe Pollizzi, a project engineer at the Space Telescope Science Institute. He noticed that the logarithmic shape of the curve resembled one used to show how decibels relate to sound. Decibels are a measure of the intensity of sound. The knee in the curve is the 3 decibel (3db) point—hence the name 3db software engineering.

REENGINEERING LEGACY SYSTEMS

We've seen the development process for new projects. It's all well and good to say that in the earliest stage of development everything is amorphous because you are starting from scratch. However, many developers' first experience with object-oriented development will not be new development, but reengineering an existing system. What we need to understand is how this process can differ from that for new development. If you are rewriting the existing system from scratch, the process is essentially the same. In fact, there are a few advantages. You should have a better understanding of your system's requirements. You can also use the existing system's functionality to help you develop scenarios. You'll want to define these scenarios as early in the process as possible. Also, the existing system should give you a better idea of what will and won't work. There are also disadvantages to starting with an existing system. Your view of the new system's structure could be colored by the functional structure of the existing system. This can make it difficult to determine the best organization of classes and their relationships. It is important to make as clean a break as possible from the old functional structure. Once your scenarios are in place, proceed as if you were doing entirely new development. Leave the old baggage behind.

What do you do if you can't redo a system from scratch? There are two approaches. The first is to create the majority of the system from scratch. Use the object-oriented portion to provide the basic architecture of the system. The next step is to encapsulate critical existing subsystems as classes or put wrapper classes in front of them. Either approach can provide a consistent and clean interface that will let you incorporate the subsystems into your architecture. This should be a limited number of subsystems. You use object-oriented technology to provide a robust system structure and supplement it with specialized existing subsystems. This is how many developers deal with legacy systems. This type of development is still very close to the process used for new development. The difference is that this time you must encapsulate existing subsystems and incorporate them into your new architecture. This requires some detailed class interface design early in the process. The architecture created by your analysis will be shaped by the existing systems, which must remain in place. Fortunately, the iterative approach supports mixing analysis and design activities, but some details must be decided upon earlier in the process.

The second approach is to create classes that encapsulate all existing system functions. With this approach there is no new underlying object-oriented architecture. The functional design drives the structure of the classes. This method of encapsulating the components of an existing system does not use the iterative approach to development. The underlying structure of the system does not change. The process is one of dividing existing functions into classes. Once this is complete, no additional analysis or design is needed. The class structures serve only to provide cleaner interfaces to the different parts of the system.

Why do some developers take this approach? Sometimes they have no choice. They want to gain the benefits of object-oriented technology but do not have the time or other resources needed to create a system from the ground up. Is their hope realistic? At best, they will gain only a marginal benefit from this approach. The system will have better encapsulation through the use of classes, which can help minimize module interactions. On the negative side, there is no improvement in the system's architecture, which is fixed by the structure of the existing system. This structure was probably created with a functional approach to design. To gain the architectural robustness promised by object-oriented technology, you must create your classes and relationships based on the problem domain. In this approach to reorganizing an existing system, you do not have such freedom. Furthermore, the problem may be complicated by the quality of the legacy system's design. Poorly designed systems with common global data and scattered operations will be difficult if not impossible to encapsulate in any useful fashion.

Which approach should you take for legacy system reengineering? It depends on your circumstances. You will gain the most benefit from object-oriented development if you can create a new object-oriented architecture. This approach will give you the greatest benefit by creating a robust maintainable system. If you want this benefit, then you must either start from scratch or minimize the number of existing subsystems you encapsulate into classes. Either way, you have to create a new class-based architecture. If you are creating a new architecture, then you should use the full object-oriented iterative approach to development.

The approach of simply encapsulating existing system functionality into classes has minimal benefits. The main advantage is the improved interfaces you create through encapsulation. You won't find much improvement in robustness or maintainability. Iteration is not used in this approach because the system architecture is fixed by the existing software's structure. Whichever approach you choose, it is important that you have a clear understanding of what benefits you can reasonably expect. This will help you choose the approach that is right for you.

SUMMARY

Developing software should be closer to evolving an organism than it is to manufacturing a product. Adaptability to changing needs is one key to successful development. It is important to understand that requirements change throughout the development process. Furthermore, not everything is known at the beginning of the process. Changes in design or implementation later in the development cycle may mean that we need to revisit earlier decisions. This not only happens frequently during object-oriented development, it is encouraged. This approach is supported by using an iterative style of development. The iterative approach best known is the whirlpool method. For the whirlpool method to work, good communication is needed at all levels of development. Many companies are organized around the highly structured waterfall approach to development. Not only are the development steps kept separate, but the people who execute those steps are segregated as well. This type of organizational structure will impede the whirlpool-development process. Those working at all stages of development must communicate, including analysts, designers, and implementors. Successful iteration is not possible without communication.

Most object-oriented methodologists recommend an iterative approach to development. They often have their own versions, but the whirlpool approach serves as a useful model for development. In the whirlpool approach, you may start with analysis, but you are free to visit other activities as needed. The typical approach is to do some analysis, do some design, and then return for more analysis. Communication between the individuals doing the work is essential. Although the process is iterative, there are techniques you can use to understand where you are in the development cycle. For example, the 3db software engineering curve can help you understand where you are with analysis and design. It shows that early development is amorphous. Everything in the system is in flux. Gradually, as you uncover your key abstraction, a structure begins to emerge. As the structure takes shape, you find there is a shift in emphasis from analysis to design. This is the 3db point on the graph. You continue iterating and working on the details until your design can support the scenarios you created to define the system's functionality. At this point it is complete.

The approach you take to reengineering an existing system into an object-oriented framework is similar to that for new development. You can redo the system from scratch, which is identical to new development. You can create a new underlying object-oriented architecture but encapsulate a few existing subsystems as classes. This lets you use the best of legacy systems while gaining some of the benefits of an object-oriented development. The final approach is to simply encapsulate existing functionality as classes. The first two approaches give you the benefit of a robust object-oriented system architecture. The third approach has minimal benefits.

Success at object-oriented development requires communication and teamwork. Organizational structures and processes that do not promote this lessen a project's chances for success. The whirlpool approach to iterative development supports both of these needs. It also helps create systems that meet users' needs. It does this by supporting the ability to adapt to changing requirements throughout the development process.

REFERENCES

1. Boehm, B. *A Spiral Model of Software Development and Enhancement.* Software Engineering Notes, vol. 11, 1986.

CHAPTER 10

StarView—
A Real Project

At last, we reach an example of a real system. This project is not a made-up problem. It is a real project with all its bumps and warts. Earlier in the book, we used our simple banking example to illustrate the concepts of object-oriented development. While it was useful for making specific points, it was too small to give you the flavor of the scope of work involved in creating a real system. Other books often have the same problem. Small projects show ideas but lack the breadth of a real project. Even large examples are often made up and lack the grit of a real development project. They are often too formal and lack the dynamics of real development. That's not the case here. In our examination of StarView, we will see how an object-oriented methodology was applied to a real problem. More importantly, we will see where it succeeded and where it needed to be supplemented by other work and documentation. This is the chapter where we can indeed roll up our sleeves and get a look under the hood of a project.

StarView is the user interface to the Space Telescope Science Institute's Hubble Data Archive (HDA), which is the archive for all of the scientific data collected by the Hubble Space Telescope (HST). All of the data are stored in jukeboxes on optical disks. The data for each observation are grouped together in a package known as a dataset. In the archive is a catalog that describes each dataset and its characteristics. The catalog is organized as a large relational database with 200 tables and 1500 attributes. In 1993, there was 1 terabyte of information on line. The archive is designed to take in information at the rate of 10 gigabytes a day, meaning that as the archive grows, its catalog is also going to grow significantly. This catalog is a large complex body of information. Scientists use StarView to query the catalog and select appropriate datasets for study. For example, a scientist may want to know what observations have been made of Mars. StarView sends the query to the archive, which returns to StarView a list of all Mars observations and additional information about those observations. The scientist then selects from the list of observations the particular datasets he or she wants to study. This request for datasets is sent to the HDA, which processes the request and returns the datasets to the scientist.

This is the simple version of StarView's purpose. The actual requirements document used in StarView's design is rather thick. Before we explore StarView's design, let's take a look at the scope of the project. Perhaps a little chronology for the original development work will help. This phase resulted in the first delivery of the system. It has since been through additional iterations. The first 6 months of the project were spent developing the requirements document, selecting tools and equipment, and getting the team trained in several object-oriented methodologies. This process ended with a formal requirements review and an official requirements document. The composition of the team influenced the type of training the team received. The team had seven developers and one technical writer. The team leader had extensive object-oriented experience. The others were experienced developers, but had no object-oriented experience. Because of the team's skills, we felt that they would be able to pick up the C++ language without a great deal of difficulty. A more important issue was that the team learn how to design robust object-oriented systems. For this reason, several team members were sent for training in different object-oriented methodologies. The team settled on Booch's methodology for the StarView project.

After the requirements were accepted, about 3 months was spent in the analysis and design phase. As you would expect, the requirements continued to evolve during this time. This phase of the work led to a number of enhancements and additions to the standard Booch methodology. The most notable of these were the event flow language and diagrams. The design was critiqued and accepted through a formal review process. After this review, an additional 12 months was spent in coding, testing, and delivery. An iterative approach was used throughout. It was an essential and much valued aspect of the development process. For example, there was a significant change in requirements just 3 months before delivery. The iterative approach supported making additional design changes with minimal impact. It is worth noting that the first phase of StarView was delivered on time and under budget. Now for a closer look at the system.

STARVIEW ANALYSIS

Let's look in more detail at the design goals for StarView. One of StarView's requirements was for it to support both text terminal and X Windows interfaces. This meant we needed to create classes independent of the display mechanism. We also needed to take a generic approach to defining the forms the user sees. To meet this goal, we created a Forms Definition Language (FDL) that would work with both interfaces. Another StarView requirement was that it should work with any relational database. In the astronomical community, there are many databases. We wanted to create an interface that could be used with more than just the HDA. To support this, we created a Data Definition Language (DDL) that defines the structure of the database with which StarView communicates. Although our initial goal was just to talk to the HDA, requirements changed and we needed to talk to another archive before development was finished. Another StarView goal was to allow the user to manipulate the results of queries in various ways. We chose to give StarView its own internal relational database for storing and navigating query results. A relational database was chosen because we wanted to allow relational operations on tables of query results.

One of the difficult tasks facing StarView was providing a way to query the 1500 attributes in the catalog. If you tie a query to a screen using predefined forms, you will have an explosion of forms if you want combinations of all items. We felt a better approach would be to let the user construct his or her own custom query. Not all users are expert database users, so it was important the user not have to understand the structure of the database or know SQL, the Structured Query Language used to query relational databases. To meet this goal, we created a class that would let the user generate ad hoc queries. The user can select an arbitrary set of attributes and our class will automatically create the correct SQL statement for the query.

Another StarView goal was to be flexible in how users can view the query results. We let the user view results either on forms or in a table/row format. The latter displays the data as a spreadsheet. We enhanced the ability to view records by providing additional navigation and manipulation capabilities. One such capability is to allow multiple simultaneous views of the information in the internal database. We also were flexible in how the user could request datasets. We provided support for requesting different data formats.

An additional StarView requirement was to make it run on multiple platforms. The initial platforms were Suns running SunOS, VAXs running VMS, and DECStations running ULTRIX. We chose to develop on multiple platforms simultaneously, feeling this approach would help us identify portability problems early in the process. We believed this would be more effective, and in the long run less costly, than developing on one platform and then porting to others. This approach worked well for us. There were many other requirements for StarView, but these should give you a sense of the high-level ones.

Let's take a closer look at the techniques used to create StarView. Earlier in the book, we examined Booch's methodology for object-oriented analysis and design. Our banking example provided an overview of the methodology, but our examination of StarView gives us the opportunity to examine in detail how the methodology helped uncover the key abstractions and mechanisms needed to meet our goals. Let's take a quick look at a few examples from StarView's design. One of StarView's key abstractions is the query model. The query model is not tied to an individual form. It has knowledge about the structure of the database StarView communicates with. It also contains fundamental knowledge about a query and its components. A query-generation mechanism is created by the interaction of the query model and the custom query generator. It allows the user to select and qualify an indeterminate number of attributes from a database. This can be done through single or multiple forms. The user needs no knowledge of the database's structure or how to create joins across relational tables. The custom query generator automatically calculates joins and generates the correct SQL. The query model populates the SQL with the constraints the user specified. This interaction produces a complete query. Another key mechanism in StarView is the Model-View-Controller mechanism created for the user interface. In StarView, this mechanism allows the user to have multiple views of the underlying database. It also provides a consistent mechanism for user interaction regardless of the view. It supports both CRT and X Window interfaces while providing a common mode of user interaction.

How did we find these key abstractions and mechanisms? We needed to move beyond the noun-verb approach in finding classes and examining their relationships. Booch discusses additional approaches to finding classes and abstractions in his book *Object-Oriented Design with Applications*.[1] These techniques provide alternative methods for looking at a problem domain. No one method can reveal all there is to know about a problem. If you use multiple techniques, you increase your chances of uncovering key abstractions and designing a robust system. Let's examine the process as discussed by Booch.

One of the key problems in developing a system is creating good classes. This is why simply learning an object-oriented language is not enough. You may create a class in a language, but how do you know its structure is any good? This is a methodology issue. So what makes a good class? Let's look at the different ways you can find classes. Booch calls this process classification. The first approach he describes is classical categorization. A good example of this approach is the classification of plants and animals. In biology, the process of fitting organisms into categories is called taxonomy. Biological organisms are classified according to Kingdom, Phylum, Class, Order, Family, Genus, and Species. Like the biologist Lineas, you determine what category an organism belongs in by asking questions and looking for similarities. You can do the same thing to find classes in a system. We ask questions about a class's characteristics and look for common properties. Properties may take a common form. An example of the latter would be classes that model attributes in the database. They are common in form because each is an attribute. They differ in the details. Graphic classes are often grouped together because they have common properties—often the methods and other aspects needed for display. These classes may have a common ancestor, which provides the rudimentary display capabilities.

Another approach to finding classes is called conceptual clustering. In this approach you create a concept for a class and then decide how close a candidate is to the concept. Groupings of classes are based on the probability that a candidate is more like one concept than another. For example, there are vehicles for land, sea, and air. Cars, pickup trucks, and vans are all different classes of vehicles, but they are most closely related to the concept of land transportation. This is not the same thing as looking at properties. During analysis the emphasis is on the concept.

Booch also discusses an approach called prototype theory. In this method, you create prototypes of categories. A prototype object represents a class. Candidates are members of a category based on how closely they resemble the prototype. Booch uses games as an example. No properties are common to all games, but games are still recognized as games. Queries are an example from StarView. Some queries may be in the form of SQL, others are not. Some queries are for a relational database, some are not. In spite of the differences, all are still queries.

How else might you find candidates for objects? We've mentioned finding nouns in a problem statement, but what kind of nouns should we look for? Most obvious are nouns for things you can touch. You can also look for concepts and use them for clustering as previously noted. Interactions are also good candidates. In our banking example, we saw how the interactions between the Person and ATM classes might be turned into a Transaction class. If you recall our earlier diagrams of the banking system, we used Booch module diagrams to show different banks involved in the transaction process. This indicates that organizations and their substructures, such as divisions, branches, etc., are candidates for classes. Organizations may be in different geographic locations. Locations are also candidate classes. If we look at the people in an organization, we see that the roles they play, such as manager, engineer, or employee, are also candidates. If you earned your living teaching seminars and wanted to create a system for scheduling them, you might quickly decide that events can also be candidates for classes. I'm sure you get the idea and can think of other candidates.

We've talked about how to find classes, but where do you search for them? Certainly you can use your requirements if you have them. If nothing else, you should write an informal description of the problem. This is especially useful when you are initially estimating the scope of a project. It's not an exhaustive approach, but it is easy to use.

You can also perform a domain analysis to look for classes. Start by picking one aspect of the problem and perform some analysis on it. Be sure to use domain experts, if they are available, to help identify key abstractions. You can also look at existing systems, if such exist. Look for their key components. If more than one system is available for examination, compare and contrast the systems. Construct a model of the system. Be generic at first. Then, as you gather more information, refine the model. Do this for one problem area at a time. When complete, you can unify the pieces into a whole at a higher level. Iterate through the refinement process to accomplish this.

Earlier, we identified the importance of determining key abstractions and mechanisms for a system's architecture. They are the key to a sound architecture and robust system. They identify the boundaries of the system and determine what its capabilities are. They also become the way you talk and think about the system—its vocabulary. Out of all of your candidates for classes, how do you find key abstractions? Booch suggests you ask specific questions. Ask how the object is created. Can it be copied or destroyed? If you cannot answer these questions, then your class is not a key abstraction.

Key abstractions may also participate in our main mechanisms. They are often the linchpins in the mechanisms. They may even participate in multiple mechanisms. Key abstractions can also be operated on by mechanisms. Finding key mechanisms is more a matter of design skill and art. The best tool to use is applying a behavioral approach to understanding the system. If you use Jacobson's approach, you can follow what happens to use cases in your system. You can also make use of the role-playing technique mentioned in the CRC approach. Notice which objects seem to interact. Generalize the interaction. If an interaction cannot be generalized, it may not be a mechanism. The MVC is a generalized user interface interaction. It was the first mechanism we identified for StarView. In our examination of StarView's class diagrams we will see others. The most important of these is the mechanism for processing queries.

It's time we take a closer look at StarView. Let's examine all of the different types of documentation created for StarView's analysis and design. We will not show every diagram created. That would take its own book. In fact, that documentation became the StarView Programmer's Reference Manual. Instead, we will show several of the class diagrams to give you an idea of what is required in designing a real system. By this we mean a system that requires more than one diagram. We will also show you some new kinds of documentation not discussed in the methodologies. Different projects have different requirements. StarView was no exception. Additions to methodologies are often made to accommodate these needs. This is not just a matter of design requirements. Each project may have different tracking and reporting needs. You may need to create your own unique documentation in order to meet reporting requirements. Sometimes, though, you need to supplement the design methodology. There are examples of both in StarView.

We began the analysis process for StarView by searching for candidate classes. We'll not duplicate the entire requirements document here. It's many pages long. Instead, we'll use a simple statement of the problem as a place to start.

Rumbaugh suggests this as a good starting place for projects. We'll then look for classes in the problem statement.

> StarView is the user interface being developed for the Hubble Data Archive (HDA). The HDA is the data archive for HST observations. It has a relational *database* catalog describing the archived data. Scientists will use StarView to *query* the catalog and select appropriate *datasets* for study. StarView will allow scientists to query the catalog through forms. StarView will retain information on the structure of the HDA and its *attributes* in its own *data dictionary*. StarView sends requests for archived datasets to the HDA, which processes the requests and returns the datasets to the user.

We can find several candidate objects in this statement. We've highlighted query, form, database, attribute, data dictionary, and dataset. Further analysis will reveal that not all of these are good classes. For example, dataset becomes a specific type of attribute. How did we come to this conclusion? As we created class diagrams and tried to define relationships, we recognized similarities and overlapping functionality in classes. When this happens, we unified these classes. Either one class incorporates the other or a new higher-level class is created. Usually, you don't just make cuts from your list, without looking at relationships, structure, and function.

As soon as we created our list of candidates, we started capturing information about their structure and function in class specification forms. As we saw earlier in the book, these are similar to Booch's templates, but with a few additions. An example of a class specification for the Help class is shown in Figure 10.1. At the top of the form we see the name of the class followed by six sections. The purpose section tells us why we need the class in the first place. In this example, the Help class is the main engine for navigating and displaying help text. The inheritance section describes what classes are ancestors to this class. This gives us an indication of the class's complexity by showing who it inherits structure and behavior from. The Help class has no ancestors. The next section is the requirements reference, which is an addition to the Booch templates. This section ties the class to the fulfillment of requirements. There are

Class Help
1. Purpose
   Access StarView help library
   Reads in help text for a given topic
   Controls navigation through topic hierarchy and between related topics (i.e., SeeAlso)
2. Inheritance
   None
3. Requirements Reference
   500.1, 500.3, 500.4, 600.1
4. Data
   helpLibraryName   //name of help library file
   currentTopicName   //name of the current topic
   topicStack   //stack containing topic names
                            // in order of viewing
   seeAlsoTopicList   //list of SeeAlso topics
5. Methods
   Public
                //constructor, read topic from help library immediately
                Help(topicName)

                //retrieve help and seeAlso text for a given topic
                Get(topicName, topicText, seeAlsoText)

   Private
                //open the help library file
                Open()
6. Testing Dependencies
   HelpForm

FIGURE 10.1. Class Specification for the Help Class

several requirements that the Help class satisfies in whole or part. The data section is next. Here you record a class's attributes. Several attributes are listed for the Help class. They may be classes in their own right. If so, this relationship is modeled by the contains relationship in the class diagram. Next in the class specification is the methods section and its subcategories. Public and private are the two basic subcategories. If you want to make your classes specific to C++, you could add a protected subcategory. Only a few of the help class's methods are listed in this figure. Note that they were written in a fashion similar to C++. This was done to ease the process of implementation. The final section is for testing dependencies. This is also an addition to the standard templates. This section is a list of the external classes necessary to fully test this class. Only the HelpForm class that does the actual displaying of help text is shown here. It is important to begin capturing testing information as early as possible. This not only supports the testing of the system, but can help you organize the order in which classes are developed. Once you've started creating your class specifications, you need to begin capturing the relationships between the classes.

This leads us to the next step in the StarView analysis and design process—class diagrams. Figure 10.2 shows the legend for the Booch notation. This is just a reminder to help as you review the StarView class diagrams. We used only the basic notation for StarView. Remember that the process of filling out class specifications and creating class diagrams is iterative. You don't do all of one and then the other. There is no artificial line between analysis and design. You iterate around the whirlpool. You may start with a class specification and then move on to some portion of a class diagram. This diagram may give you additional insights into the nature of a class and you return to the class specification to capture those. Because there is no clear distinction between when you do analysis and when you do design, we will examine the final system architecture as part of the StarView design process.

STARVIEW DESIGN

Documenting a design is a necessary, if at times laborious, process. When documenting a system, you will find some parts of the documentation more useful than others. For StarView, the Booch class diagrams gave us our most important view of the analysis and design work. We also created additional documentation to supplement the Booch methodology and fill in gaps for reporting on and tracking the design process. You may find some of these additions useful. As you work through the process of analysis and design of your own system, you should feel free to create your own additions as necessary. I offer a word of caution at this point. Don't get bogged down in documentation, just create the documentation necessary to design a good system. Different kinds of documen-

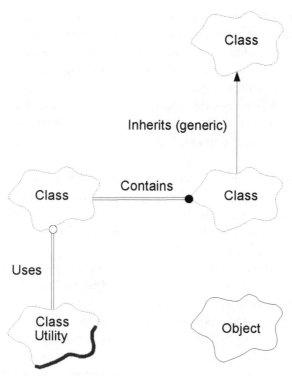

FIGURE 10.2. Notation Legend

tation are needed by different team members. General design documentation is needed by all team members. Various types of cross-reference tables are useful for comparing the design to the requirements. This type of documentation is most useful to the project leader. The cross references we show are a representative sample. Some types of documentation may be nice to have but not worth the effort to create. If the process of creating this kind of documentation can be automated by extracting information from necessary documentation, it is worth doing. If it can only be created manually, the benefits may not be worth the effort. This greatly reduces its value.

Let's begin looking at the StarView documentation by examining the StarView class diagrams. I will not show you all of the diagrams, just enough to give you a sense of the scope of the system and what a real system looks like. We see a high-level class diagram of StarView in Figure 10.3. This diagram shows the basic structure of StarView. We can examine it and identify some of the key abstractions and mechanisms that are part of StarView's design. Key classes include Form, EventHandler, and QueryProcessor. The Form class and its descendants control what and how information is displayed. The Event-Handler class understands what each form's capabilities are and responds to user input. The QueryProcessor class controls access to the underlying model in the system. Taken together, the interaction of these three classes is the basis of our MVC mechanism. Form provides the view, EventHandler the controller, and QueryProcessor the access to the model. The MVC mechanism came from the Smalltalk development environment, but it is also useful with C++. This is our own version of it.

Supporting our version of the MVC is the idea that all information is stored in models. Within StarView, different models provide different functionalities. The QueryModel class defines the structure of a query to the database. The ArchiveServices model defines the structure of a request for dataset retrieval. The Environment model holds parameters that control how StarView starts up and how it behaves. The QueryProcessor class is not only a part of this important mechanism, it is also a key abstraction. It is the linchpin between the Model's complex underworld of processing queries and the user's view of the model. It also participates in the query-handling mechanism. Queries are sent to the archive through the CatalogDB class. Returned results of a query are stored through the LocalDB class in an internal relational database. Query results are an example of a key abstraction that is operated on by a mechanism. The QueryProcessor works like a traffic cop to direct flow and ensure that everyone is properly updated. This includes properly updating the model. The Query-Model class is another key abstraction. It is also part of the query-generator mechanism. The SQL class interacts with it and the DataDictionary class to get the detailed information it needs to generate a query. Once it has this information, it generates a query on the fly. The QueryModel holds all the attributes needed for a query. The DataDictionary understands the structure of the attributes. The SQL class understands the relationships between the attributes. Together, they have all the information needed to create a query.

There are other key abstractions in StarView. The Form class is one of the most important. Form is the fundamental class for displaying information to the user. Form itself is an abstract class—only descendants are actually created. Figure 10.4 shows the Form class and its descendants. We now see our design spreading across multiple diagrams, and it's important to note how they work together. Wherever you see the Form class in Figure 10.3, you can substitute in one of its descendants. They will have the same relation to other

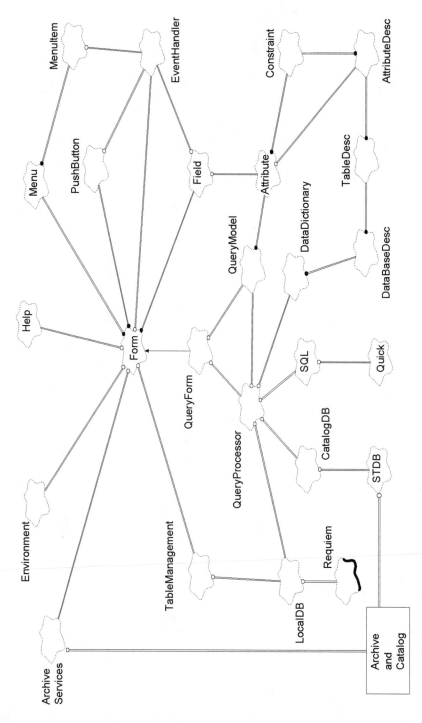

FIGURE 10.3. StarView Top Level Class Diagram

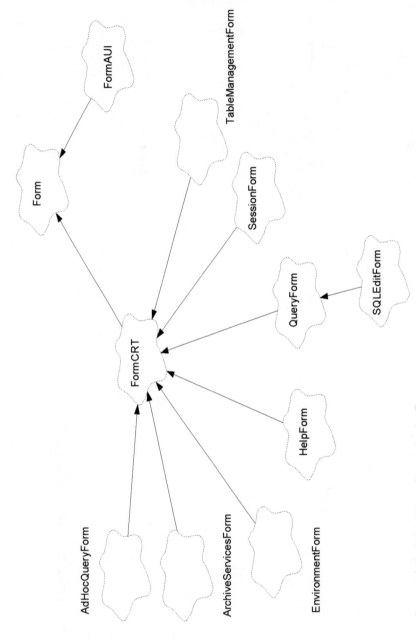

FIGURE 10.4. Inheritance Hierarchy for Form

classes that the ancestor class does. That is what is being shown with Query-Form in Figure 10.3.

The process of substitution is how you tie multiple diagrams together. This requires that a common class appear on the two diagrams you want to unite. Form is the common class for these two diagrams. It would be nice if the diagrams borrowed some concepts such as busses and off-page connectors from electrical schematics. It would simplify the diagrams and make it easier to tie them together. As we examine the Form class inheritance tree in Figure 10.4, note that the tree is deeper than it is broad. Furthermore, it is likely to grow deeper than it is broad. The proper use of inheritance for object-oriented development is an important issue. When used for generalization-specialization, inheritance can be a powerful tool for class reuse. When used in a form known as implementation inheritance, it can create long-term development problems. Implementation inheritance occurs when you use inheritance as the mechanism for code reuse without thought to the proper relationship between the classes involved in the inheritance tree. Aggregation (the contains relationship) is a better choice for code reuse when there is no generalization-specialization relationship between the classes. In this case we see an example of generalization-specialization. The children in the tree are specialized forms of the general Form class. When you use generalization-specialization as the basis for inheritance, you will gain some benefit from code reuse. In this case, deeper trees show more code reuse through the proper use of inheritance. It is one way of reducing the amount of code you write, but should not be the determining factor in using inheritance. There is another side to the benefit or reuse. There is increased complexity in the descendent classes. Finding the best balance requires an understanding of the tradeoffs.

The Field class is another key abstraction. The Field class and its descendants, shown in Figure 10.5, display the values found in the models. We see that the Field class also has a deep inheritance tree. In this case it is four levels deep. Usually, you don't see inheritance trees more than six levels deep. One reason for this is the difficulty in understanding the real complexity of the classes deepest in the tree. You often need the support of tools to understand the true structure and size of such classes. Metrics that can help ensure consistency of generalization-specialization in the inheritance tree can help you determine how deep the tree should be.

The Attribute class is the final key abstraction I want to discuss. Each field in the archive's catalog is described by an attribute. Another way of looking at

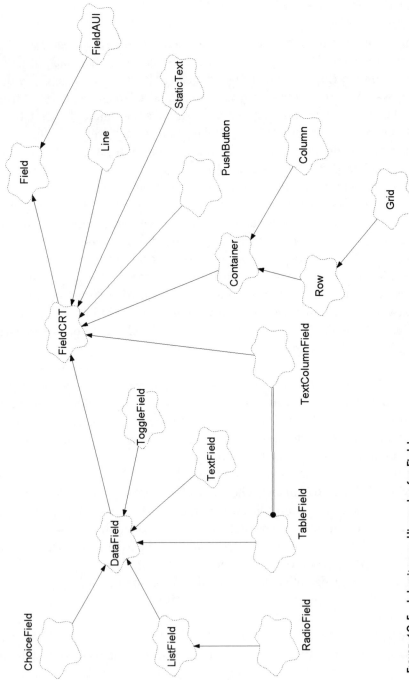

FIGURE 10.5. Inheritance Hierarchy for Field

this is to say that everything in the catalog about which you can ask a question is an attribute. Attributes model the database fields and provide all of the functionality needed to work with them. Figure 10.6 shows the Attribute class inheritance hierarchy. You can still substitute any of its dependents into the main system class diagram wherever you see the Attribute class. The attributes PositionRA (right accession) and PositionDec (declination) are good examples of the kind of functionality found in attribute classes. These attributes provide astronomical coordinates for objects in the archive. Among the capabilities these attributes have is the ability to convert from one coordinate system to another. This lets the user view coordinates in any system he or she wants, regardless of the coordinate system of the position in the archive.

So far we have shown only four of StarView's class diagrams. These should be enough to give you a sense of the scope of the project and how to tie multiple diagrams together. The top-level diagram shows most, but not all, of the basic relationships in the system. The reason to create numerous diagrams is to provide yourself with different meaningful views of your system's structure. One problem with small examples is that they don't show the difficulty you can have in combining all of the diagrams into a meaningful whole. In StarView's case, the top level diagram was useful for most discussions. The others provided supplemental views of particular portions of the system. In this example, the supplemental views showed inheritance hierarchies, but they are not the only candidates for this type of view. It is often helpful to create supplemental views for subsystems and mechanisms as well. The process of working with all of these diagrams is very much like reading a multiple page schematic or mechanical drawing. The most important factor in creating your diagrams is to organize them in meaningful chunks that support your design efforts and make it easy to discuss and understand various portions of the system.

It's time to take a look at some of the other documentation created for StarView. After the class diagram, one of the most important diagrams you'll create is the object diagram. Class diagrams show the relationships that exist between classes, but they don't provide any details about them. Object diagrams let you capture the details about the methods involved in a relationship. In Figure 10.7, we see an example of an object diagram from StarView's design. In this diagram, we see relations between fields and models or fields and attributes. Notice that named *objects* are represented in the diagrams, not *classes*. For example, there is an object named field1. It appears in two places on the diagram. Because the names are the same in both places, both object representations stand for the same instance of the same objects. The diagram also shows

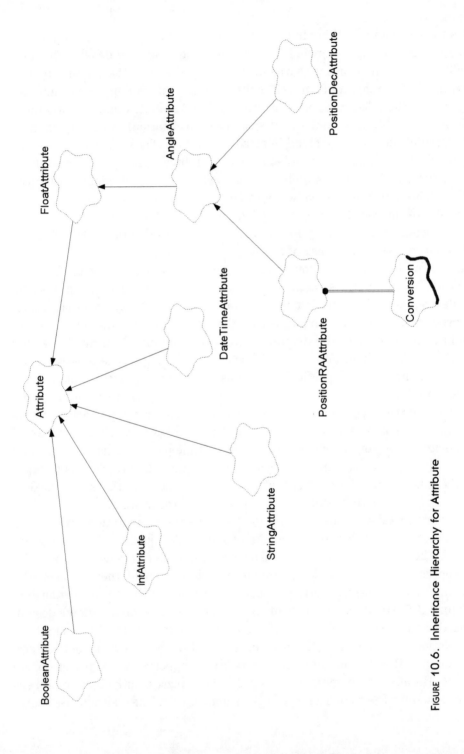

FIGURE 10.6. Inheritance Hierarchy for Attribute

two different methods in the relationship between fields and models: Set and DisplayValue. The line between objects says there is a message sent between them. This particular diagram shows one message per line. The Booch notation supports a list of messages per line. Unfortunately, the early Case tools used on this project did not. This diagram was left in this form to show how developers often have to work within the constraints of their tools. You can model all of your system's methods with these diagrams, but you may not need to. These diagrams are most useful when there are multiple messages in a single relationship. As mentioned in the chapter on Booch's notation, various adornments can be added to provide additional information in the diagram.

One tool used in traditional development is a data dictionary. One of the purposes of a data dictionary is to provide a cross reference of who uses what functions. We created our own version of this cross reference, shown in Figure 10.8. This is not a standard part of the Booch methodology. It is one of those additional types of documentation we felt would be valuable to us. These cross references are organized by class. They show which classes call the methods of the subject class. It is an additional way of organizing the information in the object diagrams. We see here an example for the Help class. Another way this table is useful is to identify testing dependencies. Classes that call the Help class's methods need the Help class to exist before they can be fully tested.

One concern for any new development project is that you provide the functionality you agreed to. One way to do this is to document which classes are used to implement specific requirements. An example of this is the cross reference shown in Figure 10.9. This table is organized by requirement to ensure that all requirements are covered. Any class that participates in meeting a requirement is listed to the left. This ensures that all requirements have been considered and tells you where to go to see how the requirement is met. This is also an addition to the methodology, but we felt it an important one. Some methodologies seem to gloss over the fact that in creating a system you are signing up to provide certain functionality. Someone must ensure that you've done all you've agreed to. In our case, the project leader was able to use this information to demonstrate where and how each requirement was met.

As part of StarView's design, we created and documented some things that are not classes, but are processed by them. For example, one of our goals in StarView was to be flexible in how we dealt with the archive's database. We know that the structure of the archive's catalog will change over time. StarView's SQL class needs to understand what the current structure is. Furthermore, the

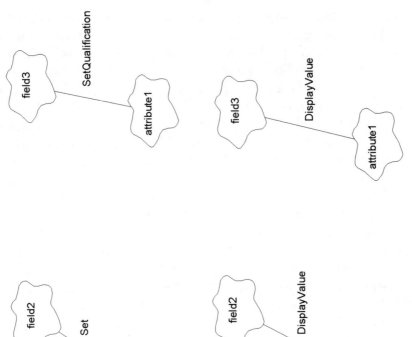

FIGURE 10.7. StarView Object Diagram

Class Method Cross Reference for HELP

Methods	Called By
constructor	HelpForm
destructor	
Read	HelpForm

Figure 10.8. Class Cross Reference Form for Help

QueryModel needs to understand the structure of the attributes in the catalog. We accomplished our flexibility be defining the catalog attributes and their structure in our own DDL. A very small portion of the DDL is shown in Figure 10.10. The DDL is read in by StarView when it starts up. This ensures that we can communicate with the latest version of the catalog without making code changes. We created additional design documentation to define the DDL's structure and proper use.

There are similar needs for the forms the user sees. Forms will change over time, because what users want to see will change. We needed to be able to change the forms without changing code. We did this by creating a Form Definition Language (FDL) to define all forms. The FDL is read on the fly by StarView as needed. A small sample of FDL is shown in Figure 10.11. Again we created additional documentation to detail its structure and use. Certainly, our DDL and FDL documentation was not covered by the methodology. They serve as an example of other documentation you often need to create in designing a system.

Requirements Implementation

Requirement	Class
100.3.1	QueryControl
210.1	CommandLineField
	Form
	Main
210.3	QueryProcessor
	QueryForm
	QueryModel
210.3.1	QueryProcessor

Figure 10.9. Requirements Cross Reference

```
SCHEMA                                     //entire   schema   for   the
DataDictionary
     DATABASE: catalog                     //the Catalog database
          TABLE: proposal                  //the proposal table
               ATTR: pro_pep_id
                    descriptivelabel: proposal_id
                    datatype: int4
                    logicaltype: int
                    constraints: >0 //should always be greater
                                    than 0
                    definition: "The proposal identifier known to
                                PEPSI"
               END_ATTR
               ATTR: pro_pi_last_name
                    descriptivelabel: pi_lastname
                    datatype: varchar(20)
                    logicaltype: char
                    definition: "The principle investigator's last
                                name"
               END_ATTR
          END_TABLE
     END_DATABASE
END_SCHEMA
```

FIGURE 10.10. Data Definition Language Example

One of the very important parts of the analysis process was creating the scenarios that covered all user interaction. They are tied to requirements and help define what the system is supposed to do. The following is an example of a scenario.

Query Scenario

Select Query from the Session Manager menu. Select a predefined query from a list of 10. The query selected has five fields from the same table: PI, Instrument, RA, DEC, and DataSetName. Ask for help on the query form. Ask for help on the PI field. Enter data into the PI, RA, and DEC fields. Submit the query. Show how the query is automatically saved. The query returns 25 records. Show how this infor-

```
TITLE "Basic Query"

MENUBAR
    MENU "File" _F
            ITEM "Refresh" _R ^L f.exec Refresh
            ITEM "Exit Starview" _X ^X f.exec Exit
    ENDMENU
    MENU "Help" _H
            ITEM "Using Help" _U f.form Help
    ENDMENU
ENDMENUBAR


WORK

ROW
    COLUMN
            FIELD catalog..instrument.config
                WIDTH 5
                LABEL Instrument:
                    QUALIFICATION WFC | PC | FOC
            ENDFIELD
    ENDCOLUMN
ENDROW

ENDWORK
```

FIGURE 10.11. Form Definition Language Example

mation is displayed. View the first 5 one at a time. Step backwards through the list for 2 records and then get the rest of the results. Do this using the same form used to create the query. Display the 14th returned record. Delete the 14th record. Change to the table-row format to view all records at one time.

It's important to show how these scenarios are tied to the requirements, because later we will use them to determine when our design is complete. Figure 10.12 shows a cross-reference table showing the relationship of each sce-

Scenario Cross Reference

Scenario	Requirement
Query	210.3
	210.7
	210.15
	210.32.3
	210.34
	210.38
	210.39

FIGURE 10.12. Scenario Cross Reference

nario to the requirements it addresses. This is done for all scenarios. This cross check also helps ensure that all requirements are covered. We use the scenarios to verify the design's completeness by demonstrating how the design supports each scenario. The scenarios also help define the user interaction for testing. They can become the basis of final acceptance testing.

The basic static system design is captured by class specifications and class diagrams. What we needed was a method of validating the sequence of events in the system to show how the design supports a given scenario. At the time of the original design, Booch had no easy way to show the flow of events through the system. His standard timing diagrams didn't show the flow clearly. We decided to create our own diagrams to show this. We called them event flow diagrams and we annotated them with an event flow language. The event flow diagram shows the flow of events from one object to the next. They illustrate what happens in the system during the execution of a scenario. The event flow language (loosely based on C++) is used to annotate the flow of events. Booch now uses Jacobson's interaction diagrams to capture this information. These will also work quite well.

An example of an event flow diagram is shown in Figure 10.13. This diagram only covers the start-up of the Query scenario. The solid cloud shapes are actual objects that have been created in the system. The numbered arrows itemize the flow of events. The arrows are numbered to show sequence. They show who calls who. An example of the event flow language is shown in Figure 10.14, a companion illustration to Figure 10.13. The event flow language looks much like C++. This was done as a convenience to us. We wanted it to closely match our implementation language. You could create your own language to match your

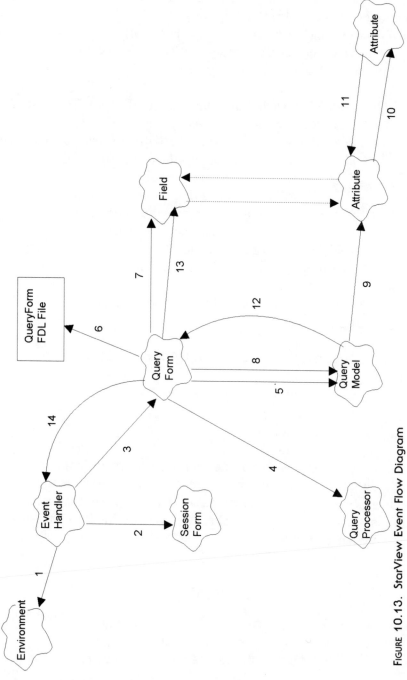

FIGURE 10.13. StarView Event Flow Diagram

```
EventHandler.PopupForm(QueryForm)
    new QueryForm(QueryProcessor, QueryModel)
        QueryProcessor.Attach(QueryForm)
        QueryModel.Attach(QueryForm)

        //Read Form Definition Language (FDL) file to construct form
        for each field in the FDL description
            field_id = new Field(form_id, attributeName, position, size)
            attr_id = QueryModel.Attach(field_id, attributeName)
                    create attribute if necessary
                    if attribute is PositionRA or PositionDec
                            create corresponding attribute
                            and attach them to each other
            field_id.SetAttribute(attr_id)
        for each menu in the FDL description
            new Menu(form_id)
        // register form level callbacks (if necessary)
        //display form

    //User enters qualifications into the PI, RA and DEC fields
    Field EditQualification()
        Attribute.Set("qualification", qual_string)
```

FIGURE 10.14. StarView Event Flow Language

own needs. One of the real values of the event flow language is that it can annotate the algorithms needed to implement methods. Since it annotates the actual steps being executed, the language is a good place to document the algorithmic specifics of a method. This is a valuable feature missing from Booch's interaction diagrams.

SUMMARY

You've now seen the basic types of documentation we created for StarView. We did not create all of the kinds of documentation allowed for in the Booch methodology. We didn't have a strong need for state, process, or module diagrams. You should always feel free to use those diagrams that are helpful to you, but be selective about what you create.

You might want to ask how the design has held up. Many claims have been made for the benefits of object-oriented design. Has this system proven to be robust? It has been through several iterations. We've made both small and large changes to the system to support new requirements. Throughout, the design has proven to be very robust. It has adapted well to the changes and additions we've needed. The basic architecture is still viable. Has the object-oriented approach provided the benefits claimed? In a word—yes. Object-oriented technology is not a magic bullet. It is a sound approach to software development. Certainly, the methodologies are still evolving. You may need to adapt or add to them based on your own needs. This is especially true for documentation not covered by the methodology. That doesn't mean the methodologies are inadequate for development. It only means that to some degree each effort is unique and the methodologies must be flexible enough to accommodate individual needs.

What about pitfalls and problems in the development process? You could view the need to create documentation outside what is covered by the methodology as a problem, albeit a small one. A more significant issue is how you manage the iterative development process. This requires that management understand where the team is in the process. We'll talk more about the issues of managing a system's life cycle and development process in the next few chapters.

REFERENCES

1. Booch, Grady. *Object-Oriented Analysis and Design*. 2d ed. Redwood City, CA: Benjamin/Cummings Publishing, 1994, pp. 145ff.

PART IV
Managing Object-Oriented Technology

CHAPTER 11

The Rest of the Object-Oriented Life Cycle

In previous chapters, we've talked about how systems evolve. There is an iterative cycle of analysis and development. This is the whirlpool approach we discussed. There is no big bang resulting from a sequence of steps. There is just evolving functionality. That's fine for development, but what about the rest of the life cycle? Does this iterative approach work when you are doing maintenance on an existing object-oriented system? Indeed it does. Iteration is the preferred way of working throughout the object-oriented life cycle.

THE MAINTENANCE LIFE CYCLE

There are three main activities in maintenance. The first is fixing defects or "bugs." "What!" you exclaim. "You mean that after all the benefits you're supposed to get from object-oriented technology, you still have bugs to fix? Don't object-oriented techniques cure all software problems?" Of course not. In spite of the hoopla, it shouldn't be mistaken for snake oil. There is both good news and bad news in using object-oriented techniques. The bad news should come as no surprise. Object-oriented technology is not a magic bullet. There are individual and process issues that still need attention. For the individual, object oriented techniques help, but they don't magically cure bad habits or sloppy work or prevent innocent mistakes. The development process can also contribute to problems. You can use techniques well or poorly. The key is to understand what you are doing. You can take steps to improve your work if you identify the problems in your process. It is wrong to assume that the first time you use object-oriented techniques, you will use them all correctly. There will always be room for improvement.

The good news about using object-oriented technology is that you will probably have fewer bugs. Anecdotal evidence from those working in object-oriented metrics indicates you typically find one-third the usual number of defects. Our experience with StarView would support this statement. Encapsulation and code reuse both contribute to a reduced number of defects. Encapsulation isolates the code. Reuse means there is less code to debug. Encapsulation makes them easier to localize and fix. Categorization of existing problems helps identify problem areas. In the case of StarView, in initial development the largest category of defects was in the area of dealing with the subtleties of C++. This was not unexpected, since it was the first C++ system for most of the developers. In spite of this being their first object-oriented and C++ system, they still had a greatly reduced number of errors.

One activity in maintenance that should not be overlooked is the work of refining in the existing system. A common activity during maintenance is identifying portions of the system that can take additional advantage of code reuse. This doesn't mean the existing software is incorrect or "buggy." It also doesn't mean that new functionality will be provided. It means that the developers have found ways in which the system can be better organized. Changes can be made to the system that allow for more code reuse through inheritance. It is quite common to find common code in classes that can be moved to a new ancestor class. This activity centralizes the common code in one place and reduces the number of places you have to work on to maintain the system. The result of such work is a system that is more robust, more amenable to change, and more maintainable. This is the best reason for doing refinement. It has a very tangible benefit. The problem is that many managers have difficulty allocating resources to this type of work because of other pressing issues.

Another activity during the maintenance phase is implementing new requirements. In many ways, new requirements are similar to defects. The system doesn't do what you want it to do, so you have to change it to get the desired behavior. This raises a number of questions. For example, how do you go about making changes to an existing system? As we shall see, the iterative approach still applies, but where do you start?

Bug fixes and new requirements come in many forms. Some are simple and others complex. For each of these we need to understand what work is required in an object-oriented system to implement the desired changes. Certainly coding and testing will be done, but what else is required? What about documentation? What do you want to keep up to date? We saw a lot of documentation created during new development. Does all of this need to be kept up-to-date? I think we can honestly say no. Many of the cross references were created to track the myriad details of new development. Usually, they are not needed as part of the maintenance life cycle. However, some of the documentation is still useful. In particular, the class, object, and event flow diagrams are still needed. It's always important to understand your system's structure. It's essential that you keep this documentation up to date so that you will know how to accommodate changes in your system. The question then becomes: What is the best way to keep documentation up to date?

Documentation should evolve with the system. It should not be left as an afterthought. Updating documentation should be a natural part of iterative development. Unfortunately, in most shops it's not that way. It is more like pulling teeth to get people to do the necessary updates. This is particularly true for bug fixes. Once a bug is fixed, most developers feel the work is complete. Once they think the work is done, they lack the motivation to make changes in documentation. Part of this attitude relates to when most documentation is created. In most systems, much of the documentation is complete before coding starts. This is particularly true in the maintenance phase. It's often viewed as lots of unnecessary work to go back and bring documentation up to date for small changes. Developers often forget that in maintenance, changes take place just as they do at other points in the life cycle. This is because the process is iterative. In initial development, it's important to capture the changes made at the coding stage. If you don't capture this information, you quickly lose track of how your system actually functions. For the same reason, it is important to capture this information during maintenance as well.

It is crucial to keep your design documentation current. You need this information to determine how to make changes to your system. That doesn't have to be painful. One new approach to keeping documentation current is to use reverse engineering techniques. Reverse engineering is not new. What is unusual is that it is not often applied to standard maintenance work. Tools are becoming available that will let this approach be used. These tools can be used to generate new class diagrams or update existing diagrams. They do not necessarily generate all the information you would want, but it is a start. This type of tool can be used in three ways. First, you can use them to update your documentation with small changes made at the coding level. The tool provides a painless way for the developer to keep documentation current. Large changes should be documented before the work is done. The second way to use this tool is to validate the design of a delivered system. Is the system you implemented the system you designed? This only happens in the ideal world. Changes occur during implementation. Not all of these get migrated back into the documentation. It is important to know what the true structure of the system is. Did you end up where you intended? The success of future changes may well rely on this knowledge. The diagrams created through reverse engineering can also serve to identify areas of misunderstanding or miscommunication. It may be that what you end up with in your system is not what you intended. On the other hand, by using reverse engineering, acceptable changes will be documented. The final way to apply this type of tool is as the name implies—reverse engineering. It is one way to create some documentation for a system that has none. This documentation can provide the basis for further maintenance work, as well as provide information for insight into a system or for reengineering a system. What it will not do is create a design where one does not exist. Poorly designed systems remain that way even when documented.

The documentation shown in the previous chapter was design documentation. The maintenance phase may actually add an additional type of documentation. We can add peer-reviewed code. Code gains value in the peer-review process, which serves several purposes. First, standards can be developed for both coding and commenting. Peer reviewing of code helps ensure conformance to development standards, which, in turn, ensures the code documents what is actually done in the implementation of the system. Peer review also improves the quality of code. This increases the chances of catching errors before the code is delivered.

We've talked about documentation during maintenance, but what about the rest of the process? It is very similar to the development process. The process

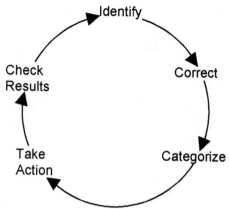

FIGURE 11.1. Maintenance Cycle

of adding new functionality is iterative as in new development. You begin by defining what you want to do to the system. Next, you iterate through analysis and design to determine how best to add the new functionality. Perhaps you will even prototype alternatives. Finally, you implement and test as needed.

The bug-fixing process is also iterative. You can use the standard whirlpool if you wish. However, some changes you make to the cycle will have a significant impact on the quality of your software. Take a look at Figure 11.1, which shows the improved maintenance cycle for defect correction. The process begins by identifying the problem to be corrected. It is often very difficult to track down problems created by unexpected interactions. Such interactions are minimized by the object oriented approach, but they can be affected by the quality of the design. The next step is to correct the problem. This, after all, is the main purpose of this activity. Included in this step is the testing and delivery of the fix. Your documentation should also be brought up to date at this point. The work isn't really complete until this is done. Most developers stop there, but it is not enough to just fix a problem. The next activity is to categorize the defect. By categorizing defects, you can identify the types of problems that will need additional work. For example, some problems may be based in poorly understood requirements. Others may be the result of design defects. Others may come from coding errors. In StarView, the greatest source of errors were coding defects associated with the subtleties of C++. This was to be expected since this was the developer's first encounter with the language. By identifying this category of problem, we were able to obtain additional training to reduce this type of problem. It's better to categorize a problem after it is fixed, because you are in a better position to know why it occurred. Categorizing defects is a step often overlooked in the maintenance process. It is important because it can contribute a great deal to improving the quality of your development process.

This leads us to the next step in the process—taking action. Look for your largest category of problems. Then, take specific action to correct it. You must be specific about your problem—it is not enough to say "we have coding errors." What kind of coding errors? Are they based on sloppiness? Are there aspects of the language the developers don't understand? Are your coding standards inadequate? Do developers become confused reading code? Identify the particular problems, and then take action to correct them. Start with the largest problem, because solving it will have the single largest impact on your quality.

Next you need to check the results of your actions. Did you take the right action? How do you know? Did you see the results you were expecting? Has this category of problem decreased? If not, perhaps different action is needed. The point is to check your results, don't just assume them. If you don't check them, you won't know if your actions were correct.

Once you've checked the results of your last actions, identify additional areas for improvement. It is a sad fact that most bugs are introduced by developers fixing other problems. This is a vicious cycle that needs to be broken. Breaking this cycle is one of the best ways of improving software quality in the long run, because you continually work to identify your largest problem areas and reduce them. The result of this iterative process of continual improvement is better software and better developers.

REUSE

Reuse is an issue in maintenance, new development, and project management. This is a rather sweeping statement. One of the problems with the word reuse is that the term is too broad. We will have to be more specific if we want to understand what reuse means in object-oriented development. There is more than one kind and level of reuse. Most people think of new projects reusing classes developed in earlier projects. This is certainly one type of reuse, but it is not the only one. At the code level, inheritance is a valuable form of reuse. It helps improve the quality of software, because there is less software to debug. With inheritance, you can reuse code that has already been tested. It is very common to find additional opportunities for this type of reuse during maintenance. These are the two most obvious types of reuse, but there are other levels of reuse that may pay even bigger dividends.

If we think beyond the class level, we can find other forms of reuse that affect the system's higher level behavior. The first thing that comes to mind are mechanisms. These can provide basic architectures for building systems. The MVC is an example of one that is reused extensively. There is a fair amount of work being done in this area. Methodologists are now referring to this as work on patterns.[1] At a higher level still are subsystems. Subsystems package a whole level of functionality. Subsystems are not constrained to a basic class level of functionality. If classes are the bricks and mortar we build with, subsystems are the walls and rooms of modular buildings. This is not the endpoint for reuse. Application frameworks provide another level of reuse. Application frameworks are more like mechanisms because they provide an underlying architecture but are more comprehensive. Many methodologists are also talking about domain reuse. This is the reuse of whole application areas. These are more than application frameworks. We are talking about building new systems out of old ones. Interfaces and interconnections between systems is the key issue. Much work remains to be done in all of these areas.

Many issues surround reuse. It is more than just a maintenance or development issue—the decision to make use of reuse is a strategic business decision. It is not just a matter of how to develop reusable components. Even more critical decisions must be made. Will you be developing code for reuse? If so, you have to treat the code as a business resource to be used. Reuse doesn't occur by happenstance. It must be planned for and resources allocated to support the effort. There are a number of associated economic issues. For example, is reuse to be rewarded over new development? When developers are judged only on the lines of code they create, there is no incentive for reuse. In fact, there is a disincentive. Companies that only look at new lines of code lose the benefit of reuse because of a short-sighted method of evaluating developers. Reuse has a broader economic benefit. If you were manufacturing a part, would you create all new nuts and bolts when standard components would work? If you do not encourage reuse, you promote wasted resources.

If you are going to develop reusable components, how can you make them available to others? Different models for this have been created by different firms. Some develop groups to collate work from different projects and promote their reuse through a common library. One of the main activities of this type of group is educating others about what is available. They also spend time generalizing the specific work done by others, which is necessary for components not originally designed to be reused.

Other firms let each development group create its own library. Each group then becomes its own advocate. The success of such libraries is partially dependent on the group's marketing efforts. This is a difficult model for those who want to reuse other's work. A lot of time can be spent seeking out what is available.

Another model uses a central repository for components but has no central advocacy group. Each development group is left to itself to add and find components. One problem with this type of model is that efforts are duplicated with slight variations. This is particularly true in the library's early life. The idea in this approach is that as the library grows, more of it will be reused and only new types of components will be added.

No one model has been completely successful—all have drawbacks. The question is which will have the greatest benefits for your organization? The model with a central library and advocacy group may produce the higher quality library. It may also be easier to reuse components from it because there are resources available to help you do just that. Unfortunately, the cost of such an approach can be high. Funding this type of support group is unpalatable to many organizations. The latter approach with a central library but no centralized support is chosen most often. It often fails because firms don't provide an incentive to contribute or reuse components from the library. It becomes nothing more than a nice idea. Another problem is the lack of standards in the library. Different groups create components differently and incompatibly. The time necessary to figure out how to use a poorly documented component is often not worth the trouble. If this model is to succeed, there have to be standards adhered to by all contributors. The firm also has to provide economic incentives to contribute and reuse components.

If you want to create reusable components, there are some basic things you can do:

> Plan for reuse from the beginning.
>
> Plan how you will let others know what you are doing and what is available.

Clearly document how to use your code. The modularity of object-oriented code will make reuse easier.

Look at what others have done.

Try not to reinvent the wheel. Certainly, there is a tradeoff between the effort needed to search for a component versus the benefit of finding it. This situation will improve as libraries become more sophisticated in their organization.

There are other options to using internally developed components. The number of third-party libraries is growing. Certainly this is an option worth considering. However, you need to be aware of issues associated with using someone else's library. The first problem you often encounter is the naming issue. There are potential conflicts when using multiple packages. For example, a library may have the class String in it. Unfortunately, String is also defined for the X Windowing system. It is best to have unique names for your own classes and those from third parties. In StarView, we created the SvString class as our version of String.

Another issue arises if you use multiple libraries. The structure of the library may require that you include most or all of it when you use some components because the more complex components are built from the simpler ones in the library. This can lead to unnecessarily bloated programs. There is also more opportunity for conflicts with other libraries. This doesn't mean that you only want to use libraries with isolated components. Those libraries have a tree structure that is broader than it is deep. Libraries structured as deep trees can be very powerful. In using any library, it's important that you be selective and understand the impact of your selection. Another problem in using multiple libraries is that it can be difficult to get them to work together. You may find that you would like to mix one class from one library with classes from another. Unfortunately, they are often incompatible.

There can also be distribution and licensing issues. Third-party libraries may impose unacceptable restrictions on what you distribute. Some libraries may require royalties. You need to understand your own expectations in this area. You must decide if you want to distribute sources or binaries. You usually can't distribute the sources to third-party libraries. This may mean that others who get your sources will have to purchase the third-party library as well. Even if royalties are not an issue, it may prove unacceptable to distribute something built with a third-party library.

If you decide to create your own classes and want them reused, there are some things you can do to make them more usable by others. The basis for these recommendations can be found in Rumbaugh's *Object-Oriented Modeling and Design*.[2] Begin by making sure your classes have one main purpose. This is called coherence. Poorly designed classes try to do too much. They become close relatives to the proverbial kitchen sink. Pay attention to the size of your methods. Most methods are fairly small. Trying to do too much in a method leads to methods that are not coherent. Like classes, methods should perform one function. The size of methods is not an absolute. Some will be large by their very nature. This is often true when you are implementing a specific algorithm. The main goal is to make the method coherent. One of the things that makes reuse difficult is creating classes that use different names for methods that perform the same function. For example, classes that need an Update method could all have one called by that name. This is reasonable if the method has the same basic purpose and functionality in all of the classes. It should also have the same parameters in the same order if possible. This is a matter of trying to make the use of classes as consistent as possible. The more consistent methods are between classes, the easier a time developers will have using the classes.

Classes usually do one of two things: implement an abstraction or serve a control or logic function. Classes that serve in a control function tell the system what to do. Classes that serve an implementation function tell the system how to do it. It is important to separate the two. Mixing these functions leads to a lack of coherence in a class. It can also lead to a lack of coherence in methods. One of the difficult things to do in designing a class is to make the methods more general. Take, for example, the function of concatenation in the String class. You may want to concatenate one string with another. You may want to concatenate a character array with a string. You may even want to concatenate two character arrays into a string. To handle all of these possibilities, you need to create methods for each of these combinations. To make a class reusable, you need to generalize its methods. Provide coverage for all reasonable inputs to the method, just as we did for string concatenation. Along with generalizing the inputs to a method, you need to generalize the methods themselves. Make a method as general as you can within the constraints of keeping the method coherent. This is another step in appropriate generalization.

You can go too far in generalizing. In an effort to generalize, some developers make the mistake of using global information. The use of global information violates encapsulation. It destroys the independence of your class. Classes should only work on internal information. This can come in the form of parameters to methods or be generated internally. Avoid references to external information, which can change without the class's knowledge. This can cause significant problems. Consistent behavior is also desirable in classes. A blatant example of inconsistent behavior can be found in text editors. Keys often change their function depending on the mode they are in. For example, it is sometimes difficult to know if you are in insert or command mode. Many find this changeable behavior confusing. Avoid having class methods change behavior based on modes. Modality makes classes hard to reuse because you don't know what a class is supposed to do. You have to know the mode before you can know the behavior.

All of these suggestions can work together to help you create classes that are more reusable. You can apply them to higher-level components as well. The main task is to keep components coherent and general. These can be conflicting desires. As with all design decisions, you will have to make compromises based on your overall goals.

SUMMARY

Maintenance, like new development, is an iterative process. The three main activities of maintenance are bug fixing, refinement, and new enhancements. Enhancements follow the normal whirlpool process. Bug fixes and refinement follow a modified cycle to help you improve the quality of your software. The key to success in this cycle is not fixing individual problems, but identifying categories of problems and working to eliminate them. This can result in significant improvements in software quality. This process is very similar to that used in process improvement and Total Quality Management.

We also saw that there are many issues associated with reuse. Reuse means different things to different people because there are different types and levels of reuse. These can be broken into two basic categories. Code reuse can be accomplished through inheritance or through reusing classes found in libraries. The second category is based on the size of component reused, which can vary from class to application domain.

Firms have developed different models for implementing reuse in their organizations. It is fundamentally important that firms understand that reuse must be considered a strategic business decision. This gives the perspective needed to make reuse a success. We finished our chapter by highlighting the issues involved in writing reusable code, which is something that needs to be planned for from the beginning. Reuse cannot simply be added on at the end of development.

REFERENCES

1. Gamma, Erich et al. *Design Patterns: Elements of Reusable Object-Oriented Software*. Reading, MA: Addison-Wesley, 1995.
2. Rumbaugh, James et al. *Object-Oriented Modeling and Design*. Englewood Cliffs, NJ: Prentice-Hall, 1991, p. 282–285.

CHAPTER 12

Managing Object-Oriented Development

We've discussed the development cycle from the developer's point of view. We've examined the work to be done and the iterative nature of the process. We now must ask how this process looks from the manager's point of view. Managers have additional reporting requirements and need to make progress clear to those who care only about results—not iteration. Managers are responsible for ensuring that resources are available and properly applied. What resources are needed for an object-oriented project? What kind of tools are helpful on such a project? We'll examine these issues to determine the resources you should have and examine ways of tracking the development cycle. We've talked a lot about documentation in previous chapters but have said little about standards. Standards can be an important tool in managing development. We'll see how standards can be applied to an object-oriented project and how this affects our documentation. We will also look at how testing and quality assurance can be integrated into and managed as part of the development process.

Is managing an object-oriented project completely different from managing a conventional one? Not at all. Concerns for good programming style, traceability, and accountability must still be addressed. The difference is the new issues that must be dealt with, which require new approaches to project management. For example, what about code reuse? How do you track reuse? Can you see how it affects development? Another issue is the way you report progress when the development process is both iterative and incremental. Because it is iterative, how do you know when to iterate and when to stop? We'll show how to use 3db software engineering to move the project forward. How do you handle ongoing integration? The waterfall model has a big bang step at the end of development. Because development is incremental, we'll see how ongoing integration can be combined with milestones to show real development progress and catch potential problems in their early stages. All of these issues have an affect on the resources needed to complete a project and the way those resources will be used. What you will find for object-oriented projects is a reduction in the total resources needed and a change in the timing of their deployment.

RESOURCES

Let's begin our look at object-oriented project management by looking at the resources we need. We can group our resources into two categories: people and tools. What kind of people do you need to successfully complete an object-oriented project? Booch suggests you have the following types of people on your team: system architects, class designers, class implementors, and application programmers.[1] You could also add a technical writer. What is the difference between these types of people? System architects are the ones who make strategic decisions about the system. They give the system its shape and focus. Class designers work at the next level down. They define subsystems and the mechanisms that make them work. Class implementors focus on the individual classes. They organize classes and implement their functionality. Application programmers take the classes created by the class implementors and connect them through defined mechanisms. Technical writers help create the system documentation, but mainly focus on the user guide or other documents to be distributed.

The distinction between these categories is somewhat artificial. In small teams, an individual may play all roles. Even in larger groups, the distinction is fuzzy. If these people work in isolation from one another, you will find you're back in the waterfall approach. Iteration is impossible without continual interaction at all levels. The technical writer is the only one whose work is distinct. Initially, the technical writer may be more an observer than a participant. One of the contributions the writer can make is to help the team focus on documented requirements as the system is being designed. The writer can also serve as a check point for system functionality. In developing a user guide, they expect to see a certain functionality based on the requirements. The questions they ask can help solidify the shape of what the user sees.

If an object-oriented project needs these functions fulfilled, how large a team do you need to do a job? Initial projects should be pilot projects with a small team of five to nine individuals. You do not want to learn a new technology while dealing with the pressures of a mission-critical project. Likewise, a number of failures in initial object-oriented projects have been reported when the project started with too large a group. One project that failed had over 100 developers. This is a management issue. People try to do more than they are ready for. They lack the experience they need to manage any object-oriented project, let alone a large one. The problems encountered in managing object-oriented development trips them up. They try to manage in the old waterfall style with little iteration. The only result they should expect from this is failure. It is better to pick an appropriately sized first project and team. This will give you an opportunity to learn and understand the differences in managing object-oriented technology, which will lay the foundation for growth and expansion. What about the duration of the project? Initial projects should take the team from 6 months to one year to complete. This lets you get early feedback on the object-oriented approach.

I offer one additional note of caution. Fred Brooks, in his book *The Mythical Man Month*, identified what he called the second-system effect,[2] which arises after the completion of a first project. The team makes the mistake of thinking they encountered all the problems and pitfalls in the first project. The result is that they make numerous new blunders in the second project because they overestimated their skills and knowledge. They also tend to bring in all of the embellishments that were carefully laid aside in the first design. This kind of overconfidence can occur in object-oriented projects. It's best to remember that there is *always* more to learn. Experience can be a useful guide if used wisely.

TOOLS

Tools, tools, and more tools—that's what developers want; or so it seems if you're the one who has to sign off on buying them. What kind of tools can you use in developing an object-oriented project? Are all of them needed? These are questions you need to answer before starting the project. We've already seen how the design process can generate lots of documentation. This is a fitting place to begin our look at tools. Certainly it is very helpful to have analysis and design tools. These tools can be used to capture your diagrams and details about the system's design. Ideally they should support you in creating documentation from analysis through implementation. They should also feed the other documentation tools you use. This last item is important if you want to integrate all of the documentation you create. Some tools will not support every aspect of a methodology. You may need multiple tools to create your documentation. You can also use a manual process instead of automated tools or supplement the tools with a manual process. CRC cards are an example of a low-cost tool that can be used either way.

If you create documentation not covered by your design tool, such as class specifications, data definition language, or scenarios, then you will need tools for text documentation. Most word processors will do. It's a definite advantage if they can support the inclusion of graphics. This becomes a requirement if you are merging your documentation into a comprehensive whole. Most word processors offer a wide range of features. Select one that covers as much of your documentation needs as possible. Think about how you want the final documentation to appear. Some make the creation of large bodies of documentation easier than others. You may also have compatibility requirements for the storage and transfer of documents.

If you create documentation such as event flow diagrams for design validation, you will need a graphic tool or a meta-CASE tool to draw them. In fact, you may need several tools depending on what you are drawing. Not all tools are created equal. For example, some word processors have limited drawing abilities, but we found they were not capable enough to draw event flow diagrams. Their capabilities were used where appropriate, but generally other tools were needed for graphics. The key is to select the appropriate tool for the task. Do you want a general drawing tool, or is a CAD program a better choice? CAD programs give you better control over what you draw, but may not be flexible enough to draw what you want. Think carefully about what you have to draw before selecting the tool.

Tables and graphs can be an important part of your documentation. Spreadsheet programs are often the best choice for these. This is especially true when tables and graphs are dealing with the same data. You can use spreadsheet functionality to keep data in a tabular format and use the tables to automatically keep your graphs up to date. We will see an example of this type of documentation used in project tracking later in the chapter. Almost any spreadsheet with the ability to do tables and graphs will do. You must consider the type of graphs you want to create. Some programs are more capable than others. You may also want to consider compatibility with your word processor. Some programs support the automatic linking and updating of information from one application to another.

These tools may meet your need for documentation, but what about development? Several kinds of tools can be used. Fortunately, object-oriented development environments are among the most sophisticated available. In object-oriented development, tools are needed for compiling and debugging. These are the bare minimum. It is also very helpful to have tools for browsing class and program structures. You could use separate tools for these, but usually you don't need to. Almost all of these can be found in a single development environment. Which environment that is depends on the language you are using. Smalltalk environments usually include class libraries, class browsers, source level debuggers, interpreters, and incremental compilers. Smalltalk development environments are among the most complete and sophisticated available. C++ environments include class browsers, source level debuggers, and compilers. Some add C++ interpreters, and program structure browsers. They are usually not quite as nice to use as the Smalltalk environments.

Supplemental tools can also be used in development. These fit into one of two categories: third-party libraries or interface builders. There can be an overlap between the categories. Libraries may be used for almost any functionality. Typical uses of libraries include math, client-server, and database access functions. Interface builders are becoming a popular tool. These are available in X-Windows, CRT, and Windows flavors. Some of these tools provide support for all. With these tools, you develop common code for your application using their library routines for the user interface. You then use the tool to create your program for a specific machine. There are potential problems with this approach. The functionality they offer may not always reflect the full capabilities of the interface you are targeting. Also, they may limit how you use an environment because they try to be generic. Investigate the capabilities of these systems thoroughly before committing to their use.

An important part of the development process is controlling what software has been delivered and what has not. This is especially important in coordinating team efforts. You don't want team members stepping on each other's toes. You may also have them working on different versions of parts of the system. You need to establish and control a baseline for code to let this development happen in an orderly way. A good way to do this is to use source code control and configuration management software. For C++ development, you don't need special object-oriented tools—numerous tools are available and will work fine. You will need special tools if you are working in Smalltalk because of the integrated nature of its development environment.

Currently, there are few tools for configuration management in Smalltalk. Those that exist are not created equal. Before picking a tool, you need to determine the scope of your project. Some tools work well for small teams. Others are appropriate for 100-person projects. They also require a different view of how you organize your application. Because of the integrated nature of the environment, you must be aware of prerequisite classes. For large systems, you must understand how this complicates organizing and incorporating specific classes into various subsystems.

One important aspect of development is assuring that the software has been thoroughly tested. It is important to understand what test methods you want to use and what you hope to accomplish with them. Are there tools to help with this? The object-oriented world is new enough that little has been done in this area. That is changing as more firms get object-oriented development experience and understand the importance of testing. New products are starting to appear. Some firms have attempted to adapt standard tools to object-oriented testing, but their success has been limited. Object orientation adds its own kinks to the testing process. For example, imagine a method that calls the Draw method of every object in a list. If you are using polymorphism, this one method call may really call many different methods. Standard testing tools have no concept of polymorphism or how it affects the thoroughness of your tests. Be sure to evaluate these tools for their ability to truly support object-oriented concepts before committing to one.

If you are working in a group, communications are important. Tools that facilitate group communication can be an important part of the development process. For example, notes conferences are a readily available tool that can be used to good effect. Blackboard software is another example of group software that is on the cutting edge for this type of application. Electronic mail is a ubiquitous tool. If properly used, it will become indispensable. The StarView project made extensive use of email for communicating within and outside the group. Electronic mail kept paper memos to a minimum and sped up communications at the same time.

Which of these tools are necessary? Certainly, the code development tools represent a bare minimum. In fact, it may be too bare a minimum. There is also a great deal of value gained from using a tool to support the design process and documentation. It can contribute much by capturing decisions and making it easy to disseminate information. Other tools such as word processors, graphics tools, spreadsheets and email are not essential. However, most developers have access to these kinds of tools and should be free to use them to support their development and documentation efforts.

We've talked about tools for developers, but what about managers? For managers, there tend to be two categories of tools: those you can have and those you really need. Unfortunately, they are often not the same. What exists today are standard project-tracking and scheduling tools. These can create Gantt and Pert charts for projects. They can also handle manpower resources and costs. There are many such tools available. A note of caution is needed, however. These tools are fine for tracking a project at a high level. They don't handle iteration, so it is difficult to track this type of process. At best, you can map out much of the implementation phase of the project. Some of these tools try to support project estimation as well. They use various standard software complexity and development models. These do not work very well for object-oriented projects. They are based on a history of structured development. They simply do not understand object-oriented development issues. They have no concept of the impact of inheritance, polymorphism, etc., on development. They don't understand the changes brought by iterative development and incremental integration. Those who have tried to use them have found them very inaccurate and not worth the effort. What is needed are tools that help estimate object-oriented projects and track quality. Unfortunately, there is little available for this. Tools are being developed, but questions abound about what is needed and what the information they generate would mean. The result is that you have to create custom tools or find ways to use existing ones. In the next section we will cover a few of the techniques you can use to estimate projects and track their development. It will not be an exhaustive list, but some techniques have proven useful in practice and satisfy basic managerial needs.

Before we leave the subject of tools, we should ask where they should run. The answer to this question will affect the choice of tools. Where you have only one type of machine available, there is no choice. However, where you have a variety of machines available, you should know that it is possible to successfully use a mix of machines and software. In StarView, for example, we mixed VMS, SunOS, Ultrix, and Macintosh platforms. We found tools that let us trade information between systems.

PROJECT ESTIMATION

There are many things a manager must do to plan a project and track its progress. Traditional approaches to both, such as counting lines of code, don't seem to work very well in object-oriented projects. Concepts such as classes, inheritance, and polymorphism don't fit in well with the usual metrics. What we need are approaches that take into account the unique features of object technology. This is true for both estimating and tracking projects. Tools that understand object-oriented concepts and automate both processes are desirable. Unfortunately, none of any value are currently available. Of the two tasks, estimating an object-oriented project appears to be the most difficult. Estimating has always been something of an art. In spite of all that has been written on the subject, experience is still more valuable than formulas. This is as true for object-oriented projects as it is for conventional ones. Does this mean you have no hope of succeeding if you lack this experience? No. Some rules of thumb have proven useful in estimating projects. Understanding how to properly use these is a good step down the road to experience. They have ranged from the ridiculous suggestion of one line of comment per class to things that are truly useful. Tom Love developed several for sizing classes and effort after reviewing several projects.[3] They are as follows:

Estimate of Method Size
Prototype class: 5–10 lines of code
Production class: 10–20 lines of code

C++ will require 2–3 times more lines of code than Smalltalk

Estimate of Number of Methods
Prototype class: 10–15 methods
Production class: 20–30 methods

Estimate of Development Time
Prototype class: 1 person-week
Production class: 8 person-weeks

Number of Instance Variables per Class
4–8

To use these rules of thumb successfully in project estimation, you will have to do a preliminary object-oriented analysis of your project. This helps you determine the scope of the project by letting you estimate the number of classes in the proposed system. Coming up with a reasonable number of classes is one key to successful object-oriented project estimation. Experience is a real factor in class estimation. Obviously, the more analysis you do, the better the number you will come up with. On the other hand, you don't want to do all of the analysis. If you do, you will have done much of the project and nullified your reason for wanting an estimate. The best approach is to take a reasonable cut at analysis. Estimate what fraction of classes are covered by the preliminary analysis. In the preliminary analysis, you will not uncover many of the support classes or see how the original classes may be split into several. You must use a multiplier to estimate the final number of classes. Depending on how good this analysis is, you should use a 2x or 3x multiplier. For StarView, we used a 2x multiplier for the project estimate. This turned out to be reasonable. Once you have the number of classes, you can use it with the rules of thumb.

Rules of thumb are just that. They are not absolutes for class and method size. At the end of StarView's first delivery, we compared the average class and method size using these rules of thumb. We were pleasantly surprised to find they fell right in the middle of the rules of thumb for production classes. That was not planned. Of course, the actual sizes of the classes were both larger and smaller than the average. All this verification did was lend confidence in using the rules of thumb for future estimations.

To see how these rules work, let's estimate a project with them. We will assume that we have estimated 100 classes for the project. We will also assume an eight-person team to work on the project. Using this number of classes and going with the average number of methods for a production class (25), this gives us an estimate of 2500 methods in the project. If we multiply this by the average lines of code per production class (15), this gives us a total of 37,500 lines of code for the project. Now comes the tricky part—estimating how many lines of code per person per day to use. Often values based on non–object-oriented languages are too low. For example, one group had many years of experience maintaining Fortran programs. Their average was 11 lines of code per day per person. When they created an object-oriented system, the average lines of code per day per person was 16. This is an important difference and can make a significant difference in the overall estimation of a project. This is why experience is still more valuable than formulas. You have to be able to correctly judge the productivity of your team.

For our example, we will use the known figure of 16 lines of code per day for C++. This gives us a total of 2344 person-days for the project. If we consider the size of the team, we can determine that the project should last about 59 weeks. This seems to be a reasonable estimate for a project with this number of classes. If we had used the 11 lines of code estimate, the project's length would be estimated at 85 weeks. This is a big difference. You will have to select numbers based on the team you are estimating for.

We should compare these numbers to those based on the rule of thumb of 8 weeks per class. This metric would put us at an estimate of 100 weeks. This is almost double our original estimate. The value you use depends on the skill of the team you are estimating for, but 8 weeks seems too high. Personally, I would be more inclined to use 5 weeks per class. This puts us much closer to our original estimate.

A better approach is to avoid lines of code and simply use weeks per class to estimate project duration. If you do this, you do not need to consider lines of code. Simply multiply the estimated number of classes by the weeks per class. This gives the total person-weeks for the project. Divide this number by the number of team members to estimate project duration. In this case with 100 classes at 5 weeks each, we end up with 500 person-weeks. Divide this by the eight-person team and we estimate a project duration of 62.5 weeks.

SCHEDULES AND MILESTONES

After completing estimates for a project, the next task a manager faces is to create a schedule for the project. You can begin this based on the information you created for your estimates. One of the challenges faced by the manager of an object-oriented project is how to show progress in an iterative process. You can show a more linear view of progress by using milestones. Let's examine the major steps in development and see what milestones might be appropriate. The preferred approach to creating milestones is to have few formal and several informal design reviews during analysis and design. This should be followed with a steady stream of prototypes or incremental releases that demonstrate increasing functionality in the system. By prototypes, I do not mean experiments, but the actual system as it evolves. The milestones demonstrate the actual state of the system at a given point in time. I use the word prototype because, until the very end, the system is incomplete. Since development is iterative, there is additional opportunity for the system to evolve and change.

Recall the key points in analysis. You know you are making progress when you see the classes start to stabilize. You will also see the key interfaces between classes stabilize. At this point you start the transition from analysis to design. This is what we called the 3db point on our 3db software engineering curve. This is the first significant point in the process, and it is a good point for an informal design review. This review is more of a sanity check than anything. You can compare your requirements with the architecture revealed through your analysis. It is difficult to estimate when you will reach this point. It depends on the experience of your team. Teams with experience or a mentor will reach this point earlier than inexperienced teams. It also depends on the scope of the project. It takes longer to reach this point in large projects. If you have a sense of how long you would spend in a structured analysis, increase that by half. As a benchmark, use the example we covered for project estimation. With a 100-class project and an inexperienced team with a mentor, you could expect to spend about 1.5 months to reach the 3db point.

There are other key moments in the design process we can use for milestones. The first is when you can trace all of your requirements to classes in the system. This milestone shows that you have captured all your requirements in the system. The next key point is when you can use your scenarios to validate your design using event flow diagrams and language. This milestone shows how the design supports all that the system is supposed to accomplish. It is also important because once this milestone is complete, you are ready for a formal design review. Once you have reached this point, you are ready to create a detailed implementation schedule.

One important goal of the implementation milestones is to demonstrate the increasing functionality of the system through incremental integration and a steady stream of prototypes. The value of these incremental releases is that you begin demonstrating the actual system's functionality early. Even though the system is incomplete until the very end, others evaluating the project have a high level of confidence that progress is being made because they can see the system grow and evolve. This is much better than waiting for the big bang of integration at the end of implementation.

To create these milestones, you will have to understand the interrelationships between classes. Let the integration milestones help determine the order of development. Start with the core classes, your key abstractions, and move on to those that use them. You can also create milestones for subsystems. Establish milestones that demonstrate important new functionality in the evolving system. Incremental milestones should reflect the completion of key aspects of the system. With these, you can show a more linear view of progress towards your goals. This view can give a meaningful view of progress to managers who aren't interested in iteration—only results.

These milestones are very valuable, but managers need even more information to track development. Milestones don't just magically happen. Likewise, if they are missed, it's not by accident. Managers need to understand the details of development so they can identify existing or potential problems. For example, was a milestone missed because the system was growing out of its original boundaries? Was new functionality added that wasn't in the initial schedule or requirements? This happens when requirements change in the middle of development. The flip side of this is to find functionality that may have been lost. This means that someone forgot to do part of the work. The conventional approach to finding these problems is to count lines of code. As we shall see, there are much better ways to track development in an object-oriented project.

The key component in object-oriented development is the class, not the line of code. By tracking the number of classes and methods developed, we can have a better idea of what is going on in the system. The basic idea is that by counting classes and methods, you can understand something about the state of development. An increase in classes and methods can show that a system is growing out of bounds. It can also be the result of poor estimation due to lack of experience. This is most often the case with first projects. A reduction in expected number may show missing functionality. An increase in classes but a reduction in methods may indicate that implementors are making more use of reuse. If you count fewer classes but more methods, it may indicate that a consolidation of classes is occurring. You can make analysis easier by grouping classes and counts by subsystem. In StarView, the actual counts were one for each method and one for the class itself. To monitor progress, we tracked the growth of classes by comparing them to estimates made at the beginning of implementation.

We can see an example of this type of metric in Table 12.1. This is the table format for the data collected in the StarView project. The Plan column shows the original projection for classes by month in different subsystems. The Forecast Delta column shows changes to the schedule or changes based on the acceptance of new functionality. Added to the Plan column, they indicate what count should be seen each month. The Actual column shows what was actually done for the month on a subsystem basis. The Actual Delta column shows the difference between the actual and the Planned plus the Forecast. This information is turned into an easier to read graph in Figure 12.1. This diagram reflects the fact that new functionality was accepted into the system during implementation. The Forecast and Actual lines show the increase over the initial plan.

In Figure 12.1, we see that the Actual was consistently greater than the Planned or Forecast. Why? As development proceeded and users saw the incremental prototypes, they requested additional functionality. The Planned line only shows the original scope of the project, not the requested changes. The Forecast reflects the changes based on requests for new functionality. On the whole, the Actual tracked the Forecast fairly closely. It might take a jump up one month if we were ahead of schedule. The next month it would often level off.

Another way to track system functionality is to use an earned value approach. In this approach, we assign value to each piece of functionality and track the value growth. What is a "piece of functionality"? Usually it is a piece of system functionality defined in your requirements. For example, the ability to generate a query was one for StarView. Another might be the ability to display a form. The system gains value as pieces of functionality are completed. The total value for a piece of functionality is counted when all work for that piece is complete. This is not synonymous with counting classes. A piece of functionality may require several classes to be complete.

In StarView, we assigned a value of 10 to each piece of functionality. An example of StarView earned value data in table format can be found in Table 12.2. The organization of this table is the same as that for class and method count. The meaning of the columns is also the same. Figure 12.2 shows the data

Table 12.1. Class and Method Count

	Forms & Fields for CRT				Networking & Services				Query Model			
	Plan	Forecast Plan Delta	Actual Plan Delta	Actual	Plan	Forecast Plan Delta	Actual Plan Delta	Actual	Plan	Forecast Plan Delta	Actual Plan Delta	Actual
Apr 92	21		1	22								
May92	12		16	38								
Jun 92	10	-10		0					67		32	99
Jul 92	88		37	125	74		-16	58	0			
Aug92	0	61	-1	60	15	16	-31	0	11	27	17	28
Sep 92	33	114	7	154	0	30	-30	0	81		55	163
Oct 92	0			0	32	-16	13	29	79	0	19	98
Nov 92	30	-7	-23	0	20			20	0			0
Dec 92	23	27		50	0	51	-51	0	8		-8	0
Jan 93		47	23	70	20	-20		0			25	25
Feb 93			289	289						69	-17	52
Mar 93		289	-287	2								
Apr 93										0	2	2
May93												
Total	217	521	62	810	161	61	-115	107	246	96	125	359

TABLE 12.1. (continued)

	Query & DB Services				Total for All Classes			
	Plan	Forecast Plan Delta	Actual Plan Delta	Actual	Plan	Forecast Plan Delta	Actual Plan Delta	Actual
Apr 92					0	0	0	0
May92	73		19	92	94	0	20	114
Jun 92	0				79	0	48	137
Jul 92	36		15	51	120	-10	-1	109
Aug92	0			0	114	16	23	153
Sep 92	0				81	118	24	223
Oct 92	14			14	158	98	39	295
Nov 92	19		-19	0	39	0	-19	20
Dec 92	0	19	-19	0	38	63	-101	0
Jan 93		19		19	43	26	25	94
Feb 93		125	56	181		241	62	303
Mar 93						0	289	289
Apr 93		0	2	2		289	-283	6
May93						0	0	0
Total	142	163	54	359	766	841	126	1743

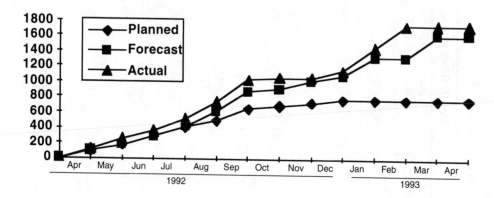

FIGURE 12.1. Class and Method Count Graph

TABLE 12.2. Earned Value

	Forms & Fields for CRT				Networking & Services				Query Model			
	Plan	Forecast Plan Delta	Actual Plan Delta	Actual	Plan	Forecast Plan Delta	Actual Plan Delta	Actual	Plan	Forecast Plan Delta	Actual Plan Delta	Actual
Apr 92												
May92	210		10	220								
Jun 92	120		160	380					670		320	990
Jul 92	100	-100		0	740		-160	580	0			
Aug92	890		370	1260	150	160	-310	0	110		170	280
Sep 92	150	610	-160	600	0	300	-300	0	810	270	550	1630
Oct 92	330	1140	70	1540	320	-160	130	290	790		190	980
Nov 92	0	150		150	200			200	0			
Dec 92	370	-190	-180	0	0	510	-510	0	80		-80	0
Jan 93		500		500	200	-200		0		80	170	250
Feb 93		470	230	700						690	-170	520
Mar 93		2890	2890	2890								
Apr 93			-2870	20						0	20	20
May93												
Total	2170	5470	520	8260	1610	610	-1150	1070	2460	1040	1170	4670

TABLE 12.2. (continued)

	Query & DB Services				Total for All Classes			
	Plan	Forecast Plan Delta	Actual Plan Delta	Actual	Plan	Forecast Plan Delta	Actual Plan Delta	Actual
Apr 92					0	0	0	0
May92	730		190	920	940	0	200	1140
Jun 92	0			0	790	0	480	1370
Jul 92	360		150	510	1200	-100	-10	1090
Aug92	0			0	1150	160	230	1540
Sep 92	0				960	1180	90	2230
Oct 92	140			140	1580	980	390	2950
Nov 92	190		-190	0	390	150	-190	350
Dec 92	400	190	-590	0	850	510	-1360	0
Jan 93		590	-400	190	200	970	-230	940
Feb 93		1250	560	1810		2410	620	3030
Mar 93						0	2890	2890
Apr 93		0	20	20		2890	-2830	60
May93						0	0	0
Total	1820	2030	-260	3590	8060	9150	280	17590

Earned Value

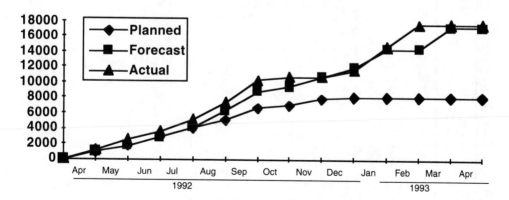

FIGURE 12.2. Earned Value Graph

TABLE 12.3. Lines of Code Count

	Forms & Fields for CRT		Networking & Services		Query Model		Query & DB Services		Totals for all Classes	
	Plan	Actual	Plan	Actual	Plan	Actual	Plan	Actual	Plan	Actual
Apr 92									0	0
May92	600	165					620	839	1220	1004
Jun 92	900	500			1000	1016	0		1900	1516
Jul 92	800		1400	2251	0		900	949	3100	3200
Aug92	1800	1616	300		200	183	0		2300	1799
Sep 92	400	790	0		2300	2490	0		2700	3280
Oct 92	1500	492	900	372	2100	427	1200	2338	5700	3629
Nov 92	0		600		0		400		1000	0
Dec 92	700		0		800		400		1900	0
Jan 93		924	1300			1155		710	1300	2789
Feb 93		718		1707		1523		365		4313
Mar 93		7399								7399
Apr 93		253		110		185		133		681
May93		-93								-93
Total	6700	12764	4500	4440	6400	6979	3520	5334	21120	29517

from this table in graph form. Again, the graph shows us that new functionality was accepted during implementation.

For StarView, the shape of the Earned Value graph of Figure 12.2 closely matches that of the Classes and Methods graph of Figure 12.1. The Earned Value graph has the shape it does for the same reasons given for the other graph.

The final tracking metric used in StarView was the infamous lines of code. We tracked lines of code because we were required to do so. Since we had to track it, we tried in several ways to see if it could be useful. We first tried estimating lines of code based on the classes and methods count. There was no correlation between lines of code and methods or functionality completed. This metric also proved useless in judging the quality of classes. The only value we could find in lines of code was as a measure of level of effort. You can use it to ask if developers are turning out code at the rate predicted. Even this use of the metric depends on how you originally estimate lines of code. It does not measure system progress. It can't tell you if the code being developed is needed or not. Most people developing object-oriented metrics agree—lines of code is a poor metric at best. The best approach is to not use it at all. If it is used, it must be used with caution. It does not give the insights into a system many believe it does. Table 12.3 shows the lines of code data counted for StarView. Figure 12.3 shows the same information in graph format.

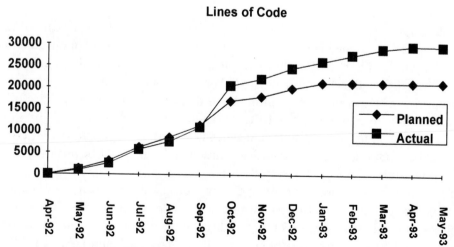

FIGURE 12.3. Lines of Code Graph

DOCUMENTATION

We've already seen many types of documentation for an object-oriented system. One issue that we have not discussed is standards. The purpose of standards is to improve the consistency and quality of work. One type of standard that is useful in object-oriented development is a standard for coding. Coding standards are necessary for quality and consistency when working in groups. Group coding standards serve several useful functions. They set expectations for the peer review of code. Everyone has a common standard for judging quality. They also clearly define what is expected of each developer. Everyone is clear about what standard they are expected to adhere to. Coding standards can also set the basic individual standard for development. They serve as the goal toward which each individual works. Coding standards make an important contribution to the maintainability of the system. They encourage a consistency of form and style that makes it easier for everyone to understand code developed by others.

Figure 12.4 shows an example of the StarView coding standard for C++ header files. An important part of this standard is that it defines the order in which items appear in the file. Things are not scattered about, but can be found in consistent places in the file. Another part of the StarView standard required comments for each attribute and method in the header file. All code was peer reviewed, and any code that did not meet the standard had to be fixed. The final peer-reviewed code became part of the standard documentation for StarView's maintenance.

You can set standards for other parts of documentation as well. One of the first standards you need is to decide what methodology and design documentation you will adopt. For StarView, we picked class and object diagrams annotated from the Booch methodology. You can select other diagrams as appropriate. State transition or interaction diagrams could be appropriate. If you are going to make changes to the standard notation, you need to agree ahead of time what is acceptable and what is not. If you use automated tools, you will be limited to the tools abilities. These may or may not be a reflection of the full notation of the methodology.

You may need standards for other documentation of your own creation. For example, we created scenarios. Before creating them we needed to define their purpose. Defining the purpose of any additional documentation you create will help you understand why you are creating it and how it should help you. What we did for StarView's DDL and FDL provides an example of this. These lan-

Class declarations should use the following format:
- prolog
- #ifndef CLASSNAME_H (bypass header to avoid multiple inclusion)
- #define CLASSNAME_H

- #include <system.h>
- #include <project/filename>
- #include "local"
- const's
- typedef's (put after const, since they may use the constant values)

- class name
- public methods (and data members - not recommended)
- protected methods and data members
- private methods and data members
- friend classes and methods (other than in overloaded operator
  declarations)

- #endif // CLASSNAME_H (bypass)

FIGURE 12.4. Sample Coding Standard

guages are fundamental parts of StarView. We created a BNF notation for each language to define how to construct and use it. This definition became a standard part of the developer's maintenance documentation.

We also created standards for the event flow diagrams and language, since these were used to validate our design. We also standardized the form of class specifications. Other documentation needed no standards per se. The numerous cross references are an example of this. They were a one-time, limited-use form of documentation.

Creating internal standards does not need to be a complex, drawn-out process. It is basically a matter of agreeing on how things will be done and specifically what will be done. They are useful because everyone can understand the work of others and can make their own work understood. Create standards only when they will be useful and can improve group communication. Standards that are an unnecessary burden will not be used.

TESTING AND QUALITY ASSURANCE

So far in our discussion of the object-oriented development process, we've talked very little about testing and quality assurance. They are as important as ever. Good development practices are still required. What we will see in object-oriented development is how the incremental approach to testing and integration supports quality development. It closely resembles the Total Quality Management (TQM) approach to continual improvement.[4] An important aspect of this approach is that it allows you to catch and correct problems early. This is important, because defects caught later in the process are much more expensive to correct.

Studies done on the impacts of the early detection of defects show that design activities introduce 50–60% of all defects.[5] Design reviews will uncover 50–75% of these design defects. These studies have also shown the cost impact of early detection. If an error is uncovered at the design stage, its cost is 1 unit. If the same error is uncovered just before testing, its cost is 6.5 units. If the error is caught during testing, its cost is 15 units. If the error is not caught until after release, its cost is 60–100 units. Clearly, catching and fixing the problems later in the development cycle is much more expensive than fixing them early. Development and testing approaches that encourage early detection and correction will need fewer resources in the long run.

What is the purpose of testing? Your answer to this question will shape the approach you take to it. Many believe the purpose of testing is to show that their software is correct. Others believe that testing shows their software has no errors. Still others believe that testing shows that a program does what it should. Each of these definitions is inadequate. How do you know your testing is thorough enough to verify your software is correct? Can testing really show that software has no errors? Glenford Myers has a better definition of testing. He says that "testing is the process of executing a program with the intent of finding errors."[6] This perspective is quite different from the others, and it leads to different methods of testing.

Think of software testing in the same fashion as a doctor ordering a medical test. You go to the doctor because something is wrong with you. The doctor orders tests to try to find the cause of the problem. It the test does not reveal the cause, the doctor does not consider the test successful, but orders other tests. A successful test is one that shows the cause of a problem. The same is true for software. Resources are often scarce. We find that we have limited time and people to perform testing. To make the best use of these limited resources, we want to find and fix as many errors as we can in the limited time we have. One way to maximize the use of our resources is to develop tests that have the greatest likelihood of finding errors. If these tests find errors, then we can fix them and improve the quality of our software. If we write simple tests that are not likely to find errors, then we are wasting our time. Every bug found and fixed improves the quality of our software. Every bug that remains hidden creates risk later in the life cycle.

The object-oriented approach to testing tries to catch problems early and minimize the introduction of new ones. One approach is to use three levels of testing. Black box and white box testing is done at each level. Black box tests know nothing about the internal structure or functioning of the item being tested. White box tests are based on a detailed understanding of an item's structure and how it functions. Both types are needed to create complete suites of tests. In all cases, we ask ourselves what subset of all possible tests has the highest probability of finding errors. These are the tests we want to implement.

The first level is unit testing. The unit being tested is a class. In this approach, each method in the class is tested. When doing black box testing on a method, two techniques are typically used: equivalence partitioning and boundary-value analysis. Equivalence partitioning is defining a set of tests where testing one value is equivalent to testing several values. Boundary-value analysis tests values at the boundaries of expected input as well as values outside the expected boundaries.

Two types of white box testing are also done. These are decision/condition coverage and multiple-condition coverage. Decision/condition coverage requires enough test cases so that for each method, each condition in a decision takes on all possible outcomes at least once, each decision takes on all possible outcomes at least once, and each point of entry is invoked at least once.[7] Multiple-condition coverage requires enough test cases so that all possible combinations of condition outcomes in each decision and all points of entry are invoked at least once. Together these tests provide broad coverage of potential problems. After implementing a class, the developer does the unit testing. Only after unit testing is complete is the code peer reviewed. Old tests are retained for regression testing for evolving classes.

The next level of testing is subsystem testing. At this level, we are concerned with the interaction between classes. This is the place to test multiclass mechanisms. Class designers usually do this type of testing. Appropriately testing mechanisms and higher levels of integration takes a lot of planning. You need not only to test for basic functionality, but you need to look for unintended interactions and ripple effects. Unintended interactions are usually the result of poorly defined interfaces or methods trying to do too much. Ripple effects result from classes too dependent on classes to which they are not directly connected. This can happen with the use of global information or when some intermediate classes are used only to pass through information. Equivalent types of black and white box tests are also constructed at this level.

The third level of testing is the system level. At this level we are looking at system-level integration. This testing may be done by a separate testing and integration team and is based on the system defining scenarios. These scenarios provide the basis for both system validation and acceptance testing. The three-level approach to testing builds confidence in lower-level abstractions first. Remember that testing and integration in object-oriented development are not the major steps they are in the traditional waterfall approach. Object-oriented testing is an iterative process. It happens throughout the whirlpool development cycle. Using multilevel testing in an iterative fashion promotes the early detection and correction of problems. It has the effect of improving quality and supporting the incremental milestones used to track development.

SUMMARY

We've covered a lot of territory in this chapter, highlighting the key issues in managing object-oriented projects. We've seen that there are many tools you can use to develop object-oriented projects. Most of the tools available are for developers. Managers also need tools, but they have fewer choices. Standard tools have limited applicability to object-oriented projects. Don't be tied down by the tools available. Use what you have in ways that will help you accomplish your goals.

We also saw that schedules for object-oriented projects are developed differently from those in standard waterfall development. In project estimation, you can use object-oriented rules of thumb to estimate the scope of the project. The 3db software engineering curve can help you to understand where you are in analysis and to design and find points for milestones. The 3db point can be the place for an informal design review. The ability to use scenarios to validate the design pinpoints the time for a formal design review. The implementation milestones are based on incremental integration. These milestones show the system continually evolving in functionality.

Standards are an important part of documentation. They promote consistency and quality in development. They can be used to set both individual and group standards. Standards need not be a burden. Use them where they will promote better communication within a group.

Finally, the object-oriented approach uses multilevel iterative testing throughout the development process. This encourages the early detection and correction of problems and improves the quality of the system using fewer resources. It also supports the incremental milestones used to track development.

REFERENCES

1. Booch, Grady. *Object Oriented Design with Applications*. Redwood City, CA: Benjamin/Cummings Publishing, 1991, p. 207.
2. Brooks, Fred. *The Mythical Man Month: Essays on Software Engineering*. Reading, MA: Addison-Wesley, 1975, pp. 53–58.
3. Tom Love in a talk at ObjectWorld 1991.
4. Berk, Joseph and Susan. *Total Quality Management: Implementing Continuous Improvement*. New York: Sterling, 1993.
5. Grady, Robert. *Practical Software Metrics for Project Management and Process Improvement*. Englewood Cliffs, NJ: Prentice-Hall, 1992.
6. Myers, Glenford. *The Art of Software Testing*. New York, New York: Wiley, 1979, p. 5.
7. Myers, Glenford. *The Art of Software Testing*. New York, New York: Wiley, 1979, pp. 43–44.

CHAPTER 13

Making the Move

We've covered a lot of ground in this book. We've talked about object-oriented technology and the benefits it can bring to software development. We have also laid the foundations for using the technology by examining the different methodologies and how they work. We've discussed how to manage an object-oriented project and examined a real project to see how it was done. Now it's time to see how to make the transition to object-oriented technology. Any fair examination of moving to a new technology must review the risks in making the move. We also need to understand the startup costs involved. Finally we will look at how to help the team make the transition.

RISKS

We've examined the benefits of object-oriented technology, but are there risks to adopting it? There are always risks when you adopt a technology you are not familiar with. That is not the same thing as saying the technology is risky.

Many of the risks come from not understanding how to correctly implement the new technology. There are also risks in *not* moving to a technology. The purpose of this book is to help you over that hurdle.

There are other issues you need to understand if you wish to implement object-oriented technology. While object oriented methodologies can be used as they are defined, you may have additional needs or requirements they do not address. For example, you may believe it is important to tie your design back to its requirements. Failure to do this could mean missed functionality in your design. Most methods have no explicit tie back to requirements. You may need to supplement the methodology with cross references or additions such as the requirements section in the class specification.

Another area where you may need to supplement a methodology is with real-time extensions. Most methodologies provide no explicit support for things such as timing and memory budgets. You will also have to decide how important it is to you for the methodology to support the capture of implementation details. Methodologies differ in their support at this level. Some offer explicit notation, while others leave it to the tool that supports the methodology.

One thing should be clear by now—there are no cookbook approaches to using a methodology. All require thought and care in their use. Object-oriented methodology is not a magic bullet. It is a powerful tool that, when properly applied, can bring considerable benefits to software development.

Other issues must be considered when starting an object-oriented project. There are potential pitfalls in the choices of language, libraries, and development tools. Integration is an important consideration for libraries. If you use multiple libraries, you may uncover incompatibilities. You can see the same problem if you try to integrate public domain software into your system. There can also be incompatibilities between libraries and development environment.

Deciding which development environment and libraries you need to use may narrow your platform selection. Not all tools are available on all platforms. Language choice and availability can also narrow platform selection or, if you are delivering for a specific platform, you may find your choice of language and tools limited. You must also consider the learning curve for a language. Some require longer learning curves than others. For example, a C programmer will be able to move to C++ quicker than he could move to Smalltalk. On the other hand, Smalltalk may be a better choice for a particular application.

What about the performance risks in object-oriented programs? There is an old claim that the cost of message passing makes object-oriented programs significantly slower. This has proven groundless. Object-oriented programs can be as efficient as any program written in a high-level language. Often it is faster to look up a dynamic method than it is to evaluate case statements. Even when using an interpreted version of a language such a Smalltalk, the language may not be the most significant performance factor. If you are using a language in conjunction with a GUI windowing system, you will find the windowing system is a greater performance hit. In fact, if you are working on an application that is mostly user interface, you may not even be able to tell the difference between using a compiled or interpreted object-oriented language.

There are other issues to watch out for with object-oriented languages. One is the explosion of message passing among layers. This occurs when classes serve as intermediaries, passing messages from one class to the next. Intermediaries may be valuable if used in a limited way. The problem occurs when messages must be passed through many layers or most messages are handled this way, which is usually the result of poor design and can degrade performance. Other issues may be related to a specific language. For example, an area that deserves close attention is the dynamic allocation and destruction of objects in C++. C++ has many subtleties. A careful understanding of an object's behavior is required to avoid memory leaks. Learning the nuances of an object-oriented language must be part of the transition plan. Training and an opportunity to gain experience with the language is the best cure for this type of problem. Your choice of language will affect how much time is needed for this issue.

You may also have to face issues of cross-platform development. It is often difficult to have compatible tools across all platforms. Furthermore, not all development environments are created equal. You may not be able to get all the tools you want on all platforms. Developers who must use the less sophisticated tools may feel handicapped in their development work. This may impede development on some platforms and can be complicated by the fact that not all compilers are created equal—not even those from the same vendor. We have seen instances where compilers produce different behavior on different platforms. This is usually the result of code that has behavior that is undefined in the language. Working with multiple compilers simultaneously quickly identifies areas where you need to create more transportable code. To be successful with cross-platform development, you must plan for it from the beginning of the project. We have found it best to work on all platforms simultaneously. This quickly identifies portability problems. The typical approach is to develop on one platform and then port to the next platform. This delays the discovery of problems, but it also makes porting more costly in the long run.

COSTS

Costs are one of the main issues you will have to deal with in starting an object-oriented project. There are several types of costs you may incur. Time and money are both factors. If the team has no object-oriented experience, it will take them about 6 months to get over the training hump and be productive. They will need time to experiment and gain experience with the technology. They will also need time to investigate tools. This does not mean that the 6 months is wasted time. It is a good time to flesh out and define system requirements.

Training can also be an important investment. I use the word investment rather than cost because it is a better reflection of how the money is used. Training represents an investment in improved productivity and better software quality. There are different types of training you can make available to the team. The two basic choices are methodology and language training. Is one more important than the other? You will certainly be developing in a particular language. The developers will need some experience with the language to be successful in development. However, there is a more important issue to consider. Just because you know how to create a class in a language does not mean you know how to create a good class. Knowing what makes a good class and good interfaces between classes is a methodology issue. Understanding what methodologies have to teach will contribute more towards a good system than will expertise in a particular language.

There are several choices for training. Team members can attend individual training classes. This is often the most convenient form of training, because classes are available year round. Once a team member has returned from training, he can share his training with other team members. Another alternative is to have training brought in house so that everyone has the same training. It can also be more cost effective than paying for many individual courses, especially when you need to train six to eight people. If your training is tailored to a specific project, the team may learn more than they would using standard exercises. Conferences represent an additional alternative. Several of these are specific to object-oriented technology and languages. They usually offer training in both methodologies and languages and represent the easiest way to get training in several aspects of object-oriented technology at one time.

Equipment is a cost you may need to factor in. The equipment you develop on may not match your delivery platform. You will need equipment capable of running the tools you purchase to support the project. For many tools, this implies workstation class computers. This is often more of an operating system issue than one of processor horsepower. Some of the best development environments are only available under UNIX. Fortunately, this is changing as sophisticated development environments start to appear on a wide variety of platforms.

In the last chapter, we discussed the kinds of tools you can use for object-oriented development. Indeed, if you don't have any tools on hand, their purchase can be a significant expenditure. In the analysis and design phases, you may want several tools. Foremost among these would be a case tool that supports the methodology you will be using. You can also use tools for creating other documentation and presentations. The main tool for this documentation will be a word processor. For creating tables and graphs, you can use a spreadsheet. You may also want various presentation and drawing tools for creating charts, graphs, drawings, and slides. Managers may also want to use project-planning and tracking tools that can create Gantt and Pert charts. These can be useful even with an iterative life cycle.

There are also various tools you can use in the implementation phase. The most important of these is the development environment. You might want to supplement this with third-party libraries or interface builders. You may even want to try multiple compilers in your work. Additionally, you may want source code control and configuration management tools. You may need to develop tools of your own to track development. These could include tools for counting classes and methods, earned value, and even lines of code. Tools that support testing are also candidates for use. Finally, you may want various group work tools, including notes conference software and email.

You can spend a lot of money buying these types of tools. Are all these tools necessary? It would be nice to have them, but it is not necessary. Figure 13.1 shows three levels of software tools.

The first level shows basic tools for object-oriented development. It is true that some projects only use a development environment. The first-level tool set represents those needed for the development of a serious project of reasonable size. These tools will give you the basic resources you need to develop a project with a small team. The second level of tools include those that add support to the development and documentation processes. The most important of these is

First-Level Tools
    Case Tool
    Word Processor
    Development Environment
    Project-Tracking Tools

Second-Level Tools
    Source Code Control/Configuration Management Software
    Additional Documentation Tools
        Spreadsheet
        Drawing Tool

Third-Level Tools
    Interface Builders
    Third Party Libraries
    Group Work Tools
    Testing Tools

FIGURE 13.1. Software Tools by Category

source code control software, which helps make the development process manageable. The third level represents those tools it might be nice to have. The use of third-party libraries and interface builders might be moved to a higher level, depending on what you need to accomplish in your project.

One reason for creating these levels of software is to help warn you away from the tool trap. Buy only those tools that will give you a real benefit. Tools are resources; they should give you value as resources. Don't waste money on tools that won't pay off for you. Also, don't become a slave to your tools. Sometimes tools demand that you do a lot of preparatory work before you get to the point where you can use them for what you need. Often this extra work is unrelated to what you need to accomplish. Use a tool for how it can work for you. Avoid tools that require unnecessary work. Use only those parts of tools that contribute to your goals. Design tools are particularly tricky in this respect. Don't warp your design to match what the tool can do. Create the design you need. If the tool won't support what you need, abandon it.

TRANSITIONING

What are the steps you actually need to take to make the transition to object-oriented technology? The first step is to pick a project of the appropriate size—this means a project that will take the team no longer than a year to complete, not including training time. After you have selected the project, it is time to put the team together. The team for this project should be small—no more than six to nine people. If the team is new to object-oriented technology, you will have to allow time for them to learn the technology and get some experience with it. This should take no longer than 6 months. During this time you can begin both individual and team training. By team training, I mean getting experience as a team sharing and practicing what they have learned in individual training. During training, you may find that the team has a "hump" they have to get over to understand object-oriented technology. This hump is different for each individual, but there is often difficulty in making the conceptual leap to thinking and working with objects.

There are several typical problems. The first is difficulty in understanding just what an object is. This happens because people are still thinking about functions rather than who performs a function. Another problem is that new developers often have difficulty seeing how objects work together. They may understand the structure shown in a class diagram, but they have no idea of how the system works or why it has the structure it does. Following a scenario through the system helps here. This can be supplemented with an event flow diagram to help them understand how information moves through the system and how work is accomplished. Another common area of difficulty is making the connection from analysis to implementation. Once they understand the structure of the system, they still may not understand how to turn a design into actual code. Studying a simple example like our earlier banking example may help the team members make the necessary leap. It shows the front-to-back connectivity without a lot of the confusing details.

One of the best ways to speed the team through the transition process is to have a mentor working with the team. This can be a consultant, trainer, or someone who simply has used the technology before. The team will benefit by using the best mentor you can find. A mentor supports the transition process by helping the team avoid the pitfalls and dead ends that can derail a project. How long you need to use a mentor depends on how you want to help the team. For early projects, it is useful to have a mentor throughout the analysis and design phases. If it is a first project, you may want to use a mentor all the way through the initial software delivery.

While the team is in training, they can also be working on the requirements for the project and selecting tools for use. If you have the tools available, the team can spend time working with them. One way to build team expertise during training is to work on a simple problem. They can go through all the stages of development up to the actual implementation. If their development environments are available, they may want to do some prototyping. This helps them test their understanding of the design while giving them experience with their tools. Another important activity for the training phase is planning for the development process. If you have existing tools, such as those for configuration management, you will need to plan on how to integrate them into your work. You can also plan on how you will use your project-management and tracking tools. You can build the ones you need at this time. In fact, they may be excellent candidates for the team to start cutting their teeth on. Use their development for training. The result is a better trained team and a useful tool. Once the training phase is complete, the team is ready to begin work on the assigned project.

Teamwork is essential to object-oriented development. The traditional dividing lines between analysts, designers, and coders are no longer valid. Analysis, design, and implementation require input from all levels. Although the focus shifts throughout the process, the need for iteration to other levels continues. To make iteration work, you have to break down the walls between groups. Good communication is the key to successful development. This is the foundation for teamwork. This doesn't mean you won't have different people performing different functions. It does mean that the barriers between the different activities must fall.

SUMMARY

Throughout this book, we've talked about the many benefits that object-oriented technology offers. These are real benefits that lead to more robust maintainable systems. Object technology offers a true conceptual break from structured analysis and design. As we've examined the various aspects of object-oriented technology, we've tried to offer practical insights into how to use and manage the technology. Let practicality be your guide in using object-oriented analysis and design. Don't be a slave to a methodology. Supplement the methodology where needed to meet your needs. Object technology is one that can be managed. The whirlpool approach provides a model for iterative and incremental development. Concepts such as 3db software engineering provide new tools for project management and control. There are always risks and costs involved in moving to a new technology. In the case of object technology, the benefits far outweigh the risks. A practical approach to transitioning to the technology minimizes risk. The long-term benefits of the object-oriented approach will favor those that use it. Isn't it time for you to make the move?

INDEX

Explore the leading methodologies

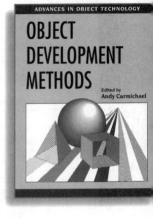

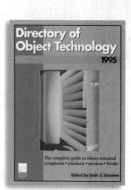

SIGS BOOKS ORDER COUPON

YES! Please rush me the following books:

☐ ___copy(ies) of **Inside the Object Model** (ISBN: 1-884842-05-4)
at the low price of $39 per copy.

☐ ___copy(ies) of **Object Lessons** (ISBN: 0-9627477-3-4)
at the low price of $29 per copy.

☐ ___copy(ies) of **Directory of Object Technology** (ISBN: 1-884842-08-9)
at ☐ $69 (Individual Rate) per copy.
  ☐ $169 (Corporate Library Rate) per copy.

☐ ___copy(ies) of **The Dictionary of Object Technology** (ISBN: 1-884842-09-7)
at the low price of $55 per copy.

☐ ___copy(ies) of **Object Development Methods** (ISBN: 0-9627477-9-3)
at the low price of $39 per copy.

☐ ___copy(ies) of **Objectifying Real-Time Systems** (ISBN: 0-9627477-8-5)
at the low price of $44 per copy (including diskette).

RISK-FREE OFFER! *If you are not completely satisfied with your purchase, simply return the book within 14 days and receive a full refund.*

Total Purchase

Inside the Object Model	$_____
Object Lessons	$_____
Directory of Object Technology	$_____
The Dictionary of Object Technology	$_____
Object Development Methods	$_____
Objectifying Real-Time Systems	$_____
Postage	$_____
NY Resident Sales Tax	$_____
TOTAL	$_____

Risk-Free Offer!

METHOD OF PAYMENT   ☐ Check enclosed (Payable to SIGS Books)

☐ Charge my: ☐ Visa   ☐ MasterCard   ☐ AmEx

Card#:_____ Exp. date: _____

Signature: _____

SEND TO:

Name _____

Company _____

Address _____

City/State _____

Country _____ Postal Code_____

Phone _____

Fax _____

Postage and handling per Item: U.S. orders add $5.00; Canada and Mexico add $10.00; Outside North America add $15.00. Note: New York State residents must add applicable sales tax. Please allow 4-6 weeks from publication date for delivery.
Note: Non-U.S. orders must be prepaid. Checks must be in U.S. dollars and drawn on a U.S. bank.
PBA1

Distributed by Prentice Hall. Available at selected book stores.

RETURN ORDER TO: SIGS Books, P.O. Box 99425, Collingswood, NJ, 08108-9970, USA.
Fax: 609-488-6188   Phone: 609.488.9602